I0815423

PRESENTED TO
FROM
DATE

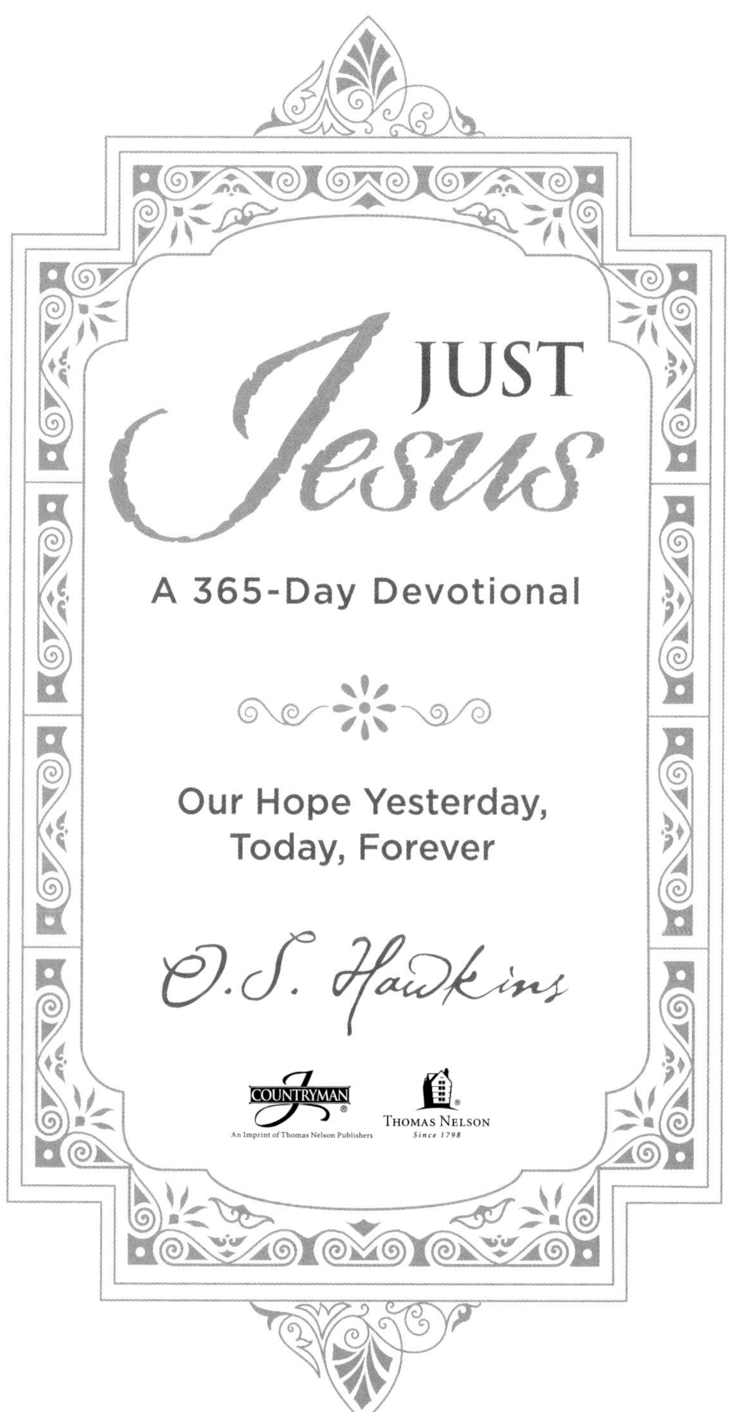

JUST Jesus

A 365-Day Devotional

Our Hope Yesterday, Today, Forever

O. S. Hawkins

COUNTRYMAN
An Imprint of Thomas Nelson Publishers

THOMAS NELSON
Since 1798

Just Jesus

© 2025 Dr. O. S. Hawkins

The text in this book has been drawn from the following books by Dr. O. S. Hawkins: *The Bible Code, The Prayer Code, The Promise Code, The Connection Code, The Spirit Code, The Passion Code, The James Code,* and *The Jesus Code.*

All rights reserved. No portion of this book may be reproduced, stored in a retrieval system, or transmitted in any form or by any means—electronic, mechanical, photocopy, recording, scanning, or other—except for brief quotations in critical reviews or articles, without the prior written permission of the publisher.

Published in Nashville, Tennessee, by Thomas Nelson. Thomas Nelson is a registered trademark of HarperCollins Christian Publishing, Inc.

Thomas Nelson titles may be purchased in bulk for educational, business, fund-raising, or sales promotional use. For information, please email SpecialMarkets@ThomasNelson.com.

Unless otherwise noted, Scripture quotations are from the New King James Version®. Copyright © 1982 by Thomas Nelson. Used by permission. All rights reserved.

Scripture quotations marked ESV are from the ESV® Bible (The Holy Bible, English Standard Version®). Copyright © 2001 by Crossway, a publishing ministry of Good News Publishers. All rights reserved.

Scripture quotations marked KJV are from the King James Version. Public domain.

Scripture quotations marked NET are from the NET Bible®. http://netbible.com. Copyright © 1996, 2019 by Biblical Studies Press, L.L.C. Used by permission. All rights reserved.

Scripture quotations marked NIV are from the Holy Bible, New International Version®, NIV®. Copyright © 1973, 1978, 1984, 2011 by Biblica, Inc.® Used by permission of Zondervan. All rights reserved worldwide. www.zondervan.com. The "NIV" and "New International Version" are trademarks registered in the United States Patent and Trademark Office by Biblica, Inc.®

Any italicized Scripture is the author's emphasis. It is not italicized in the original Scripture.

Any internet addresses, phone numbers, or company or product information printed in this book are offered as a resource and are not intended in any way to be or to imply an endorsement by Thomas Nelson, nor does Thomas Nelson vouch for the existence, content, or services of these sites, phone numbers, companies, or products beyond the life of this book.

Cover design: Left Coast Design
Interior design: Kristy Edwards

ISBN 978-1-4002-5090-5 (HC)
ISBN 978-1-4002-5092-9 (audiobook)
ISBN 978-1-4002-5091-2 (eBook)

Printed in Malaysia

25 26 27 28 29 PJM 10 9 8 7 6 5 4 3 2 1

To the multiplied hundreds of thousands of readers of
the Code series of devotionals, including
The Joshua Code, The Jesus Code, The Bible Code,
The Promise Code, The Spirit Code, and a dozen others.

The royalties from every book you have purchased have gone to support retired pastors and their wives and widows living at or near the poverty line through Mission:Dignity. Like all the "Codes" before it, the proceeds from Just Jesus *go to these good and godly people as well.*

INTRODUCTION

The idea for the title of this volume, *Just Jesus*, came to me while looking at the nativity set my wife, Susie, displays every Christmas season on our mantel. It is an olive wood carving we purchased decades ago in Bethlehem complete with angels, wise men, shepherds, sheep, Mary and Joseph, and, of course, the baby Jesus.

I have a feature on my iPhone that enables me to take a picture and then crop out what I might not want from the top, bottom, or sides of the picture. Some time ago we took a family picture with Susie and me in the middle flanked by our six grandchildren, with their parents standing on either end. I have a confession to make. I cropped the parents out of the picture and now have a favorite photo with just us and the grandkids!

Have you ever thought about what happens when you "crop" the nativity? When you look at the entire scene, it is a worship service. The whole place is exploding with worship. Angels hover above like drones singing "Glory to God in the highest"; shepherds and wise men are bowing down. When you crop the scene a bit you find in the middle a family: Joseph, Mary, and Jesus. It is a reminder that God is pro family. He entrusted His own Son to a human family. But "crop" the scene once more and, in the very middle of it all, it is . . . just Jesus!

One of the most informative scenes in Scripture occurs in the seventeenth chapter of Matthew when our Lord ascended the Mount of Transfiguration with Peter, James, and John. There, for a moment, He was transformed before them into His glorified self and His face shone like the sun before them. Moses and Elijah came from heaven to join Him there. Suddenly a bright cloud enveloped them, and

Scripture says, "When they had lifted up their eyes, they saw no one but Jesus only" (v. 8). Some see no one but Moses only. That is, they are consumed with the legalism and the law he came to present. Some see only Elijah and are consumed with future prophecies yet to be fulfilled. It is better to see Moses and Elijah *in* Christ than to see them *with* Him. They "saw no one but Jesus only." When all is said and done, it is . . . just Jesus!

This volume of daily devotions is designed to help us all bring focus to our lives, to put aside so many of the peripheral issues that tend to get in the way of our Christian growth, bringing us to the point where we close the book each day for a year with the thought, *Today help me to focus on Him alone. It is just Jesus.* At the end of each day's reading there is a takeaway question. I always find it helpful at the end of my own daily devotions not to rush away but to "be still" before the Lord for a moment and listen to what He says to my heart in His "still small voice" (Psalm 37:7 NIV; 1 Kings 19:12). I call it the *prayer of communion*. It goes beyond mere words and ushers me into a time of simply listening to Him apart from the noise and nonsense of the day's happenings. I encourage you to take each of these takeaways and spend a moment meditating on them as He speaks to your heart in a moment of communion between just you and Jesus.

His presence is with us always—yesterday, today, and forever. When you crop all the hustle and bustle out of your life and all is said and done, you will get down to the amazing reality that it is . . . *Just Jesus.*

JANUARY

JANUARY 1

THE ETERNAL QUESTION

I am the way, the truth, and the life. No one comes to the Father except through Me.
JOHN 14:6

It has been said that leadership can be characterized by certain punctuation marks. Some speak with the period: Go here. Do this. Do that. Others communicate with the exclamation point, expressing enthusiasm, expectancy, optimism. But most often, true leaders are characterized by the symbol bent in humility: the question mark.

The Lord Jesus frequently asked questions. The Gospels record more than one hundred. One day, He got to the heart of His own exclusivity when He asked His disciples, "Who do *you* say that I am?" (Matthew 16:15). Today He asks us the same question. For each of us, this is the question of eternity.

When asking this question in the language of the New Testament, the "you" is placed for emphasis at the beginning of the sentence, as if Jesus were asking, "What about you? You and you only? Who do *you* say that I am?" God bless the impulsive Simon Peter for giving the right answer: "You are *the* Christ, the Son of the living God" (Matthew 16:16).

Who do *you* say Jesus is?

JANUARY 2

Trees Walking

So He took the blind man by the hand and led him out of the town. And when He had spit on his eyes and put His hands on him, He asked him if he saw anything. And he looked up and said, "I see men like trees, walking." Then He put His hands on his eyes again and made him look up. And he was restored and saw everyone clearly.

MARK 8:23–25

Most of Jesus' recorded healing miracles were instantaneous. He spoke the word and healing happened. But here, in Mark's account of this blind man, the healing is intentionally in two stages. Since physical sight is often a metaphor for understanding, Jesus' two-part healing reflects the gradual unveiling and understanding of the disciples. It was a miracle with an intended message for the disciples and for us. When Jesus touched this blind man, he could see. But his vision was so blurry he could not tell if he was looking at a man or a tree.

Like this blind man, we need the second touch of our Lord. Until then we will continue seeing people not as individuals who are loved by Jesus with unique needs, heartaches, and hurts but as "trees" walking. This second healing touch is what enables us to see each other clearly through the eyes of Christ.

When has Jesus helped you see clearly concerning a person or a situation in your life?

JANUARY 3

Place Your Trust in God

Trust in the Lord *forever, for in* Yah, *the* Lord, *is everlasting strength.*
ISAIAH 26:4

Our eternal connection with Jesus works out experientially. He is sensitive. He never orders, compels, coerces, or commands us to relate positively to Him. He appeals to us on the basis of His love. Second, He is submissive. He submitted Himself to a vicious and vicarious execution in order to demonstrate His love and make a way out of no way for us. He is also supportive. He stands by our side and calls us His own children. He never leaves us or forsakes us. And when we are in a saving relationship with Him, one day He will stand by our side, as our advocate, supporting us before His Father's throne of judgment. Finally, Jesus is sensible. We should be too. It just makes sense to place our faith and trust in Him. And unless we do, we will never know how valuable we are, nor will we ever sense our highest level of self-worth or self-love.

How has placing your faith in God and trusting Him made a difference in your life?

JANUARY 4

Who Am I?

But Moses said to God, "Who am I that I should go to Pharaoh, and that I should bring the children of Israel out of Egypt?"
EXODUS 3:11

We cannot depend on the physical for a proper self-image. How we look should not determine our self-worth. All the positive thinking and pumping ourselves up will never provide a healthy or accurate sense of worth. We must discover who we really are: a spirit being led by God's own Spirit (Romans 8:14). Only in Christ will we find true self-worth.

Think about Moses. This timid, stammering, reluctant man went away from that burning bush to become the great emancipator of God's people and the leader of a great nation. This same man who began by asking, "Who am I?" in Exodus 3:11 is last seen on the Mount of Transfiguration amid the glory of Jesus Himself.

Understanding who he was because of God's power and grace gave Moses confidence and strength for the task he was called to do. Similarly, when our spirit connects with the Holy Spirit, then we will have an accurate and healthy self-image, for "Christ in you [is] the hope of glory" (Colossians 1:27).

Why shouldn't you allow your physical attributes to determine your self-worth?

JANUARY 5

The Prayer of Intercession

Praying always with all prayer and supplication in the Spirit, being watchful to this end with all perseverance and supplication for all the saints.
EPHESIANS 6:18

When praying according to God's Word, we follow the pattern of confessing our sin, giving thanks, and offering praise. Next, we move to the prayer of intercession, where we approach the Lord on behalf of someone else. Here we pray for our family members, pastors, missionaries, friends, political leaders, and even our enemies.

We also pray for those who do not know the Lord. The person without Christ is blind to the things of God, for "if our gospel is veiled, it is veiled to those who are perishing, whose minds the god of this age has blinded, who do not believe, lest the light of the gospel of the glory of Christ, who is the image of God, should shine on them" (2 Corinthians 4:3–4). Therefore, realizing that "the weapons of our warfare are not carnal but mighty in God for pulling down strongholds" (2 Corinthians 10:4), we intercede to pull down strongholds of pride, prejudice, presumption, procrastination, or any stronghold in which we discern they may be held, freeing them to choose Christ.

Who are the people you regularly intercede for, and what answers to prayer have you seen?

Stress Is Predictable

Beloved, do not think it strange concerning the fiery trial which is to try you, as though some strange thing happened to you.

1 PETER 4:12

Experiencing stress is not an *if*; it's a *when*. Stress is predictable: It is inevitable, inescapable, unavoidable.

Nowhere in the Bible will we find the promise that we're immune to stress or sickness, exempt from trials or tribulations. Some teach falsely that if we're living the Spirit-filled life, we'll have only smooth sailing on the sea of God's will. But our Lord Himself warned, "In the world you will have tribulation; but be of good cheer, I have overcome the world" (John 16:33).

We can't avoid stress, but it can actually be good for us. Stress can be a motivating factor to make changes in our life. However, too much stress coupled with not knowing how to deal with it can be detrimental mentally, spiritually, and physically, leading to depression or serious health issues.

Although stress is predictable and can have ramifications, it does not have to be our foe. God never calls upon us to work harder than He did in the creation event—and He took the seventh day off!

How does it help you to know that stress is a normal part of a believer's life?

JANUARY 7

Present Your Petition

If we ask anything according to His will, He hears us. And if we know that He hears us, whatever we ask, we know that we have the petitions that we have asked of Him.

1 JOHN 5:14–15

The first level of prayer is *presenting a petition.* We are to "ask." This little word is one of the most important ones in life. Salespeople ask for purchases. Politicians ask for votes. Doctors ask about symptoms. Much of what we have learned in life we now know because we asked questions.

Jesus was aware of this. He reveals that the first level of prayer is simply to "ask." When this is done "according to His will," He promises our petitions will "be given" to us (Luke 11:9). This does not mean that whatever we ask for we will receive. Sometimes we ask God for things not in our best interest. Anyone who has raised children understands this. I am thankful God has not granted everything I asked for because I realized later He had something better for me.

When we pray on the level of presenting a petition, the key is knowing and having assurance of the will of God. And when we do, we "ask, and it will be given" to us.

Since God knows all things, why do you think He wants us to ask for what we need from Him?

JANUARY 8

Promises Kept Mean the Most

Let us hold fast the confession of our hope without wavering, for He who promised is faithful.
HEBREWS 10:23

Promises made are always appreciated. But promises kept are what mean the most. It is one thing to make a promise and quite another to keep it. Every one of us can attest to the validity of this truth. We all have had our own experiences of promises that were made and never kept. However, there is Someone to whom this does not apply. Did you know that the Bible is replete with promises God has made . . . to *you* . . . and that He has a perfect record of keeping all His promises? He does!

Throughout centuries of the Christian experience, the promises of God have sustained His people. When all hope seemed lost, believers have held to the promises of God. If there was ever a day the family of God needed to leave their explanations behind and cling to the promises of God's Word, it is today.

When has someone made a promise to you and kept it? How did that make you feel?

JANUARY 9

ACTS CONTINUES

The former account I made . . . of all that Jesus began both to do and teach.
ACTS 1:1

Did you catch the words of today's scripture? They teach us that the Gospels are only the account of what Jesus *began* to do. He is not finished. He is still active. He continues to use the Holy Spirit—and you—to accomplish His work.

The book we call the Acts of the Apostles is really about the acts of the Holy Spirit, which He is still accomplishing today in and through you and me. Luke's gospel tells us what Jesus did in His physical body. Acts tells us what the Holy Spirit continues to do in and through His spiritual body, the church. What an encouragement to know that Jesus is still at work through us, presenting to the world a picture of Himself today.

The book of Acts ends rather abruptly. This is because the story continues, all the way to today. And you and I are part of it. We represent Jesus in the world, and by the Holy Spirit, He is working through us.

How does it encourage you to know that Jesus is still at work through us today through the power of the Holy Spirit?

JANUARY 10

Justified and Forgiven

For whom He foreknew, He also predestined to be conformed to the image of His Son, that He might be the firstborn among many brethren. Moreover whom He predestined, these He also called; whom He called, these He also justified; and whom He justified, these He also glorified.
ROMANS 8:29–30

It is one thing to be forgiven but quite something else to be "justified." The word means to be declared to be right, to be made pure, as though we have never sinned. Christ is not our Justifier because we are worthy of being justified. We are worthy because we have been justified by Him through faith. It is not *our* works that justify us. It is *His* work—His finished work—on the cross that enables us to stand in His righteousness alone and one day to be presented faultless before His Father's throne.

A human court may acquit someone of a crime. It can pardon someone from their trespasses. But it can never *justify* anyone's crime. But Jesus can and does because faith in Him is "accounted for righteousness" (Romans 4:5) to those who believe. Paul framed it best when he said we were "*justified freely* by His grace through the redemption that is in Christ Jesus" (Romans 3:24).

How does your salvation compare to being pardoned by a court of law, and why is it much better?

JANUARY 11

A Dangerous Conception

When desire has conceived, it gives birth to sin; and sin, when it is full-grown, brings forth death.
JAMES 1:15

Sin is the result of a selfish desire left unchecked and our deliberate choice to act on that desire. Eventually, desire "gives birth to sin." This Greek phrase suggests a child in the mother's womb. The evil desire cannot stay hidden within forever. That desire will "give birth." If the root of sin is left untouched in the heart, the shoot will emerge sooner or later. "Your sin will find you out" (Numbers 32:23).

The Greek meaning behind the English word *sin* means "to miss the mark." In the physical dimension, it describes an archer who aims at the target, lets go of the arrow, and misses the bull's-eye. In the mental dimension, it describes a student who takes a test and fails to get the answers right. In the spiritual dimension, it describes someone who knows a certain standard of behavior yet falls below it.

There is an obvious progression here: conception, then growth, followed by a birth. But note what James said about this birth: This sin "brings forth death"! It is stillborn.

How does understanding the progression of sin—from conception to growth to birth to death—change the way you think about sin?

JANUARY 12

No Competition

Let nothing be done through selfish ambition or conceit, but in lowliness of mind let each esteem others better than himself.
PHILIPPIANS 2:3

Relationships built on competition never win in the long run. Everyone ends up losing. Take, for example, a husband and a wife. He constantly orders her around the house. He coerces and controls. After a while, her resentment is sure to build. For years he thinks he is winning. But one day he wakes up to see she has had enough and is gone. And in the end, they both end up losing. This can also happen with parent-child relationships, when a parent thinks he or she has to win every argument, keep a thumb on the young person, and control them by withholding. The child leaves home one day and seldom returns, and everyone ends up in the loss column.

Those who play the game of relationships in a spirit of competition—the win-lose principle—never are real winners in the long run. When the final whistle blows, everyone ends up losing.

Why do you think relationships built on competition end up in the loss column?

JANUARY 13

God Finds Joy in Giving

Thanks be to God for His indescribable gift!
2 CORINTHIANS 9:15

You and I give gifts to those we love because we believe they will benefit and bless the ones who receive them. It is the same with God's gift to us. Salvation is His "indescribable gift," and He gives it to benefit us and to bless us. Paul wrote about God's gift of salvation by grace through faith in Ephesians 2:8–9. Then he continued, "For we are His workmanship, created in Christ Jesus for good works, which God prepared beforehand that we should walk in them" (v. 10).

When you receive God's gift of eternal life through faith, you become a new creation. You become His "workmanship." He so fashioned and formed you that no one else has your specific DNA. You are unique and indescribably valuable to Him.

Next time you exchange gifts with your family or friends, instead of watching the recipient, catch a glimpse of the joy on the face of the giver as he or she watches the one they love open the gift. So it is with God.

What is your favorite gift-giving memory?

JANUARY 14

God Lets Go but Doesn't Give Up

If I ascend into heaven, You are there; if I make my bed in hell, behold, You are there.
PSALM 139:8

In the parable of the prodigal son (Luke 15:11–32), we see the father with an open hand. He let the boy go. He was wise enough to know that the way to keep his children was to let them go, and the way to lose them was to hold them too tight. He could have guilted the young man ("Are you trying to break your mother's heart?") or played the comparison game ("Why can't you be like your older brother?"), but he didn't. He let him go, but he never gave up on him.

Likewise, your loving heavenly Father has an open hand toward you. You are not a puppet. And so, He lets you go . . . because the love you can voluntarily return to Him is indescribably valuable to Him. He may let you go your own way, but He will never stop loving you and never give up on you. He knows the way to keep you is to open His hands and release you.

Have you ever chosen to go your own way, apart from God—and discovered His love for you in the process? What happened?

JANUARY 15

A Model of Repentance

For I acknowledge my transgressions, and my sin is always before me.
PSALM 51:3

In the first six verses of Psalm 51 David takes *personal responsibility* for his sin. Some people never find a place of new beginnings because they refuse to take personal responsibility for their sin. Their failures are always someone else's fault. Most of us know the story. David saw beautiful Bathsheba, Uriah's wife, bathing on the rooftop of her home below his palace. He summoned her, and an adulterous affair ensued. David knew he was responsible for his sin and undeserving of God's grace and forgiveness, so he made his appeal on the basis of God's mercy. Note the intensely personal pronouns in this prayer: "*My* transgressions . . . *my* sin. . . . *my* iniquity."

David realized that sin hounds us: "My sin is always before me" (v. 3). Everywhere he turned he saw the ghost of his guilty and wicked past. He also was keenly aware of how sin haunts us: "Against You, You only, have I sinned" (v. 4). His sins were not just against Uriah, or Bathsheba, or their baby who died; his sins were primarily against God. He unloaded his confession before God, never once offering any self-justification for his wrongs. He modeled for us the road back to God.

How can you use Psalm 51 as a model for your prayers?

JANUARY 16

Rich in Faith

Listen, my beloved brethren: Has God not chosen the poor of this world to be rich in faith and heirs of the kingdom which He promised to those who love Him? But you have dishonored the poor man.

JAMES 2:5–6

We should guard against dishonoring anyone, especially those whose dignity is about all they have. Let us keep in mind that Jesus said, "Inasmuch as you did it to one of the least of these My brethren, you did it to Me" (Matthew 25:40). In the same spirit, to paraphrase today's scripture, "Don't deny their dignity; don't steal their honor."

Have you noticed that the poor often seem to grasp the gospel in greater numbers than the rich and more privileged do? In general, those who have materially less are more aware of their powerlessness, so it is easier for some of them to recognize their need for salvation. Often the rich and powerful, however, see no reason to have Christ in their lives. Frequently, the greatest barrier to reaching the wealthy with the gospel is their pride, while the greatest barrier to reaching the poor can be their self-pity and bitterness.

Ask God to help you view people around you today through His eyes. You just might see a few folks differently than you have in the past.

Have you known anyone who is materially poor but "rich in faith"? What have you learned about God from this person?

JANUARY 17

The Way Forward May Be Back

I am sending him—who is my very heart—back to you.
PHILEMON V. 12 NIV

Often the way forward is back. Back—to admit I was wrong in ways I always insisted I was right. Back—to make a previous wrong right. This is one of the great paradoxes of the Christian life. In God's economy, the way up is down, and the way down is up. Paul added an additional paradox to the equation that the way forward is back when he let Philemon know that he was sending Onesimus back to him. Onesimus, who had previously ripped off Philemon, met Paul in a Roman prison cell and came to faith in Christ through the apostle's bold witness. Now Onesimus is headed back in repentance to make restitution, and Paul sends this letter ahead of him to prepare the way. It was along these lines of seeing that the way forward is back that Jesus said, "If you bring your gift to the altar, and there remember that your brother has something against you, leave your gift there before the altar, and go your way. First be reconciled to your brother, and then come and offer your gift" (Matthew 5:23–24). Do you see it? This is one of life's great paradoxes—the way forward is back!

In a situation in your life, how might you find the way forward by going back?

JANUARY 18

What Makes Jesus Unique

Now when He had said these things, He cried with a loud voice, "Lazarus, come forth!"
JOHN 11:43

It was a sad and somber day in the little village of Bethany on the eastern slope of the Mount of Olives as Jesus stood beside a brokenhearted family at the grave of their brother, Lazarus. Looking into their sorrowful faces, including those of Lazarus's sisters, Mary and Martha, He made one of the most astounding promises in all the Bible: "I am the resurrection and the life. He who believes in Me, though he may die, he shall live. And whoever lives and believes in Me shall never die" (John 11:25–26). Then, to prepare His disciples for His own resurrection, He called Lazarus forth from the grave with the words of today's scripture.

The resurrection of Christ is what separates Him from a thousand other gurus and self-proclaimed prophets who have appeared time and again across the centuries. And it is His resurrection that assures our own in that coming great day.

How does knowing that Jesus is unique among other gurus and so-called prophets encourage you in your faith?

JANUARY 19

The Danger of Discouragement

And the people spoke against God and against Moses: "Why have you brought us up out of Egypt to die in the wilderness? For there is no food and no water, and our soul loathes this worthless bread."

NUMBERS 21:5

It's easy to forget not just where we have been but also where we are going. When we only have eyes for the "now," discouragement comes easily.

These chosen people of God complained about the way they were being *led*. They began to murmur against Moses, but the real object of their complaint was God Himself. Moses was simply following God's lead and relaying God's instructions to the people.

Their other complaint was the way they were being *fed*. The manna fell fresh every morning—a picture, we later learn, of the sustaining life we can have in Jesus Christ, the Bread of Life. The manna the people hated was God's gracious gift of sustenance.

When discouragement comes, it has a dastardly way of diverting our focus away from God and His blessings. Are you discouraged today? Look to Jesus. He has brought you out of your own Egypt to take you into His promised land.

What wilderness experience are you currently going through, and how can you look to Jesus in the midst of it?

JANUARY 20

THE LORD'S TABLE

For as often as you eat this bread and drink this cup,
you proclaim the Lord's death till He comes.
1 CORINTHIANS 11:26

We refer to Communion as the "Lord's Supper" because it is His, not ours. He does the inviting, and we are His guests at His table. First Corinthians 11 offers four important reminders about this important meal.

First, there is a *word of explanation.* Paul insisted that he was simply passing on what he had "received from the Lord" (v. 23).

We also note a *word of exaltation* (v. 24). Times of Communion call for thankful hearts.

When we receive the bread and the cup, we also express a *word of expectation.* When we partake of this meal, we "proclaim the Lord's death till He comes" (v. 26). It is not just a look backward but a look forward. He is coming again.

Finally, there is a *word of examination.* Based on verse 28, times of Communion can be seasons of refreshing in the presence of the Lord when we examine ourselves and find cleansing and a new beginning through confession and repentance.

When you take the Lord's Supper, how often do you think of Christ's return? Why is it important to do so?

JANUARY 21

Confess, Crown, Claim

And the disciples were filled with joy and with the Holy Spirit.
ACTS 13:52

I awoke this morning with the incredible realization that the Holy Spirit is alive *in me*. His desire is not to simply indwell us today but to fill us each moment of every day with His presence and power.

First, *confess* your sins to Him. Come clean. "If we confess our sins, He is faithful and just to forgive us our sins and to cleanse us from all unrighteousness" (1 John 1:9).

Next, *crown* Jesus Lord of your life. Take yourself off the throne and put Him there. "For to this end Christ died and rose and lived again, that He might be Lord of both the dead and the living" (Romans 14:9).

Finally, *claim* this truth: "Whatever things you ask when you pray, believe that you receive them, and you will have them" (Mark 11:24).

What is more important: what God says or how you feel? Don't equate feelings or the absence of feelings with being filled by the Spirit. You are filled according to your faith.

What do you need to do to be filled with the Holy Spirit right this moment?

JANUARY 22

Teach Us to Pray

Now it came to pass, as He was praying in a certain place, when He ceased, that one of His disciples said to Him, "Lord, teach us to pray, as John also taught his disciples."

LUKE 11:1

Prayer, the ability to fellowship with God, is one of the awesome privileges of the Christian experience. The only thing the disciples ever asked Jesus to do was teach them to pray. They heard Him preach powerful sermons, but they did not ask Him to teach them to preach. They watched Him engage in personal evangelism, but they never asked Him to teach them to evangelize. They heard Him teach the most marvelous life lessons, but they never asked Him to teach them to teach.

For three years they witnessed the intensity and frequency of His personal prayer life with the Father. They watched Him as He went up into the mountains to pray through the night and as He prayed before every great undertaking and after every great victory. They knew if they could ever capture the essence of prayer, they would have no problem preaching, teaching, or performing any of the other tasks their ministries would need.

If you had been one of Jesus' disciples during His time on earth, what would you have asked Him to teach you?

JANUARY 23

WHO IS YOUR PILOT?

Look also at ships: although they are so large and are driven by fierce winds, they are turned by a very small rudder wherever the pilot desires. Even so the tongue is a little member and boasts great things.

JAMES 3:4–5

The Greek word translated in today's scripture as "little member" can also mean "melody; the music to which a song is set." God intends our tongues to give life a melody. If the tongue is out of tune, life has no melody.

The real issue is not the bit in the mouth or the rudder on the ship, but the one who is in control. When oil tankers are still some distance from shore, a small boat goes out to meet them. On that boat is a person called the "bar pilot." He or she boards the massive vessel, and the captain who has piloted that huge ship across the ocean steps aside and surrenders the wheel to the bar pilot to guide the ship into port. Jesus is our bar pilot, yet too many of us are trying to steer our own ships into the harbor. We need to step aside and surrender to Him. The tongue may be a "little member," but we can use it to do great things for God when we surrender it to His control.

In what areas of your life do you need to surrender control to Jesus?

JANUARY 24

Openness Helps Build Bridges

Perfume and incense bring joy to the heart, and the pleasantness of a friend springs from their heartfelt advice.
PROVERBS 27:9 NIV

In relationships, we will do one of two things with others: We will build a bridge, or we will build a barrier. When we build bridges instead of barriers, we will have more loyal and lasting friendships.

The best way to start building bridges is to be open with others. To encourage building bridges is not to suggest letting anyone and everyone cross over into the private turf of the hidden things of the heart. Openness with others is no call to reveal every single detail about our lives to anyone who will listen. We all have our private moments that are no one else's business. We are talking about bridges here, not some wide-open Autobahn or interstate highway. We are talking about the need to be open in our relationships with one another. Something wonderful happens when two people connect with each other in openness and honesty. Openness has its own way of building bridges in relationships.

How can you be more intentional about being open to others as you build bridges in your relationships?

JANUARY 25

The Three Judgments

I saw a great white throne and Him who sat on it. . . . And I saw the dead, small and great, standing before God, and books were opened. . . . And anyone not found written in the Book of Life was cast into the lake of fire.
REVELATION 20:11–12, 15

The subject of a final judgment for everyone can be confusing unless we understand the different judgments delineated in the Bible.

The first judgment for believers has already taken place—the *judgment of sin*. Jesus said, "He who hears My word and believes in Him who sent Me has everlasting life, and shall not come into judgment, but has passed from death into life" (John 5:24).

Then there is the *judgment of sinners*, the "great white throne" judgment awaiting those who died without trusting Christ as their Savior. They will give account of their lives and then be pronounced guilty and cast into a dark, godless eternity.

Believers will stand before the "judgment seat of Christ" immediately after His return at the *judgment of the saints*. Our works will be judged, not our sins, which Christ paid for on the cross. Here, our rewards will be determined and Christ, our judge, will step down from the bench, stand by our side, and plead our case.

How does this explanation of the different judgments increase your joy in your salvation and encourage you to share Jesus with others?

JANUARY 26

Just One Book

The grass withers, the flower fades, but the word of our God stands forever.
ISAIAH 40:8

On a cold winter afternoon in 2002, we buried my ministry father, W. A. Criswell. As he had requested, when the casket closed on his lifeless body, lying open on his chest was a copy of the Bible, God's Holy Word, opened to his favorite verse, Isaiah 40:8.

Dr. Criswell often closed a message on the Bible with the story of Sir Walter Scott. As the great Scottish poet lay dying on his deathbed, he turned to his son-in-law, Lockhart, and said, "Son, bring me the book." Lockhart replied, "Father, what book? There are thousands of books in your library. What book?" "Oh," the great wordsmith replied, "there is just one book. Bring me the book." Lockhart went to the library and picked up the Bible, brought it back, and laid it in the hands of Sir Walter Scott. And the great man died with the Bible clutched within his hands.

Yes, there is just one book! And "the word of our God stands forever" (Isaiah 40:8).

How would you describe the way you value God's Word?

JANUARY 27

Your Divine Advocate

My little children, these things I write to you, so that you may not sin. And if anyone sins, we have an Advocate with the Father, Jesus Christ the righteous.

1 JOHN 2:1

Among my fondest childhood memories were the Saturday morning football games on the old vacant lot. One boy was the one everyone wanted on their team because of his size and speed. When he was on your side, you knew you were on the winning team.

In the game of life, you have Someone very powerful on your side—the Holy Spirit. Jesus said, "I will pray the Father, and He will give you another Helper, that He may abide with you forever" (John 14:16). With the Spirit helping you, you are on the winning team.

The Greek word used here for *Helper* describes someone who is "called alongside" you ("Advocate" in 1 John 2:1). Picture yourself being charged with a crime and taken before the judge. Then a person approaches the bench and speaks on your behalf, brilliantly pleading your case. You have just such an advocate on your side!

Jesus was saying, "I am leaving you, but the Holy Spirit is coming to be on your side and by your side. He will never leave you."

When have you experienced the Holy Spirit acting as your helper or advocate?

Sincere, Secret, and Simple

When you pray, you shall not be like the hypocrites. . . . And when you pray, do not use vain repetitions as the heathen do. . . . For your Father knows the things you have need of before you ask Him.
MATTHEW 6:5, 7–8

In today's scripture God assumes the believer will have a consistent prayer life. Jesus repeatedly states, "When you pray," not, "If you pray." Prayer should not be an afterthought or emergency escape mechanism for any believer who knows the Lord intimately. Being in constant communion with God should be like breathing—a natural response to our love relationship with Him.

Jesus mentions two types of individuals. The hypocrite, who "love[s] to pray standing in the synagogues and on the corners of the streets, that they may be seen by men," prays to impress people (Matthew 6:5). And the heathen, who prays with "vain repetitions . . . for they think that they will be heard for their many words," prays in a feeble attempt to try to impress God (v. 7). At times, we may find a bit of the hypocrite and/or the heathen in ourselves. But the Lord says, "Do not be like them" (v. 8). God has a way of honoring sincere, secret, and simple prayers.

How could your prayers become more sincere, secret, and simple?

JANUARY 29

Refresh Someone's Heart

Yes, brother, let me have joy from you in the Lord; refresh my heart in the Lord.
PHILEMON V. 20

Just as Paul asked Philemon to refresh his heart, you and I can set out to refresh someone's heart this week. Do something for someone. Include them. Perform some act of kindness. Do someone a favor. Pay someone a sincere compliment. Smile. Build a bridge or open a door.

Refresh the heart of someone who regularly serves you at a local restaurant this week. Pay a compliment. Rise to his or her defense. Give an extra tip.

Refresh the heart of your husband or wife. Be objective about it. Give without expecting anything in return. Do a good deed that may even be out of character for you. Buy her flowers. Prepare his favorite meal.

Refresh the hearts of your children. Let them know how much you believe in them to do the right thing. Tell them you are proud of them and help bring out the very best in them.

There are all kinds of ways to refresh someone's heart, and most people will appreciate it.

How can you refresh someone's heart today?

JANUARY 30

Iron Gates and Open Doors

When they were past the first and the second guard posts, they came to the iron gate that leads to the city, which opened to them of its own accord; and they went out and went down one street, and immediately the angel departed from him.

ACTS 12:10

Today's scripture highlights the fact that, in answer to the church's prayers, an angel of the Lord visited Peter in prison and led him out. There are many doors in life we can open ourselves, but there are also some iron gates, meaning human impossibilities where there is no hope unless God supernaturally opens the door. Some of us beat on these gates until our knuckles are bloody and bruised, when the only thing that opens them is "constant prayer" (Acts 12:5).

From prison, Peter ran to the home where the church was meeting and began to knock on the door. When he identified himself, they still did not open the door. Inside, they were in constant prayer. The lessons we learn from this story are that sometimes we must depend on God to supernaturally open doors for us, and sometimes there comes a time for us to stop praying, believe, and go open the door.

In what situation in your life do you need God to open an iron gate for you? In what situation might it be time for you to stop praying, believe, and open the door?

JANUARY 31

Jesus Gives Us Rest

Oh, that I had wings like a dove! I would fly away and be at rest.

PSALM 55:6

Many of us would echo the words of today's scripture. We live in a restless world where we are moved and motivated by overachievement and long hours, rushing around until we are depleted of much of our energy and effectiveness. Our busyness is compounded by our desire for immediate gratification. "Give it to me, and give it to me right now" is our command and cry. Many of us are exhausted.

For such a time as this, Christ offered a promise: "I will give you rest" (Matthew 11:28). Jesus originally spoke these words to a people burdened by the impossible task of attempting to keep the Jewish laws and the standards they imposed. They were at the point of exhaustion. No matter how they tried, they could not measure up. In feeble attempts to alleviate their anxiety, they kept trying harder. Sound familiar? Jesus came to them, and to us today, with a proposition to stop trying and start trusting Him. That's how we will find the very thing we're searching for: "rest for our souls" (v. 29 NIV).

How can you find rest for your soul today?

FEBRUARY

FEBRUARY 1

Use the Power of Synergy

How could one chase a thousand, and two put ten thousand to flight?
DEUTERONOMY 32:30

Consider two pencils. If you hold one in your hands, it is relatively easy to break it in two. However, if you put them together, it becomes exponentially more difficult to break them. This is *synergy*, when two or more agents produce an effort greater than the sum of their separate parts. With synergism, one plus one does not equal two; it equals three or more.

As believers, we need each other, and we become exponentially valuable and strong when we are together. This is synergism in action. Jesus once said, "If two of you agree on earth concerning anything that they ask, it will be done for them by My Father in heaven" (Matthew 18:19). The wisest man who ever lived, King Solomon, said it like this: "Two are better than one. . . . For if they fall, one will lift up his companion. . . . If two lie down together, they will keep warm. . . . Though one may be overpowered by another, two can withstand him. And a threefold cord is not quickly broken" (Ecclesiastes 4:9–12).

When have you seen the power of synergy in action?

FEBRUARY 2

PRAYING SELFLESSLY

Stretch out your hand to heal and perform signs and wonders through the name of your holy servant Jesus.
ACTS 4:30 NIV

The believers in the early church were far more concerned with honoring Christ than their own reputations. They were cautious not to take any credit for their accomplishments, acknowledging, as we see in today's scripture, that it was only "through the name of your holy servant Jesus" that their victories were achieved. We never find the early believers approaching God on the basis of their own merit, but solely in the name of Christ. They knew that the Father did not grant their requests on the basis of who they were or what they had done but on the basis of who the Lord Jesus is and what He has done.

These early believers asked God to give them a new boldness in confronting their problems. And they gave Him glory when He answered. If you will pray with power, He will give you the grace to deal with any problem. Seek Christ's highest good, that in and through all things He will be glorified.

What recent victory have you had for which God deserves the credit and the glory?

STRESS—SYMPTOMS AND SOLUTIONS

But he himself went a day's journey into the wilderness, and came and sat down under a broom tree. And he prayed that he might die, and said, "It is enough! Now, LORD, *take my life, for I am no better than my fathers!"*
1 KINGS 19:4

The prophet Elijah's story illustrates the common symptoms of stress. The first is *detachment*. Fearing for his life, Elijah ran away and isolated himself. Another is *despondency*. He sat under a juniper tree and even contemplated suicide. Then came *defeat*, a feeling of worthlessness and self-deprecation, followed by *deception*. He believed he was the only person still standing for God.

God showed Elijah and us both *practical* and *physical* solutions to his stress. The first thing Elijah did was to get some sleep and have a meal. Adequate sleep and proper eating go a long way in enabling us to deal with stress. But the solution wasn't simply physical; it was also *personal*. God asked Elijah, "What are you doing here?" (1 Kings 19:9). Many of us lose the joy of life by doing nothing. Whatever way God asked the question, Elijah heard that "still small voice" (1 Kings 19:12) calling him to new heights of faith. Our stress does not have to be a dead end; it can simply be a turn in the road.

If you've ever felt like giving up, as Elijah did, how did God help you persevere?

FEBRUARY 4

WHY, GOD, WHY?

Gideon said to Him, "O my lord, if the LORD is with us, why then has all this happened to us?"
JUDGES 6:13

Gideon was about to battle the Midianites against seemingly insurmountable odds. Then an angel appeared and said, "The LORD is with you, you mighty man of valor!" (Judges 6:12).

In times of discouragement, it is not unusual for some well-meaning "angel" to say something similar to us. You've just lost your job. Your husband left. Your wayward teenager is in trouble. You are sick. And a friend says, "The Lord is with you!" And we are prone to echo Gideon: "If the Lord is with me, why has all this happened to me?"

Look for the *cause.* Why does God allow discouragement? Paul indicated it is often to break us down. Why? In order to build us up so that "we should not trust in ourselves but in God" (2 Corinthians 1:9).

Maybe some little victory comes our way, and we begin taking some of the credit and trusting in ourselves. Our Bibles remain closed. Prayer is pushed aside. Then something happens that makes us realize once again that "we should not trust in ourselves" but in the Lord.

How has God used discouraging situations to draw you back to Himself?

The Riches of Christ

To me, who am less than the least of all the saints, this grace was given, that I should preach among the Gentiles the unsearchable riches of Christ.
EPHESIANS 3:8

Throughout Ephesians we find the concept of the "riches" of Christ. Paul said, "In Him we have redemption through His blood, the forgiveness of sins, according to the riches of His grace" (Ephesians 1:7). Next, he prayed that your understanding would be enlightened "that you may know what is the hope of His calling, what are the riches of the glory of His inheritance in the saints" (v. 18). He continued, "But God, who is rich in mercy . . . raised us up together . . . in the heavenly places in Christ Jesus, that in the ages to come He might show the exceeding riches of His grace in His kindness toward us in Christ Jesus" (2:4, 6–7).

These riches reveal that we have redemption. *Right now.* The verb used in Ephesians 1:7 is in the present, active, indicative form. We don't need to wait for redemption. We have it "in Him." Our world is looking for immediate gratification, but true gratification comes in discovering the unsearchable riches of Christ here and now.

How does knowing that you are already redeemed encourage you?

God Keeps His Promises

For all the promises of God in Him are Yes, and in Him Amen, to the glory of God through us.
2 CORINTHIANS 1:20

Though we are good at making promises, we often become lax when it comes to keeping them. But this never happens with God. Whether we keep our promises or not is based on the content of our character. An unrepentant, repeat thief may appear before a judge and promise never to steal again. But his trustworthiness, based on his past recurring behavior, does not attest to his sincerity. Because of the thief's lack of character and trustworthiness, a judge would never declare such a man innocent. So, how can we trust God and the promises He has made to us? Because of His character and the fact that the Bible declares that it is "impossible for God to lie" (Hebrews 6:18). His Word is His bond. Your Bible is laced with promises He has made to you—promises He wants you to claim as your very own. It is one thing to read the Bible and struggle with its precepts and quite another thing to believe the Bible and stand on its promises.

When has God kept a promise to you, and what did that reveal about His character?

FEBRUARY 7

Can You Call Him "Father"?

Let us therefore come boldly to the throne of grace, that we may obtain mercy and find grace to help in time of need.
HEBREWS 4:16

Prayer is to the Father (Matthew 6:9). All true prayer begins when I claim my personal relationship with Him and begin to know and love Him in the intimacy of Father and child. For me this relationship began when I was seventeen and trusted in Christ as my personal Savior. Since then I have grown to know Him as my heavenly Father. He is the source of my prayer life.

The only way God can be called "Father" is if we have been born again spiritually into His family through what Jesus called in John 3:7 being "born again." It might surprise some of us to know that we are not all God's children.

More than seventy times, Jesus began in prayer using the word *Father.* What a privilege for you and me to acknowledge that He is the source of prayer by addressing Him as Father. When we pray, we are not trying to appease a demanding parent, but we are children who, because of our relationship with Him, can come boldly before our Father's throne.

What does it mean to you personally to be God's child?

FEBRUARY 8

Choose Compassion over Comfort Zone

As you did it to one of the least of these My brethren, you did it to Me.

MATTHEW 25:40

Comfort zones . . . we all have them, and many of us never venture out from them.

Jesus told the story of a Samaritan, a member of a race despised by the Jews of His day, who came upon a traveler who had been beaten, robbed, and left bleeding on the side of the road. Some religious types had passed earlier and walked by on the other side of the road. But the Samaritan felt compassion, stopped, applied first aid, took the wounded man to an inn for extended care, and paid the bill (Luke 10:30–37).

Consider today that you were that wounded one. Jesus saw you beaten by sin and lying on the side of the road. Overwhelmed by compassion and love for you, He left His comfort zone of heaven, came into your world, clothed Himself in human flesh, and reached out to touch you. Like the Samaritan, He took you to a place of refuge, deposited you in His church, and promised that when He came back He would settle all accounts.

How often do you leave your comfort zone to connect with those who are different from you?

FEBRUARY 9

EMPOWERED FOR CHRISTIAN LIVING

He who believes in Me, the works that I do he will do also; and greater works than these he will do, because I go to My Father.
JOHN 14:12

When you awaken to the Holy Spirit's power in you, a new dimension of Christian living will greet you. We will not just *equal* what Jesus did, but we will *exceed* His works.

The key to Jesus' meaning is found in John 14:16: "I will pray the Father, and He will give you another Helper, that He may abide with you forever." Jesus promises, "I will not leave you orphans; I will come to you" (John 14:18). And come back He did, in the power of the Holy Spirit, who accomplishes greater works in us, never leaves us, and empowers us to live the Christian life.

After Jesus ascended, the disciples waited "for the Promise of the Father" (Acts 1:4). They didn't wait until they were worthy to receive Him. Who of us is worthy? The Holy Spirit fell upon them and they—and we—have never been the same since.

In what ways have you tried to live the Christian life in your own strength only to fail and realize you need the Holy Spirit's empowerment?

FEBRUARY 10

Our Prize

Brethren, I do not count myself to have apprehended; but one thing I do, forgetting those things which are behind and reaching forward to those things which are ahead, I press toward the goal for the prize of the upward call of God in Christ Jesus.
PHILIPPIANS 3:13–14

No New Testament letter besides Philippians contains such a razor-sharp focus on what Paul called "the prize," which he identified as "the upward call of God," found in Christ Jesus our Lord. In Philippians, Jesus is our Prize. The ability to obtain and then maintain focus is one of the key elements necessary for spiritual growth in the Christian life.

Focus. This one word holds the key to success in so many endeavors of life. Focus—seeing Jesus as our Prize—is the source of successful living. It helps us begin our tasks with the end in mind. What is the goal toward which you are striving? What is in the crosshairs of your scope? When we begin to focus on Christ alone, we find that He will put our priorities in order, He will give us a forward look, He will bring a new passion to our lives, and He will let us clearly see the end from the beginning.

How does focusing on Christ alone help you put your priorities in order each day?

FEBRUARY 11

THE TRUE SOURCE OF DEATH

For the wages of sin is death, but the gift of God is eternal life in Christ Jesus our Lord.

ROMANS 6:23

Ever since the garden of Eden, physical death has been the destiny of every human being. But the wages of sin can also mean the death of dreams, relationships, ambitions, reputations, opportunities, and so much else that is good. Sin never brings anything good into our lives.

In this verse death means "separation." In physical death, the spirit is separated from the body. In eternal death, the spirit of a person is separated from God for all eternity.

When we take the bait of temptation, most of us never think of the possible consequences. Sin separates us from so much that is good and, all too often, results in the death of hopes, health, homes, and happiness.

It isn't a sin when an impure thought passes through your mind. It becomes a sin when you don't allow it to pass through and instead give it a room in your heart. Stand strong in the Lord and against temptation. Keep in mind that "[God] will not allow you to be tempted beyond what you are able" (1 Corinthians 10:13).

When have you experienced the separation that results from sin?

LOSE-WIN RELATIONSHIPS

The woman then left her waterpot, went her way into the city, and said to the men, "Come, see a Man who told me all things that I ever did. Could this be the Christ?" Then they went out of the city and came to Him.

JOHN 4:28–30

Some relationships are built on compromise. They can be referred to as lose-win relationships. Some people have such low feelings of self-worth that they feel the only way they can maintain a relationship is always to let the other party win and sacrifice their own desires, hoping that, in turn, they will be accepted. They think allowing the other party to win every argument and dominate every situation will somehow help them maintain the relationship.

Relationships built on compromise (lose-win) don't get very far. The woman of Sychar played this game. She possessed such low self-esteem that she felt the only way to get any attention was to play in the loser's bracket, allowing the men of the town to win by using her. But one day she met a Man at a well and learned how to play win-win. She went back to those very people and introduced them to this One who had changed the way she thought about herself. And everyone in Sychar ended up winning.

How does knowing Jesus teach us to play win-win in relationships?

FEBRUARY 13

JESUS, THE GOOD SHEPHERD

I am the good shepherd; and I know My sheep, and am known by My own. As the Father knows Me, even so I know the Father; and I lay down My life for the sheep.

JOHN 10:14–15

Through Jesus' promises to us in John 10 we see how He cares for us like a shepherd cares for his sheep. These words of His are packed with principles and promises. He knows us—everything about us—past, present, and future. He gives us eternal life, the greatest of all gifts. He promises that we shall never perish. And He reminds us that we are securely held in His strong hand, so much so that nothing and no one can snatch us from His grasp.

This analogy of the shepherd and his sheep is not unique to the New Testament. Millions through the ages have heard these words of the psalmist King David: "The LORD is my shepherd" (Psalm 23:1). Along with the familiar John 3:16, these are the words whispered by many a soldier in a foxhole on a foreign battlefield on some star-filled night, or formed by the chapped lips of dying saints on their deathbeds of affliction. The Lord is your Shepherd. What a comfort.

In what ways have you experienced the Lord as your Shepherd?

Power vs. Influence

Now behold, an angel of the Lord stood by him, and a light shone in the prison; and he struck Peter on the side and raised him up, saying, "Arise quickly!" And his chains fell off his hands.

ACTS 12:7

Some believers today seem to be confusing two important words in our Christian vocabulary—*influence* and *power*. We pride ourselves on influence, particularly when it comes to the arena of politics. On every front, it seems we are seeking to influence those in high places. We picket and protest, pass resolutions and sign petitions.

People in the early church faced plenty of challenges. Too often, they were trying to keep from being burned at the stake or thrown to wild animals in one of Caesar's venues. When you think about it, it makes our problems—like fighting Washington to keep our tax-exempt status intact—relatively mundane.

These early believers did not have enough *influence* with the authorities to keep Peter out of prison (Acts 12), but they had something better. They had access to the *power* of the Holy Spirit to pray him out . . . and they used it!

The Holy Spirit living in you has far more power to get things done than any influence you could ever hope to wield.

How can you focus less on being influential and more on praying for the Holy Spirit's power to make a difference for Christ?

FEBRUARY 15

"SIN" AND "SINS"

If we say that we have no sin, we deceive ourselves, and the truth is not in us.

1 JOHN 1:8

There is a distinction between the root (our sin) and the fruit (our sins). Our sin (singular) nature is dealt with on the cross (1 John 1:7). When you were converted, you didn't have to confess all your "sins" simply to be saved.

While our "sin" is dealt with at the cross, our "sins" should be dealt with in continual confession (v. 9), not to be saved but to be in fellowship with the Father. Believers cannot break their relationship with Christ, but unconfessed sins can cloud our fellowship with Him.

In court, when a guilty person confesses, they are condemned and sentenced. But when we confess our sins to God, we find complete and total forgiveness. Your sin has already been punished in the body of Christ on the cross, and "He is faithful and just" to forgive you (v. 9).

When our daughter was young, she took piano lessons. She would practice a new piece and make a mistake in the first few lines, then start all over . . . until she got to the same place and made the same mistake. Then start over again . . . and again. Some of us have tried to start over in life so many times. We don't need a new and louder beginning. We already know those first bars of the Christian life by heart. We need to confess, keep going, and finish the song.

How does the idea of continual confession give you hope?

FEBRUARY 16

THE ROYAL LAW

If you really fulfill the royal law according to the Scripture, "You shall love your neighbor as yourself," you do well; but if you show partiality, you commit sin, and are convicted by the law as transgressors.

JAMES 2:8–9

People who discriminate are presumptuous. They presume that discrimination is not sin, is not significant, and is not serious. But like the stilts a clown stands on, these false presumptions are easily knocked down.

James was very straightforward about that fact: "If you show partiality, you commit sin, and are convicted by the law as transgressors." The Bible calls discrimination a sin. God is as serious about the sin of partiality and prejudice as He is the sin of perversion and promiscuity. So if we are guilty of discrimination, we should deal with it like we deal with every other sin: Confess it and forsake it.

James commanded us to abide by Jesus' command: "Love the Lord your God with all your heart, with all your soul, and with all your mind. . . . Love your neighbor as yourself" (Matthew 22:37, 39). This great commandment is called the *royal law* not only because it is given to us by the King of kings but also because it is the law that governs citizens of His kingdom.

What sort of discrimination have you suffered, and how did it make you feel?

FEBRUARY 17

The First Step Forward Is Repentance

Repent therefore and be converted, that your sins may be blotted out, so that times of refreshing may come from the presence of the Lord.
ACTS 3:19

There is always hope for anyone who will admit to being the offending party in a relationship. When we do, we're in good company. Moses, the highly revered emancipator of the Jewish people, was a murderer. But after forty years on the back side of a desert, he went back and delivered a nation. King David stole the affections of another man's wife, got her pregnant, and even orchestrated her husband's demise and death. But later, plagued with remorse and repentance, he discovered the way forward was back (Psalm 51). Simon Peter, the fisherman, did what he insisted he would never do. He denied he ever knew the Christ. But he, too, discovered the life-changing principle that the way forward is back. He went back, met Christ on the seashore in genuine repentance, and then did he ever go forward. Just read of his exploits in the book of Acts. When we go back, God forgives. And then we can move forward to our greatest days.

Do you need to repent in order to move forward? Why not do it now?

FEBRUARY 18

"I AM"

And God said to Moses, "I AM WHO I AM." And He said, "Thus you shall say to the children of Israel, 'I AM has sent me to you.'"
EXODUS 3:14

Note that God instructed Moses to tell the captive children of Israel in Egypt that "I AM has sent me to you" (Exodus 3:14). When Jesus said, "I am," all those within the sound of His voice recognized this as an affirmation of His deity, that He was not a mere man; He was God Himself, clothed in a garment of human flesh. His "I am" declarations are recorded eight times in John's gospel (6:35; 8:12; 10:7, 11, 14; 11:25; 14:6; 15:1).

The most fundamental element of the Christian faith is that Jesus was not just some astute teacher or another one of the prophets; He was God incarnate. It was at this very point that the apostle Paul said, "He is the image of the invisible God. . . . All things were created through Him and for Him" (Colossians 1:15–16). It was this deep assurance and steadfast holding to this promise that would later lead Paul—and most all the disciples—to a martyr's death. They all insisted, "Jesus is Lord!"

As a believer, what does it mean to you that Jesus is God in human form?

FEBRUARY 19

Pray with a Sincere Heart

Take heed that you do not do your charitable deeds before men, to be seen by them. Otherwise you have no reward from your Father in heaven.

MATTHEW 6:1

In today's scripture, our Lord introduces the Sermon on the Mount with a stern warning. Pride and vanity are two of the greatest hindrances to God-honoring prayers. The prayers God honors are those that emerge from a sincere heart with pure motives.

Public prayers bring with them a temptation to fall into this trap. Most of us can recall hearing someone pray in public with a tone that is entirely different from their normal speech pattern. But private prayers are also susceptible to this temptation to allow pride to find its way into our prayers. For some it is difficult to fast or pray through the night without eventually telling someone about it. God invites us into His throne room of prayer, and at no time in our Christian life should we approach a matter with more sincerity of heart than when we are in sweet fellowship with Him alone. He honors sincere prayers from the heart.

When have you prayed prayers to impress people instead of sincere prayers to God alone?

FEBRUARY 20

Our Creator God

He is the image of the invisible God, the firstborn over all creation. For by Him all things were created. . . . All things were created through Him and for Him. And He is before all things, and in Him all things consist.

COLOSSIANS 1:15–17

Jesus did not just appear on the scene in Bethlehem. He has been here all along. We even find Him in the creation story. In Genesis 1:1 the Hebrew word for "God" is *Elohim* and is in the plural form, hinting that God is really three persons in one: Father, Son, and Holy Spirit.

But this was not the beginning of everything: "In the beginning was the Word" (John 1:1), and the Word is Jesus. Jesus was there in creation and is the Creator God Himself. There is a huge difference between creating something and making something. Many of us have *made* things, but none of us have ever *created* something out of nothing.

Jesus is not only our Creator; He is our sustainer. He continues to hold all things together or everything would virtually disintegrate. The true purpose and meaning in life is found only in Jesus, our Creator.

How does this explanation of Jesus' role in creation expand your view and worship of your Savior?

FEBRUARY 21

A Song in Our Heart

Oh, sing to the Lord *a new song! Sing to the* Lord, *all the earth.*
PSALM 96:1

The *inward* evidence that you are being filled with God's Spirit is "singing and making melody in your heart to the Lord" (Ephesians 5:19). This is what separates Christianity from other religions. When we are filled with God's Spirit, the first evidence is an inward joy, a song in our hearts. People of other faiths may have impressive temples and mosques, mantras and chants, but they have no song in their hearts.

Note it is "melody" and not rhythm or harmony that is the evidence of the Spirit. Rhythm appeals to the flesh. Harmony appeals to the realm of our emotions. But melody? It appeals to the Spirit, that part of us that will live as long as God lives, which is forever.

You will know you are being filled with God's Spirit when you have a joyous song of melody unto the Lord welling up within you.

What joyous melody is welling up in you right now as you reflect on being filled with the Holy Spirit?

Two-Way Communication

If you abide in Me, and My words abide in you, you will ask what you desire, and it shall be done for you.
JOHN 15:7

Prayer is two-way communication. It is not one-sided. To have a positive and productive relationship with the people in our lives, there must be verbal communication. Yet some believers think they can go days or weeks without communicating with God in prayer and still lead effective and fruitful Christian lives.

Prayer is the talking part of our personal relationship with the Lord. And, just think about it . . . He initiates it. He invites you to "call to Me" (Jeremiah 33:3).

And when we make this call to Him, we have His promise—"I will answer you!" No ifs, ands, or buts. No voicemail. No being put on hold. He picks up every single time you place a call.

The Lord knows far better than we do the deepest needs of our hearts. It is prayer that makes God real to us. Just as reading our Bible gives direction to our prayers, our prayers bring a new dynamic to our Bible reading. God speaks to us through His Word, and we speak to Him through prayer.

How would you assess your communication with God?

FEBRUARY 23

A Destructive Fire

And the tongue is a fire, a world of iniquity. The tongue is so set among our members that it defiles the whole body, and sets on fire the course of nature; and it is set on fire by hell.

JAMES 3:6

James reminds us that the tongue is destructive like fire or poison. Behind every spoken word of divisiveness or filth or rumor or anger is Satan himself. This enemy delights in using uncontrolled tongues to destroy hearts, homes, and hopes.

Uncontrolled fire can destroy, but fire itself isn't bad. When controlled, it is beneficial. In the same way, we can use our words to bless or to blast, to direct or to destroy. We've all had times when we wished we hadn't said something, and then watched the little spark result in a raging fire we couldn't control.

We may find ourselves gossiping (saying behind someone's back what you would never say to his or her face) or flattering (saying to someone's face what you would never say behind his or her back). And both are wrong. So let's join David in asking God to "set a guard . . . over [our] mouth [and] keep watch over the door of [our] lips" (Psalm 141:3).

When have you experienced the destructive power of someone's tongue?

Jesus Is Open

Therefore receive one another, just as Christ
also received us, to the glory of God.
ROMANS 15:7

We all know what it is like to attempt to build a relationship with someone who was not open to us. We could never seem to penetrate their facade. They left us feeling shut out of some of the deeper parts of their lives. They simply would not commit to deeper relationship with us. They could not seem to take even the first step of openness. Thankfully, Jesus is not that way.

In fact, openness is what made Him so winsome and warm in His interpersonal relationships with others. He was transparent. He had no hidden agenda. He traveled daily with His friends. He ate with them. He prayed with them. He wept with them on occasion. He was a people person. He got involved in their personal struggles. He allowed people to look into His heart and get to know Him. He told others of His own needs. And though it was risky, for some did reject Him, many others were drawn to this One who extended a bridge of openness to them.

How have you experienced Jesus' openness toward you?

FEBRUARY 25

The Second Coming

For the Lord Himself will descend from heaven with a shout, with the voice of an archangel, and with the trumpet of God. And the dead in Christ will rise first. Then we who are alive and remain shall be caught up together with them in the clouds to meet the Lord in the air. And thus we shall always be with the Lord. Therefore comfort one another with these words.

1 THESSALONIANS 4:16–18

Today we think about our soon-coming King. In Thessalonians, Paul drove four strong stakes into the ground of revelation regarding His coming. First, Christ Himself will descend from heaven, just as He promised in the upper room (John 14:3) and as the angel promised at His ascension (Acts 1:11). Second, Jesus will return with a loud shout and with the voice of an archangel and with the trumpet of God blasting forth. Next, all those who have died in Christ will rise first from their graves to meet Him in the air. Finally, those of us who are alive at this great event will be miraculously changed and caught up with them in the air to meet the Lord and be ushered away into the endless ages of eternity.

So what are we to do in anticipation of the return of the Lord Jesus Christ? We are to wait, watch, and work.

How are you waiting, watching, and working as you anticipate Christ's return?

FEBRUARY 26

Seeking God's Will

Teach me to do Your will, for You are my God; Your Spirit is good. Lead me in the land of uprightness.
PSALM 143:10

We know that praying according to God's will is the key to effective prayer. But what about those matters for which you are praying but are uncertain of God's will? You are to "seek, and you will find" (Matthew 7:7). When you don't know His will, seek it until you find it. This is a mature level of prayer because it puts self aside and is motivated by a deep desire to want to know the will of God in a matter. It involves an intense search for the heart of God coupled with a regular pattern of Bible reading. This is why the apostle Paul admonished us to "let the word of Christ dwell in you richly in all wisdom" (Colossians 3:16). We most often find God's will through His Word.

We are to keep seeking with an intensity that goes far beyond our simply asking and receiving. God does not veil His will from us. In fact, He is more interested in our finding His will for our lives than we are.

Why is seeking God's will a mature level of prayer?

FEBRUARY 27

Our Personal Prayer Partner

The Spirit also helps in our weaknesses. For we do not know what we should pray for as we ought, but the Spirit Himself makes intercession for us. . . . He makes intercession for the saints according to the will of God.
ROMANS 8:26–27

Would you like to have a confidential prayer partner you totally trust and with whom you could share your deepest prayer needs? You already do—the Holy Spirit.

I don't always know how to pray about a matter. But the Holy Spirit in me does, and He always prays "according to the will of God." The word Paul used to describe how the Spirit helps us means literally to "lend a helping hand." Picture two people carrying a log, one on either end, each dependent upon the other to hold up his end. The same Greek word appears in Luke 10:40, when Martha appeals to Jesus to get her sister, Mary, to help her in the kitchen. In the same way, we need the Holy Spirit to lend us a helping hand with our prayers.

There is a powerful synergy at play when we recognize we have a personal prayer partner in the Holy Spirit—One who is not just by our side and on our side, but alive inside us.

Why is it encouraging to know that the Holy Spirit is your personal prayer partner?

FEBRUARY 28

WHAT KIND OF FRIEND ARE YOU?

This is My commandment, that you love one another as I have loved you.
JOHN 15:12

Ask yourself these questions today: Are you a committed and loyal friend? Are you open with others in your inner circle, or do you too often keep your guard up? Do you build barriers with others, or do you build bridges? Do you sense an obligation to anyone? Have you stood up for anyone recently? Are you objective, or are you too quick to forget the investment others have made in your life? Are you slow to reciprocate? Do others see you as optimistic?

Building positive and productive relationships with others goes back to making sure we are firmly connected to Jesus through personal relationship with Him. Jesus has made a commitment to you. He died on the cross to relate to you. He is open. He always builds bridges, never barriers. He defends you and will be your advocate before the Father in the coming day of judgment. He is objective, no respecter of persons. And in His optimism, He brings out the best in us.

What kind of friend are you to the people in your life?

FEBRUARY 29

Jesus Offers Us Himself

Come to Me, all you who labor and are heavy laden, and I will give you rest. Take My yoke upon you and learn from Me, for I am gentle and lowly in heart, and you will find rest for your souls.

MATTHEW 11:28–29

Jesus' invitation in Matthew 11:28 is simple: "Come to Me." He simply offered us Himself. A little child learning to walk can understand this word, *come*. Christ called us to come not to some plan, program, principle, or procedure but to a Person. "Come to Me." Note all the personal pronouns in this promise. Five times in these short verses He referred to Himself—Me, I, My, Me, I.

How can we find rest for our souls? Come to Jesus. He is the only One who understands, because there is nothing about our journey He hasn't already experienced. No matter my need, I can come to Jesus. When I am in sorrow, I can come to the One who was Himself "a Man of sorrows and acquainted with grief" (Isaiah 53:3). His promise to give us rest is a simple one. Anyone can do it. "Come to Me." Come to Jesus.

In what ways or from what situations does your soul need rest? In the midst of the pressures you face, do you know that Jesus is the only person who can give you rest?

MARCH

MARCH 1

Fellow Soldiers

Yet I considered it necessary to send to you Epaphroditus, my brother, fellow worker, and fellow soldier, but your messenger and the one who ministered to my need.
PHILIPPIANS 2:25

This passage in Philippians is one of two times where Paul adds an element to describe an external connection. Paul considered Epaphroditus his "brother, fellow worker, and fellow soldier." He also referred to Archippus as a "fellow soldier" in Philemon verse 2. In Greek, this is an expressive term that carries with it the idea of being a fellow combatant, a comrade in arms, one who faces the same dangers and fights in the same foxhole as another in the same conflict.

As believers, we are all members of the same regiment. Some of us do not see ourselves in the same struggles, looking toward the same victories as others. There seem to be a lot of one-person armies in the marketplace today. Too often in our world, when someone gets wounded in the battle, it is his so-called friends who finish him off with criticism, gossip, or judgment. People in longtime relationships are not only family and friends but "fellow soldiers" in the daily fight.

Who are the fellow soldiers in your life?

MARCH 2

We Live by Bible Promises

His flesh was restored like the flesh of a little child, and he was clean.
2 KINGS 5:14

In the kingdom of God we do not live by explanations; we live by promises. Naaman, the commander of the king's armies of Syria, contracted leprosy and tried every possible cure, to no avail. In a desperate, last-ditch attempt, he approached the prophet Elisha. This man of God instructed him to immerse himself seven times in the Jordan River with the promise that he would then be cured.

Infuriated by what he considered an absurdity, Naaman got back in his chariot and sped away. However, his servant pointed out that he had nothing to lose. So the proud conqueror approached the Jordan River, took off his royal robes, and submerged himself seven times. When he emerged after the seventh dip, he was clean. Naaman obeyed the promise and found his cure. Like some of us, he almost missed the opportunity for healing because he was looking for an explanation—when God had given him a promise. In God's kingdom we do not live by explanations; we live by Bible promises.

Among God's many promises in the Bible,
which ones mean the most to you?

MARCH 3

Change Your Mind

From that time Jesus began to preach and to say,
"Repent, for the kingdom of heaven is at hand."
MATTHEW 4:17

Repentance has become one of the forgotten words in our English vocabulary. Yet it was the message of all the prophets. It was the message John the Baptist preached in the Jordan Valley. It was the message of Jesus as He commenced His ministry with the words of today's scripture. It was the message that birthed the church at Pentecost and the message of all the apostles.

Repentance is not remorse, being sorry for our sin. The rich young ruler went away "sorrowful" but didn't repent (Matthew 19:16–22). It is not simply regret, wishing that some moment could be lived over again. Pilate washed his hands, regretting his evil deed, but he didn't repent (Matthew 27:24). Repentance is not reform, trying to turn over a new leaf. Judas reformed by returning the silver coins but didn't repent (Matthew 27:3).

Repentance means "to change one's mind," which results in a change of will, which in turn results in a change of action. This is the evidence of repentance.

What is the danger of mistaking remorse, regret, or reform for true repentance?

MARCH 4

Retrace Your Steps

So the man of God said, "Where did it fall?" And he showed him the place. So he cut off a stick, and threw it in there; and he made the iron float.

2 KINGS 6:6

When Elisha came upon the scene where one of the prophets had dropped an ax-head in water, his first words were, "Where did it fall?" The young man "showed him the place." After all, the place to start looking for something is the place where we last had it!

If you have lost the cutting edge in life, the first step to getting it back is to admit it. You must then go back to the place where you lost it. Did you lose your cutting edge when your busy schedule squeezed out your morning quiet time? Or when the Bible you once opened each night remained closed on your nightstand? Perhaps you lost your cutting edge when you judged another person or when bitterness took root in your heart. Or maybe you lost that ax-head in the waters of worldliness or the pools of pride. The place to recover the cutting edge is to go back to the place where you last had it.

Where did you lose your cutting edge,
and how can you recover it?

MARCH 5

The Mediator Between God and People

For there is one God and one mediator between God and mankind, the man Christ Jesus.
1 TIMOTHY 2:5 NIV

Of the many names for Jesus in the Bible, one we should hold close is Mediator. On almost every page of the Gospels, we find Jesus mediating conflicts. In Mark's gospel alone, we find others in conflict with Him twenty-six times. There was conflict in His hometown. There was conflict with His family. There was conflict with the religious Pharisees. There was conflict with His best friends. Conflict seemed to swirl around Jesus everywhere He went. And in every instance, He attempted to mediate those conflicts and reconcile others to God.

Consider humanity's relationship with God. We were in conflict with Him, with His purpose and plan for our lives. We had a good start in a perfect paradise. But we chose to go our own way and do our own thing. All of us "have sinned and fall short of the glory of God" (Romans 3:23). Then Jesus came, our personal Mediator, to resolve our conflict and bring us into a restored relationship with the Father.

How can Jesus' role as a mediator help you deal with conflicts in your life?

MARCH 6

Count It All Joy

My brethren, count it all joy when you fall into various trials.
JAMES 1:2

When James wrote "count it all joy," he wrote in a tense that indicates exactly when we are to do the counting: when the trial is in the rearview mirror. James wasn't saying the trial itself should be considered a joy. The word *consider* (sometimes translated *count*) literally means "to think ahead, to think forward." This is exactly what Job was doing when he said, "When [God] has tested me, I shall come forth as gold" (Job 23:10). Job did not consider his losses to be joyful, but he looked forward to the joy he knew would follow his trial.

Our Lord Himself looked beyond His painful circumstances and intense suffering. Hebrews 12:2 says that "for the joy that was set before Him [He] endured the cross, despising the shame, and has sat down at the right hand of the throne of God."

James was not telling us to try to find some kind of superficial joy during life's trials, but to look beyond them, for "joy comes in the morning" (Psalm 30:5).

Looking back on the trials you've endured,
which ones can you now count as joy?

MARCH 7

PRAYING IN THE SPIRIT

But you, beloved, building yourselves up on your most holy faith, praying in the Holy Spirit.
JUDE V. 20

Effective, powerful prayer is "by one Spirit." If the Father is the source and the Son is the course, then the Spirit is the force behind it all. It is the Holy Spirit praying in us and through us that empowers us to pray with results. Jude reminds us that we are built up in our most holy faith when we are "praying in the Holy Spirit."

It is the Holy Spirit who "helps in our weaknesses. For we do not know what we should pray for as we ought" (Romans 8:26). We can read the great prayers of saints down through the ages. We can recite prayers by rote from memory. But without the Holy Spirit we will never be effective in our prayer journey. It is only through Christ and "by one Spirit" that we can touch the Father in prayer.

Access to the Father is the goal of all prayer. He is the source. We must go through His Son and be empowered by His Spirit.

When have you noticed a supernatural quality to your prayers, and what was the result?

MARCH 8

Sensitivity and Submission

Yet for love's sake I rather appeal to you—being such a one as Paul, the aged, and now also a prisoner of Jesus Christ.
PHILEMON V. 9

A submissive spirit and attitude are indispensable to all worthwhile relationships. Love always seeks the other person's highest good. Love is always equated with action in the Bible. In Philemon verse 9, Paul could have exerted his apostolic authority or appealed on the basis of his elder statesmanship, directing his friend Philemon in the process or restoring his relationship with Onesimus, but he was sensitive and submissive enough to choose the path of love. He was also wise enough to know that lasting relationships are never built on competition—the win-lose approach—but on the basis of love, resulting in a solution where everyone involved can claim victory.

Paul wrote to Philemon in Greek and chose a strong word that we translate into the English word *appeal*. Appearing more than a hundred times in the New Testament, it is often translated as "plead," "strongly urge," or "encourage." He was sensitive to the situation and submissive in his approach to bring reconciliation to the relationship between Philemon and Onesimus.

In what situation in your life do you wish someone had demonstrated sensitivity and submission?

MARCH 9

Don't Stop the Flow

Stephen, full of faith and power, did great wonders and signs among the people.
ACTS 6:8

One of my favorite songs as a young Christian was "Fill My Cup, Lord." But the more I got to know the Holy Spirit as a person, the more I realized that my relationship with Him was more like a garden hose that continued to fill me and flow through me to bless others rather than a cup filled for my own benefit.

One example of being filled in this manner is Stephen, one of the early church's first deacons. He was "a man full of faith and the Holy Spirit" (Acts 6:5). When he was on trial, the people "saw his face as the face of an angel" (v. 15). As he was being stoned to death, "being full of the Holy Spirit, [he] gazed into heaven and saw the glory of God, and Jesus standing at the right hand of God" (Acts 7:55).

It is one thing to have the Holy Spirit *in us* and another for Him to have us so He might fill us and flow *through us.*

When you think of the Holy Spirit's power flowing through you to help others, who comes to mind, and how might you help them?

MARCH 10

PRAY IN SECRET

When you pray, go into your room, and when you have shut your door, pray to your Father who is in the secret place; and your Father who sees in secret will reward you openly.

MATTHEW 6:6

There is something about keeping our prayer life between us and God alone that He seems to honor. Jesus says to keep ourselves from the temptation to be "seen by men" when we pray.

The public life of any Spirit-filled believer rests on the private life, the hidden life. There are so many object lessons revealing this truth. The beautiful high-rise office structures emerging from our city centers stand tall and firm because of their hidden life. Deep below the surface is a foundation of concrete and steel that has been dug deep into the bedrock, enabling great buildings to glisten in the sun due to the hidden life of a solid foundation. The same is true of fruit trees from which we enjoy apples and peaches. These juicy delicacies are made possible due to the hidden life of the tree, the roots that dig deep into the earth until they find a water source through which their public life thrives. So it is with us. God honors not only sincere prayers but also secret prayers.

How is your private prayer life with God evident in your public life?

MARCH 11

A Personal God

My sheep hear My voice, and I know them, and they follow Me. And I give them eternal life, and they shall never perish; neither shall anyone snatch them out of My hand.

JOHN 10:27–28

How wonderful it is for us to know that our God is personal. We can know Him personally and intimately. When David wrote Psalm 23:1, he didn't write, "The Lord is *a* shepherd." No! Look closely. "The LORD is *my* shepherd." That little two-letter, one-syllable possessive pronoun, *my*, makes a huge difference to life's circumstances and situations. We may get word that someone's little child is deathly sick, and we have compassion and feel sorrow. But what a difference it would make if it were *my* child. This is not just any shepherd. This is personal. This is *my* Shepherd.

The awesome discovery that the God of this universe and of all created order is concerned about me personally gives purpose and meaning to my short sojourn on this speck of a planet in His vast expanse. Unfortunately, however, not everyone can say this and claim the promise of today's scripture. Christ's sheep know His voice, and they follow Him. He is personal. He is your God, and you can say with confidence, "He is *my* Shepherd."

How have you experienced God as your personal Shepherd?

MARCH 12

God Delights in Forgiving Sin

Who is a God like you, who pardons sin and forgives the transgression of the remnant of his inheritance? You do not stay angry forever but delight to show mercy.

MICAH 7:18 NIV

God delights in forgiving our sin. In fact, God delights more in healing our hearts and our homes than we do ourselves, for it appropriates His sacrifice on the cross and does not render His death in vain in our concerns. He is willing, waiting, and longing to be faithful to His promise when we come to Him on His conditions.

If my daughter and I had a misunderstanding or she had done something to break our fellowship, my heart would long for restoration. If she came to me in brokenness and humility, asked for forgiveness, and looked lovingly into my face, how do you think I would respond? Of course I would forgive and welcome her into my open arms with an open heart. How much more will your heavenly Father respond to you in such a way?

Have you ever considered the fact that God delights to forgive sin? Does understanding this truth about Him change the way you think about Him?

MARCH 13

The Seriousness of Sin

For whoever shall keep the whole law, and yet stumble in one point, he is guilty of all.
JAMES 2:10

Let these words sink in. Without the mercy of God and the grace of the Lord Jesus Christ, one sin—no matter how small it may seem—is enough to condemn a person. Only we rank sins' severity.

This should put to rest the idea that any of us can get to heaven on the basis of good works, a solid reputation, or our relative morality. Some think they can stand before the Judge of the universe and appeal to Him on the basis of the sins they have not committed. That will go about as far as standing before a judge with a speeding ticket pleading for leniency because you have never robbed a bank or committed murder.

To be a lawbreaker, one does not have to break all the laws—only one. But followers of Jesus are saved by God's grace (Ephesians 2:8). So what is our relationship to the law? The law is our tutor, our teacher, to show us how futile it is to think we could get to heaven through our good works.

Why do you think it's so appealing for some people to try to be justified by their good works rather than accept Christ's gracious offer of forgiveness?

MARCH 14

The Promised Helper

I will pray the Father, and He will give you another Helper, that He may abide with you forever—the Spirit of truth.
JOHN 14:16–17

The key to understanding the true identity of the Holy Spirit in Jesus' promise to His disciples and to us is wrapped up in the word *another.* There are two Greek words translated into our English word *another.* One, *heteros*, means "another," but of a different kind. The other word, *allos*, means "another" of the exact same kind. For example, if I showed you a fountain pen and then showed you another pen—a cheap plastic pen—it would mean "another," but of a different kind. However, if I showed you a black Mont Blanc pen and then another one identical to it, then it would mean "another" of the exact same kind.

The latter is the word Jesus used in describing this Helper to come. Jesus was saying, "I am leaving, but I am coming back to abide in you forever. The Holy Spirit is *Me, the same make and model*!" Jesus kept His promise, and His Spirit comes to live in us and never leaves us.

How would you describe your relationship with the Holy Spirit?

MARCH 15

You May Be the Key to Reconciliation

You meant evil against me; but God meant it for good.
GENESIS 50:20

The rift between Joseph and his brothers had lasted for several years (Genesis 37–50), but his brothers were ultimately filled with repentance. How would he respond to them after all that time?

Joseph was always looking beyond his trials. When revealing his identity to his brothers, he said, "You meant evil against me; but God meant it for good, in order to bring it about as it is this day" (50:20). Did Joseph "count it all joy" to be abandoned and sold by his own brothers? Of course not. But Joseph trusted in the Lord. He knew God's hand was in his circumstances, and he was thinking ahead to a better day.

From the human standpoint, most of what had happened to Joseph was bad. Now he, like all those who have been offended, found himself as the key to reconciliation. If he did not do his part, no matter how repentant his brothers were, it would be to no avail. When he finally revealed himself to his brothers, he spoke these words: "Do not therefore be grieved or angry with yourselves because you sold me here; for God sent me before you to preserve life" (45:5). God was in it all—and for a purpose. He meant it for good, and Joseph saw His hand behind it all.

In what situation might you be the key to reconciliation?

MARCH 16

Do You Believe?

I am the resurrection and the life. He who believes in Me, though he may die, he shall live. And whoever lives and believes in Me shall never die.
JOHN 11:25–26

At the conclusion of the eternal promise found in today's scripture, the Lord paused and asked a question of those around Him. In fact, it is life's bottom-line question, "Do you believe this?" I wonder where Jesus put His inflection in this question. Did He ask, "Do *you* believe this?" After all, the question is intensely personal. Or perhaps He asked, "Do you *believe* this?" It is a very pointed question, centered in where our faith and trust are placed. His interest is not in whether we give intellectual assent to His claims, but have we placed our faith in Him and in Him alone? Perhaps He asked the question in this manner: "Do you believe *this*?" That is, this promise of victory over death.

You are the only one who can answer this bottom-line question for yourself. Thankfully, I addressed this question long ago by placing my trust in Christ and declaring, "Yes, Lord, I believe that You are the Christ, the Son of the living God!" How about you? Do you believe this?

Do you believe Jesus is the Son of God and that those who believe in Him will never die?

A Symphony of Prayer

If you ask anything in My name, I will do it.
JOHN 14:14

Prayer is like a symphony. The Bible is the score. The Holy Spirit is the conductor. You and I are the instruments. As we immerse ourselves in God's Word, the Holy Spirit directs and leads us in our prayer lives.

Jesus is always our example. This includes our time alone in prayer with our heavenly Father. If He who never sinned realized the need to pray so often, how much more do we, sinful as we are, need to call on Him and rest in His promise that He will answer our prayers? Jeremiah 33:3 is one of hundreds of prayer promises we find in the Bible.

But there is more. God says in Jeremiah 33:3, "Call to Me, and I will answer you, and show you great and mighty things, which you do not know." He will not just answer your prayers in some nebulous way. He is waiting and willing to *show* you "great and mighty things."

What "great and mighty things, which you do not know," are you asking God to show you?

MARCH 18

A Bitter Spring

Out of the same mouth proceed blessing and cursing. My brethren, these things ought not to be so. Does a spring send forth fresh water and bitter from the same opening? Can a fig tree, my brethren, bear olives, or a grapevine bear figs? Thus no spring yields both salt water and fresh.
JAMES 3:10–12

When our words are contentious, they can destroy relationships built over decades or give someone a crippling burden of pain for a lifetime. James also addressed those words that are contradictory and can deceive not only others but ourselves as well. This kind of person has been called by some a person who spoke with a "forked tongue." This person said one thing at one time and in one place and the opposite thing at another time and in another place.

Our tongues speak words that spring from our inner nature, revealing who we really are deep inside. Just as it is impossible for salt water and sweet water to come from the same source and for olives to grow on a fig tree, it is impossible for our tongues to produce what is not in our hearts. If we bless and curse at the same time, something in our heart is desperately out of order. Evil speech emanates from an evil heart. A heart that truly loves God doesn't fuel lies, slander, gossip, curses, or the like.

When have you experienced someone speaking to you with a "forked tongue," and how did it make you feel?

MARCH 19

Is It Time to Take a Risk?

Now there were four leprous men at the entrance of the gate; and they said to one another, "Why are we sitting here until we die?"
2 KINGS 7:3

Four lepers were sitting at the city gate of Samaria asking the question posed in today's scripture. This got me thinking about how much sitting we Christians do—in church services, committee meetings, or Bible studies.

There are two senses that should characterize every believer: common sense and uncommon sense. We need both to be effective. But some of us exhibit only uncommon sense, or faith, meaning we become so otherworldly that we no longer connect with reality. This perversion of faith keeps us less involved in the world and ultimately confuses true faith with wishful thinking.

Then, there are people who use only common sense or logic, becoming so practical in their approach to life and ministry that there is little spiritual dynamic involved.

Are you watching the disintegration of your own hopes and dreams—and just sitting there letting it happen? Uncommon sense—faith in God—is important. But common sense is important too. Is it time to be realistic? Is it time to take a risk?

Where are you sitting back in your hopes and dreams?

MARCH 20

The Final Word

God, who at various times and in various ways spoke in time past to the fathers by the prophets, has in these last days spoken to us by His Son.

HEBREWS 1:1–2

God spoke to us in "various times" throughout Scripture. He revealed to Adam that Christ was coming to crush the Serpent's head (Genesis 3:15), to Abraham that Christ would come through a nation He would birth (12:1–3), and to Jacob that Christ would come through the tribe of Judah (49:10). He revealed to David that Christ would be crucified and pierced but would rise again (Psalm 16, 22). Furthermore, He revealed to Isaiah that Christ would be wounded for our transgressions (Isaiah 53:5) and to Zechariah that Christ would be betrayed for thirty pieces of silver (Zechariah 11:12–13).

God also spoke "in various ways." He spoke at Mount Horeb to Moses through a burning bush (Exodus 3:1–6) and at Mount Sinai through thunder and lightning (19:16–20). He spoke to the prophet Elijah through a still small voice (1 Kings 19:11–13) and to Jacob through an angel (Genesis 32:22–30). Today He has spoken to us "by His Son." Jesus is the final word. Period.

When you think of the Bible's fulfilled prophecies, how does it encourage you that everything God promises will come to pass?

The Ultimate Sacrifice

For He made Him who knew no sin to be sin for us, that we might become the righteousness of God in Him.
2 CORINTHIANS 5:21

For three hours total darkness enveloped the earth as Jesus hung on the cross. From the darkness came the piercing cry of the most haunting of all Christ's words from the cross: "My God, My God, why have You forsaken Me?" (Matthew 27:46). This question has perplexed the minds of believers for centuries. Did a loving Father forsake His only Son in His greatest moment of need? No! Then why this strange cry escaping the bleeding lips of our Lord?

The prophet Habakkuk reminds us that God the Father is so holy He cannot look upon sin (Habakkuk 1:13). On the cross Jesus took our iniquity, or sin, in His own body, suffering our shame, humiliation, agony, and death, all consequences we deserved. And for that period of time, the Father turned His face away, darkness enveloped the earth, and Jesus fought and won the battle of sin in our place. No wonder the Bible says, "Thanks be unto God for his unspeakable gift" (2 Corinthians 9:15 KJV).

How does knowing that Jesus understands what it's like to feel separated from God comfort you?

MARCH 22

God's Abundant Pardon

Let the wicked forsake his way, and the unrighteous man his thoughts; let him return to the Lord, and He will have mercy on him; and to our God, for He will abundantly pardon.

ISAIAH 55:7

In civic life, a pardon exempts someone from punishment for a crime they have committed. It rests solely on an executive decision and is not subject to any judicial review. The Creator of the universe has broad pardon powers, but pardons are not granted to everyone. They are available to those of us who "seek" Him, "call" to Him, and "return" to Him.

Our God does not simply promise to pardon us but to "abundantly" pardon. He goes above and beyond a pardon to justify those whom He pardons. Romans 8:30 says that those "whom He called, these He also justified." This is something altogether different from a pardon and is wrapped up in the thought of His promise to not only pardon us but to do so abundantly. No court of law can justify someone's offense. A court may acquit someone, or even pardon someone, but it cannot justify someone. They cannot make the particular offense as if it never happened. But God can—and God does.

When have you experienced God's abundant pardon?

MARCH 23

The Promise of a Successful Life

This Book of the Law shall not depart from your mouth, but you shall meditate in it day and night, that you may observe to do according to all that is written in it. For then you will make your way prosperous, and then you will have good success.

JOSHUA 1:8

The word *success* is viewed in a contradictory sense by many in the Christian world today. For some it carries with it the idea of accumulated possessions or aspiring positions. But in God's economy, He desires for His followers to be successful in the purest sense of the word, which is to find the will of God for your life and then to do it. His will for Joshua was for him to have "good success." Nehemiah returned from Babylonian captivity to rebuild the broken walls of Jerusalem with this promise: "The God of heaven will give us success" (Nehemiah 2:20 NIV). It is said of Joseph, "The LORD was with Joseph, and he was a successful man" (Genesis 39:2). The Lord does not define success as the world does. Success is conditional on two emphases related to His Word. Successful people, in God's eyes, are those who *read it* and those who *heed it.*

What is your definition of success, and how does it compare to God's?

MARCH 24

God's Presence and Power

And when they had prayed, the place where they were assembled together was shaken; and they were all filled with the Holy Spirit, and they spoke the word of God with boldness.

ACTS 4:31

The early church faced their difficulties not with protests or politics but with prayer that resulted in powerful living. The place where they had gathered was "shaken." They knew God was in their midst! Note the order of the prayer and the shaking. Only when they had prayed did the place shake. They didn't begin to pray when the place was shaken.

Maybe we do not sense God's presence because we wait until something around us is shaken before we begin to pray. It is possible to become so involved in doing good things that we lose the sense that God is near. But when we pray as the early believers prayed, it becomes atmospheric. God's power in our lives comes through prayer.

Much of what happens in our churches today can be explained with human plans and programs. But our greatest need is power. And power comes only through prayer.

When have you felt the power of God's presence when praying?

MARCH 25

Our Divine Healer

Is anyone among you sick? Let him call for the elders of the church, and let them pray over him, anointing him with oil in the name of the Lord. And the prayer of faith will save the sick, and the Lord will raise him up. And if he has committed sins, he will be forgiven.

JAMES 5:14–15

In Greek, the word translated as *sick* here means "without strength" or "to be weak." This includes sickness in spirit, soul, or body. The sick are to call the elders to pray for them and anoint them "with oil in the name of the Lord." When we pray, we must believe, asking "in faith, with no doubting" (James 1:6). This prayer is always offered with two things: God's Word and God's will.

There are two Greek words for *anoint*. One refers to an outward anointing, a "rubbing down with oil," found in the story of the Good Samaritan who bandaged up a wounded stranger. The other refers to a ceremonial anointing, as when the Spirit "anointed" Jesus to preach the gospel (Luke 4:18).

We should use the best medicine known to us and support the efforts of the medical community while still giving priority to the prayer of faith. All healing is divine. Medicinc, proper diet, and exercise alone don't heal. Jesus heals! Are you sick? Seek prayer and anointing in Jesus' name.

In what ways do you see Jesus healing people today?

MARCH 26

How to Appropriate God's Riches

You have lived on the earth in pleasure and luxury; you have fattened your hearts as in a day of slaughter.
JAMES 5:5

God owns all the wealth in the world; He wants it in circulation, and it will one day belong to us, who are joint heirs with Christ. The way we are to appropriate God's riches is to give, and that is very countercultural. We live in a world where accumulation is the name of the game. But one day we will answer for what we did with what God gave us along this life journey.

The fundamental danger of accumulated wealth is that it has a way of keeping our focus on this world. Too often, once we begin to possess wealth, it has a devious way of beginning to possess us. We must get our money honestly, guard it loosely, and give it generously to Christ's causes.

The Bible says, "Do not be deceived, God is not mocked; for whatever a man sows, that he will also reap" (Galatians 6:7).

If someone examined your bank accounts, what would they reveal about your heart?

MARCH 27

BEHOLD THE LAMB

But if we walk in the light as He is in the light, we have fellowship with one another, and the blood of Jesus Christ His Son cleanses us from all sin.

1 JOHN 1:7

We find a poignant picture of our coming Savior in Exodus 12 when the Passover celebration was instituted to commemorate the Israelites' freedom from death and deliverance from Egyptian bondage. God had sent a series of plagues on Egypt, where His people were enslaved. The most devastating plague came on the night the death angel passed over every home in Egypt, bringing death to the firstborn of every family.

The Jews were instructed to take a little lamb—perfect and without blemish—slay it, and spread its blood over the doorposts of their homes so that when the death angel came, he would "see the blood" and "pass over" that particular residence (Exodus 12:13). The firstborn in those homes would be saved by the blood of the sacrificed lamb.

It is no wonder that fifteen hundred years later, when Jesus appeared in the Jordan Valley, John the Baptist pointed in His direction and shouted, "Behold! The Lamb of God who takes away the sin of the world!" (John 1:29).

What does it mean to you to have a personal relationship with the Lamb of God?

The Wisdom of Preventive Medicine

How much better to get wisdom than gold! And to get understanding is to be chosen rather than silver.
PROVERBS 16:16

Every year I have an annual physical. My physician makes certain everything is in proper working order and seeks to detect any abnormalities or possible problems developing. Along with my annual exam, I try to watch my diet and exercise regularly. This is called *preventive medicine*, and I am a big believer in seeking to practice it, just as I practice preventive maintenance on my house and my car. This is part of living with wisdom.

Much of what goes wrong with my automobile, my house, or my body does so because of one word: *neglect*. No checkup. No maintenance. No accountability. *Accountability* is an important word. If it is good for cars, homes, and bodies, why is it a forgotten discipline in our personal relationships? It is good for husbands and wives to push the pause button occasionally, sit down, focus, and check up on their relationship with one another. It is good for parents to do the same with their children and for friends to stop long enough to perform some preventive maintenance on long-standing relationships.

Which relationships in your life need some preventive maintenance?

MARCH 29

EASY AND LIGHT

For My yoke is easy and My burden is light.
MATTHEW 11:30

In Matthew 11:28–29, Jesus promised we would find "rest for [our] souls." He continued with the words from today's scripture. The yoke of the law was heavy, unmanageable, burdensome, too much to bear up under. But Jesus frees us from the law, puts us under His grace, and bears our burdens for us. The yoke He offers us is one of grace. Its burden is light. John framed it like this: "For this is the love of God, that we keep His commandments. And His commandments are not burdensome" (1 John 5:3). His commandments to us are twofold: Love God . . . love others! (Matthew 22:37–39).

The offer from God still stands: "Come to Me. Trust in [Me] with all your heart, and lean not on your own understanding . . . and you will find rest for your souls" (Proverbs 3:5; Matthew 11:28–29, author's paraphrase).

It all begins in a simple act of coming to Jesus.

Are you living under a difficult yoke or a heavy burden? What is it, and how could coming to Jesus lighten your load?

MARCH 30

His Own Special People

You are a chosen generation, a royal priesthood, a holy nation, His own special people, that you may proclaim the praises of Him who called you out of darkness into His marvelous light.

1 PETER 2:9

Had we been at Caesarea Philippi the day Jesus said in Matthew 16:18, "I will build My *church*," we might have heard Him emphasize the word *church*. The church is not a high-steeple, stained glass, Greek-columned edifice. The Greek word for church means "the called-out ones." We are a *peculiar church* in the sense that God has called out a people for His own from every tribe, nation, and people. This is why Peter refers to us in today's scripture as "His own special people." We are the called-out ones. From generation to generation to generation across this church age, Christ has been building His church. There is coming a day when the final living stone will be put in place. The building will be completed, and Christ will come again to receive us unto Himself so that where He is, we will forever be also. Until then, we have and hold to His precious promise, "I will build My church."

What does it mean to you personally to know that you are part of God's church, one of "His own special people"? How will this influence the way you live?

MARCH 31

God Makes Known the Path of Life

You will show me the path of life; in Your presence is fullness of joy; at Your right hand are pleasures forevermore.

PSALM 16:11

If Christ lived with a passion for direction in life, how much more should we? We already have the promise of God's direction for our lives. He promised that He would "show . . . the path of life" for each of us. We are not a group, nor a collection of saints. We are individuals, with unique fingerprints and DNA, who are each, in our own way, indescribably valuable to God. There is something you can do that no one else can do quite like you can. God has a path, a direction for you to take, and when you find it and walk in it you have an additional promise of "fullness of joy" accompanied by "pleasures forevermore." Who of us could not use a little more of that kind of fullness in our lives? The Lord is more interested in your finding His will for your life than you are yourself.

Do you believe the Lord is more interested in your finding His will for your life than you are? Why or why not?

APRIL

APRIL 1

Forever Faithful

I will never leave you nor forsake you.
HEBREWS 13:5

During His intense struggle on the cross, our Lord spoke seven times as He hung suspended between heaven and earth. The strangest of these cries was, "My God, My God, why have You forsaken Me?" (Matthew 27:46). He knew well what it meant to be forsaken. In Galilee, He was forsaken by His family (Matthew 13:57). In Gethsemane, He was forsaken by His friends when they ran away after He was taken by the mob (Mark 14:50). And at the end of the journey, at Golgotha, while bearing our sins, He was forsaken for a time by His Father so that we might never be forsaken.

Many today know this reality. Those who are left at the altar despite promises made. Countless children abandoned by their fathers and/or mothers.

Jesus truly knew the meaning of "forsaken." But He didn't give up. He reached up! This is a help and a hope for any of us who have been forsaken. He understands. Don't give up. Reach up.

When you feel alone, how can you resist the temptation to give up and choose to reach up instead?

APRIL 2

Jesus Builds Bridges

Jesus answered and said to her, "Whoever drinks of this water will thirst again, but whoever drinks of the water that I shall give him will never thirst. But the water that I shall give him will become in him a fountain of water springing up into everlasting life."
JOHN 4:13–14

Remember the woman at the well in Samaria, the one Jesus met on a hot day and asked for water? Everyone in her village had criticized her and built barriers between themselves and her, and she had spent a lifetime building barriers between herself and other people—until the day she met Him. Her past was marred with many haunting choices she sorely wished she could make over again. She had known so much rejection that she was scarred by a lack of self-worth and self-respect. But when she met a Man who told her of the living water He could provide to her and told her everything she had ever done, He broke down every barrier and built a bridge to her. She crossed over, opened up, and in so doing found a true friend for life. This simple one-on-one encounter became the bridge that brought her entire village to faith in Him (John 4:30).

How can you build a bridge to someone who has spent a lifetime building barriers?

APRIL 3

THE EXCHANGED LIFE

Knowing this, that our old man was crucified with Him, that the body of sin might be done away with, that we should no longer be slaves of sin.
ROMANS 6:6

The great preacher Dr. R. G. Lee and his tour group went on a Holy Land pilgrimage. When they came to Golgotha, the place of the crucifixion, Lee ran ahead. When the others arrived, they found him on his knees, with tears streaming down his cheeks. "Oh, Dr. Lee," one exclaimed, "I see you have been here before."

"No," he replied, then quickly corrected himself, "Yes, I have. Two thousand years ago." Then came the words of Galatians 2:20: "I have been crucified with Christ; it is no longer I who live, but Christ lives in me."

As our Lord hung on the cross, the crowd saw only one man. But the Father saw not just Christ but you and me and all others who would put their faith in Christ. When we come to Jesus, God takes our old life from us ("I have been crucified with Christ") and puts a new life in us ("Christ lives in me"). The Christian life is not a changed life. It is an *exchanged* life.

When you think about the price Christ paid on the cross for your sins, how does it make you feel?

APRIL 4

TRIALS REFINE US

Knowing that the testing of your faith produces patience.
But let patience have its perfect work, that you may
be perfect and complete, lacking nothing.
JAMES 1:3–4

Stress can help produce *purity* in our lives. James spoke of the "testing" of our faith that happens in the process of stress. This same word is also translated *purging.* Picture a piece of precious metal being heated until it is liquid and its impurities rise to the top and are scraped off. Only pure metal remains. Our stressful trials are for a purpose. They have their own way of refining us.

Stress can also produce *perseverance*, which means "to stand up under." Only trials can prove the depth of our faith and the strength of our character. Know that there is a purpose in your trials. God is perfecting you, enabling you to "stand up under" whatever comes your way.

Stress can also lead us to *perfection*, which means "to carry to its end, to become full grown, to mature." Our goal in Christian living is spiritual maturity. Tests come along the way, and they are there to bring us to fruition and maturity.

Which trials have helped strengthen your faith in the areas of purity, perseverance, and perfection?

APRIL 5

Faith Before Love

Hearing of your love and faith which you have toward the Lord Jesus and toward all the saints.

PHILEMON V. 5

In the art of building relationships, order is important. Genuine faith in our Lord precedes true love for our friends. Behavior does not come before belief. What we genuinely believe will determine how we generally behave. Philemon verse 5, which appears in Paul's introductory paragraph of his letter to Philemon, was written in the present tense, which indicates that faith and love were not simply manifested in Philemon's past but were ongoing traits of his life.

Once Paul had affirmed his friend's loyalty to the faith, he then affirmed his love for others. When our faith is authentic, it always manifests itself in love, which becomes the glue that holds together all lasting relationships. Belief determines behavior, for what we do is a response to who we are. When believers display true love for another, it is because of their discovery of how much God loves them. Philemon's love for all the saints was an authentication of his faith in the Lord Jesus Christ.

Who in your life displays faith in God and love for others? How do they express this?

APRIL 6

Life Is About Relationships

Jesus said to him, "'You shall love the Lord *your God with all your heart, with all your soul, and with all your mind.' This is the first and great commandment. And the second is like it: 'You shall love your neighbor as yourself.'"*

MATTHEW 22:37–39

Life, from beginning to end, is all about relationships. Life is about our relationship with God. It is about our relationship with ourselves. And it is also about our relationships with others. Think of what Christ did in order to connect with us in a vital relationship. He laid aside His glory in heaven. He humbled Himself and came down here where we are. He clothed Himself in a garment of human flesh and for thirty-three years walked among us. He talked with us. He ate with us. He traveled with us. Yet He was never contaminated by our sin. And why did He come? To bring us into a relationship with the Father. This is why Paul had said to the Corinthians that God "has reconciled us to Himself through Jesus Christ, and has given us the ministry of reconciliation" (2 Corinthians 5:18). Getting right with God, being reconciled to Him, is the initial step in building positive and productive relationships with others.

Which relationships in your life are in need of reconciliation?

APRIL 7

EXPLOITATION OF WORKERS

Indeed the wages of the laborers who mowed your fields, which you kept back by fraud, cry out; and the cries of the reapers have reached the ears of the Lord of Sabaoth. . . . You have condemned, you have murdered the just.

JAMES 5:4, 6

James began this section with an accusation of *exploitation*. Never does the Bible condemn the acquisition of wealth by legal and legitimate means. James was calling out those who acquired their wealth through illegal or illegitimate means. A man who had contracted to pay his employees a certain amount exploited them by refusing to pay them what was owed. James called it what it was: fraud.

Next, this man is guilty of *expropriation*. In accusing him of "condemning" his workers, James borrowed a judicial term for the manner in which the rich pervert the legal system to accumulate wealth. Their money buys them power to use the courts to take away someone else's means of support. This landowner thought he had the power to control the system and prevent his workers from opposing him. As he deprived them of what was theirs, it was as if he murdered them.

There are still those around today who are looking for any and every loophole to defraud others. But, as James warned, God, the righteous Judge, is listening and looking.

What examples of exploitation from employers have you experienced or witnessed?

APRIL 8

Paid in Full

He said, "Father, 'into Your hands I commit My spirit.'"
LUKE 23:46

After the darkness while Jesus hung on the cross, two more words escaped His lips, a request to meet His own physical need: "I thirst!" (John 19:28). He was God, yes. But He was encased in a body of human flesh. He knew hunger, pain, thirst, emotions. Now, a simple plea. He was thirsty. But we should not fail to note that this cry of a personal need never came until after the battle of Calvary was fought and the darkness had turned back to light.

Jesus' next words came in rapid succession: "It is finished!" (v. 30). The Greek word for *finished* here means that the debt is paid in full . . . your sin debt . . . mine . . . paid up, in full! Finished. Over. Done. Some seem to think that Jesus went to the cross and made a little down payment for our sin, and we have to work and earn our way the rest of the way home. No, never. He paid your sin debt in full.

In what ways do you find yourself trying to pay the price for your sins when Jesus has already paid it all?

APRIL 9

PERFECTION AND CORRECTION

Then Jonah prayed to the LORD his God from the fish's belly. And he said . . . "But I will sacrifice to You with the voice of thanksgiving; I will pay what I have vowed. Salvation is of the LORD." So the LORD spoke to the fish, and it vomited Jonah onto dry land.

JONAH 2:1–2, 9–10

God allows things to happen that He uses to perfect our faith: *storms of perfection* and *storms of correction.* Jesus' disciples were in the middle of God's will and still got caught in a storm of perfection (Matthew 14:22–24). He then used the storm to teach them a valuable life lesson, and He perfected their faith.

Years before Jesus and the disciples were caught in their storm of perfection, the prophet Jonah found himself in a storm of correction. God had instructed him to go in one direction, but, unlike the disciples on the Sea of Galilee, Jonah headed in the opposite direction. Because of his direct disobedience, he wound up on a ship in a storm at sea, during which he was thrown overboard and swallowed by a great fish. Storms of correction come when we are out of God's will. After three days, Jonah began to thank God, and he was delivered. Giving thanks always and in all things can have a liberating effect.

What storms of perfection and correction has God allowed in your life, and what lessons have they taught you?

APRIL 10

A Double Meaning

Do you think that I cannot now pray to My Father, and He will provide Me with more than twelve legions of angels? How then could the Scriptures be fulfilled, that it must happen thus?
MATTHEW 26:53–54

Most of us have been caught in a "Freudian slip," an inadvertent mistake in speech revealing an unconscious thought.

Having stripped Jesus naked, beaten Him with a whip, and battered His head with a reed, His enemies began to mock and spit upon Him. Then a Roman soldier spewed out sarcastically, "Hail, King of the Jews!" (Mark 15:18). They even nailed those words in a sign over His head (Matthew 27:37). Meaning this as a cruel joke, they unwittingly never spoke or wrote greater truth.

The religious types added their ignorance to the barrage of double meaning around the cross: "He saved others; Himself He cannot save" (Matthew 27:42). Unknowingly, they blurted out for all posterity the substitutionary aspect of Jesus' death. He could not save Himself and save us at the same time.

The thief hanging next to Him said, "If You are the Christ, save Yourself." Then he added, "and us" (Luke 23:39). Jesus could not do both. He died so we might be saved.

What does it mean to you that Jesus sacrificed Himself instead of saving Himself—for you?

APRIL 11

Bible Promises Find You

Faith comes by hearing, and hearing by the word of God.
ROMANS 10:17

We live the life of faith by living by the promises of God. Today's scripture teaches that we develop faith as we hear God's Word. Finding God's promise to you in His Word and standing on it is what produces your faith, the kind of faith God says can move mountains (Matthew 17:20).

But let me be clear: You don't find a Bible promise. It is not like playing Russian roulette with the Word of God by simply opening your Bible, closing your eyes, and letting your finger fall on a particular verse to claim. No, you don't find a Bible promise. Bible promises find you! In the normal traffic pattern of your daily Bible reading, God has His way of reaching down by His Spirit and quickening a verse to your heart so you know that it is His special promise just to you—in your own snapshot in time—and right at the point of your particular need.

When was the last time a Bible promise "found" you?

APRIL 12

A Firm Yes or No

But above all, my brethren, do not swear, either by heaven or by earth or with any other oath. But let your "Yes" be "Yes," and your "No," "No," lest you fall into judgment.
JAMES 5:12

When James said, "Do not swear," he was not talking about using profanity. He was saying that we should be careful about taking oaths, such as, "I swear I'm going to do this or that." When we say yes, we should mean yes. In James's first-century world, people rarely signed contracts as we do today. They swore oaths to each other instead. James's point was that a believer should be such a person of integrity that an oath was unnecessary.

Still, confusion may surround the oath we take when we have jury duty or serve as a witness in a trial. James wasn't forbidding the taking of oaths in a court of law. In our fallen and imperfect world, oaths are used in court to help guard against perjury. Taking those oaths is a concession we believers make in the secular world. However, in church, oaths should be unnecessary. If we profess to follow Christ, we ought to truly mean what we say.

How careful are you with your words? Do you mean what you say, or do you need to improve in this area?

APRIL 13

Ask, Seek, Knock

Ask, and it will be given to you; seek, and you will find; knock, and it will be opened to you.
MATTHEW 7:7

The prayer that gets results is the prayer prayed in accordance with the will of God. First John 5:14–15 reminds us that we can have confidence in the Lord: "If we ask anything *according to His will*, He hears us. And if we know that He hears us, whatever we ask, we know that we have the petitions that we have asked of Him."

Our Lord taught us three levels of prayer, each directly related to the will of God for our lives. First, He instructs us to "ask." When we know the will of God for a situation, we are to simply ask and "it will be given to you." If we do not know the will of God for a matter, we are to "seek" His will. And when we do, He promises we "will find" it. Finally, if we are certain of God's will but have yet to see the answer, Jesus summons us to "knock," to keep on knocking, and "it will be opened" to us.

In what ways will your understanding of asking, seeking, and knocking help you when you pray?

APRIL 14

"AND PETER"

He is not here; for He is risen, as He said. Come, see the place where the Lord lay.
MATTHEW 28:6

When the women arrived at the tomb early on the third day, they found it empty! An angelic being informed them that the Lord was not there but that He had risen, then said, "Go, tell His disciples—*and Peter*—that He is going before you into Galilee" (Mark 16:7).

Why didn't the angel say, "Go, tell the disciples—and Pilate," or Herod, or others who played a part in Jesus' indictment? Or, "—and John"? After all, John was the lone disciple standing at the foot of the cross. But our Lord knew Peter's heart. He was the one who had so blatantly denied Christ in the hour of testing and was in dire need of a word of encouragement, a new beginning, a second chance. These two words make all the difference: "and Peter"!

Many of us need a second chance. Perhaps you need these two little words today: "Go, tell the disciples—*and* [your name]." One failure doesn't make a flop. You can have a new start, a new life, a new beginning.

What do you specifically need to hear from Jesus today?

APPEALING IN AGAPE LOVE

I appeal to you, brothers and sisters, in the name of our Lord Jesus Christ, that all of you agree with one another in what you say and that there be no divisions among you, but that you be perfectly united in mind and thought.

1 CORINTHIANS 1:10 NIV

When we try to build or mend relationships, win friends, or influence others, the manner in which we make our appeal is of utmost importance. Some of us waste valuable time appealing to others strictly on the basis of reason. Others make their appeals on the basis of merit, who they are, or where they may be coming from. Still others seek to convince others that they have earned the right to make their case because of their experience. Paul could have appealed to Philemon on the basis of each of these, but he instead chose love. In Philemon verse 9, Paul said, "Yet for love's sake I rather appeal to you." And when he wrote that, he chose the highest level of love, *agape* love. This type of love was defined by William Barclay: "No matter what someone may do to us by way of insult or injury or humiliation, we will never seek anything else but their highest good." This is God's love. This is submissive love that seeks the other's best interest.

Who has shown agape love to you, and what were the circumstances?

Faith Without Fruit

But someone will say, "You have faith, and I have works." Show me your faith without your works, and I will show you my faith by my works.

JAMES 2:18

The church today faces what could be called the "ethical effect," or, as James might have put it, "a faith without fruit." As the world watches, too many Christians profess one thing but practice another, faking their faith and forfeiting any fruit. In the not-too-distant past, the church was the most respected and influential institution in virtually every American community. Now, the church has little influence in our culture. While we are still vocal about proclaiming our faith, much of the world shouts back at us with the question of James 2:14, 16, which essentially asks, "What good is all this talk about faith?"

The church is losing its voice as our culture also suffers from this ethical effect. An integrity crisis is running rampant in every aspect of our society. Time and space keep us from illustrating here how the ethical effect has touched government, politics, business, law, medicine, sports, and, unfortunately, religion. The ethical effect has brought down high-profile individuals in every professional field. Our world needs people whose lives match their lips, whose walk matches their talk.

What are some examples of how the church's "faith without fruit" behavior has contributed to its loss of credibility in the world? What can you do to change this?

APRIL 17

The Gospel Changes Hearts

At that hour of the night the jailer took them and washed their wounds; then immediately he and all his household were baptized.
ACTS 16:33 NIV

The Philippian jailer, after having beaten Paul and Silas on their backs with a whip until they were striped with deep lacerations, securely locked them in the depths of the prison. At midnight as Paul and Silas were praising God, an earthquake sent the prison doors flying off their hinges. Knowing his fate would be death if the prisoners escaped his care, the jailer was about to fall on his sword when he realized that Paul and Silas were still there, though they could have easily fled. He fell on his knees before them, asking, "What must I do to be saved?" (Acts 16:30). After they told him, he was converted.

A beautiful encounter ensues before this story ends: This redeemed jailer "took them and washed their wounds." Just hours earlier he had lashed their backs until they were bloody; now he gently washed the wounds he had inflicted. Only the gospel can instantaneously change our hearts like this.

How has the gospel changed your heart?

APRIL 18

A Desperate Prayer

O Lord, how long shall I cry, and You will not hear?
HABAKKUK 1:2

Habakkuk asked the question in today's scripture, and it was born out of a "burden" that consumed him (Habakkuk 1:1). How could a holy and loving God—who had called Israel the "apple of His eye" (Deuteronomy 32:10)—now allow the pagan, godless Babylonians to besiege and ultimately destroy the city of Jerusalem?

If we are honest, most of us have felt like this at one time or another. We, too, have been burdened by what seems the inactivity of our God on our behalf.

If a good and all-powerful God really does exist, we ask, why doesn't He answer our prayers for what we are convinced are good and right requests? Why does He continue to allow so much evil and suffering?

God has not stood idly by. He has done something dramatic about the problem of evil in our world. He did the costliest and the most loving thing possible: He sent and surrendered His own Son to die in the place of sinful human beings like us.

How has meditating on God's gift of His Son helped you when you have experienced anguish, as Habakkuk did?

APRIL 19

Finish the Race

And I said, "Should such a man as I flee?"
NEHEMIAH 6:11

It's not just how we start a race that matters. How we finish is what's most important.

Nehemiah was not a prophet or a preacher. He was a layman, a civil servant, burdened with the reproach of Jerusalem's broken-down walls and burned gates. He was granted permission to return from Babylonian exile to be the rebuilder of Jerusalem. He assembled a competent and committed team, cast a vision, and managed the huge task. After a long six weeks of hard work, the completion was in sight. But before we read that "the wall was finished" (Nehemiah 6:15), Nehemiah came to a crossroads and was tempted to abandon the entire project in the last moment. He speaks to us, so many centuries later, of the importance of "finishing strong" in our own God-given assignments in life.

Maybe you have stumbled in some way as you've run your race. Get up and finish the race. Get back in the game. Our Lord is standing at the finish line with His arms outstretched. Keep running toward Him!

How does Nehemiah's example encourage you to keep going when you face challenges as you run your race in life?

The Desire in Your Heart

Delight yourself also in the Lord, and He shall give you the desires of your heart.
PSALM 37:4

There's an important word involved in seeking God's will for your life: *desire*. God will not lead you in a certain direction without first planting a desire in your heart to go in that way (Psalm 37:4). Those who know Christ can sense the Spirit's leading and are immersed in God's Word; He will be the One who has implanted those very desires in your heart. God does not want to veil His path and plan for you. He is far more desirous of your finding it and walking in it than you are yourself.

God has a plan, a path, a direction for you to go in life where along the way you will find fullness of joy. Pause a moment and recall the first day you came to know Him. Yield to His Spirit and search His Word, because so often we find His promises to us right there in black and white, on the printed pages of the Bible. Finally, join Jesus in praying, "Not My will, but Yours, be done" (Luke 22:42).

What are the desires of your heart?

APRIL 21

Our Shepherd Protects and Leads Us

I am the good shepherd. The good shepherd gives His life for the sheep.
JOHN 10:11

The very nature of a shepherd is to be protective. Without him the sheep could not find their way to water and life's necessities. The shepherd guards his sheep against wild animals or other dangers that could harm them. We remember the shepherd mentioned in Luke 15:4–7 who left the fold to search out the one lost sheep until he found it and carried it back, rejoicing all the way.

If you have ever witnessed a shepherd at work, he is always in front of the flock. He, unlike a cattle rancher, is not found behind his stock driving and whipping them. A shepherd leads the flock. Jesus will never force you to follow. He will never drive you. But, like a shepherd, He is leading you—even now. According to John 10:27, His sheep hear His voice . . . they know Him . . . and they follow Him. And what a promise: "They shall never perish; neither shall anyone snatch them out of My hand" (John 10:28).

How has God protected and led you?

APRIL 22

Worldly Wisdom

But if you have bitter envy and self-seeking in your hearts, do not boast and lie against the truth. This wisdom does not descend from above, but is earthly, sensual, demonic. For where envy and self-seeking exist, confusion and every evil thing are there.

JAMES 3:14–16

James left no doubt about the origin of worldly wisdom. It "does not descend from above, but is earthly, sensual, demonic." This unholy trinity of spiritual enemies is called the world, the flesh, and the devil. One thing is sure: Worldly wisdom is not from God.

Following the wisdom of the world results in envy, defined as "the displeasure we take in someone else's good fortune."

Another outcome of worldly wisdom is "self-seeking" or selfish ambition. People will plot, scheme, connive, and use any means necessary to gain their end result.

Confusion and disorder are also natural results of the world's wisdom. Instead of bringing people together, it divides and tears apart.

We don't have to teach our children the wisdom of the world. They were born with a sin nature. That's why we have to teach them to obey, talk kindly, and share. We have to teach them the better way, the wisdom that comes from above, the wisdom of the Word.

When have you witnessed the outcome of worldly wisdom, and when have you witnessed the results of the wisdom of the Word?

APRIL 23

STAY CONNECTED TO GOD

I am the vine, you are the branches. He who abides in Me, and I in him, bears much fruit; for without Me you can do nothing.
JOHN 15:5

Paul spoke with authority regarding interpersonal relationships because he was well connected. After his conversion, he related well and winsomely to others because he possessed a positive self-image found through his personal relationship with Jesus Christ. He found his source of strength in the *paternal* One (Father) and saw himself as a member of God's forever family. He found his source in the *prominent* One (Lord) and thus viewed himself as one who was under a higher authority. And he found himself in relationship with the *Promised* One (Christ), and this set him free to find his own identity in what he described as "Christ in you, the hope of glory" (Colossians 1:27). This eternal connection brought to Paul indescribable value as an individual and a high sense of self-worth. If we are not properly connected to God, our source, the light will never shine through us and into the lives of others.

How can you stay connected to God today so His light will shine through you to others?

APRIL 24

Seek the Lord to Meet Your Needs

Seek the Lord *and His strength; seek His face evermore!*
1 CHRONICLES 16:11

All throughout Scripture we are called to seek the Lord. Perhaps you need power to overcome something that has entered your life. It does not come in seeking power but in seeking Him: "I sought the Lord, and He heard me, and delivered me from all my fears" (Psalm 34:4). Perhaps you are financially challenged and in need of monetary help. Instead of seeking increased financial resources, seek the Lord, who said of Uzziah, "As long as he sought the Lord, God made him prosper" (2 Chronicles 26:5). Are you looking for happiness and contentment? You may be looking in all the wrong places. The Bible promises that those who seek the Lord will rejoice and be glad (Psalm 70:4). It might be that wisdom is your need of the day. "Those who seek the Lord understand all" (Proverbs 28:5). Whatever you need, seek the Lord. He meets every need we have (Philippians 4:19).

What do you need today? In what ways might you seek the Lord more diligently?

APRIL 25

GOD IS LOVE

Again, a new commandment I write to you, which thing is true in Him and in you, because the darkness is passing away, and the true light is already shining. He who says he is in the light, and hates his brother, is in darkness until now. He who loves his brother abides in the light, and there is no cause for stumbling in him.

1 JOHN 2:8–10

The word *love* appears thirty-four times in the three brief letters written by John, often called the "apostle of love." He provided us with the best definition of our Lord using only three words, "God is love" (1 John 4:8).

True love is now expressed in the "new commandment," which calls on us to love as Jesus loved: unconditionally. On our own, we are completely incapable of loving on that level. The only way this kind of love becomes possible for us is through experientially knowing the love of Christ in our own hearts by faith. Once we receive His love into our hearts unconditionally, we are then able to release it to others in the same way. In order to love as Jesus did, we are to love one another not only unconditionally but also with a love that is unlimited. Because Jesus' love for us has no limits.

When have you given or received the unconditional love of Jesus?

What Do You Want Me to Do?

Lord, what do You want me to do?
ACTS 9:6

Paul, who took the gospel to the far reaches of the known world and left us half our New Testament, began as the antithesis of what we know of him today. As a Pharisee he saw the Jesus movement of his day as a threat to all he had been taught, and he persecuted those who followed Christ.

While traveling to Damascus to stamp out a Christian uprising, the risen Christ miraculously appeared to him, transforming his life and purpose. Then, "trembling and astonished," he asked, "Lord, what do You want me to do?" This became the burning desire of his life—to do what pleased the Lord. Whether he was shipwrecked, stoned, beaten, imprisoned, or finally beheaded outside the city gates of Rome, this prayer became his driving motivation.

Every believer should be constantly asking, "Lord, what do You want me to do?" There is something that no one else can do quite like you can, a purpose for your life that existed before you took your first breath (Jeremiah 1:5).

What can you do that no one else can do in the same way to serve God?

APRIL 27

Waiting Patiently for His Return

Therefore be patient, brethren, until the coming of the Lord. See how the farmer waits for the precious fruit of the earth, waiting patiently for it until it receives the early and latter rain.

JAMES 5:7

Waiting periods in farming—and in life—are not without testing and trials. All a farmer can do is stay calm and trust the Lord to bring in the harvest. As believers, we should await the Lord's coming in the same way: by looking up and remaining calm. A farmer can't control the weather, and we can't control Christ's return.

We should look expectantly toward this great day of our Lord's coming without running after every so-called prophet who cries, "The sky is falling." The early church lived daily with the hope of His return. They greeted each other saying, "Maranatha!" ("The Lord is coming"), living each day as if it were their last opportunity to live for Christ before He returned.

We should live as if Christ died yesterday. We should also live as if Christ rose this morning. And we should live as if He is coming back tomorrow. And, always, "Be patient . . . until the coming of the Lord."

What would you do differently if you knew the Lord would return this week?

APRIL 28

ACCOUNTABILITY IN RELATIONSHIPS

As iron sharpens iron, so a man sharpens the countenance of his friend.
PROVERBS 27:17

Accountability plays a significant part in all we do in life. It is strange that, although we daily practice accountability in virtually every area of life, when it comes to personal relationships with friends, many of us seem to see no need for it.

If accountability is imperative for government, education, athletics, health, and business dealings, it is also an imperative incentive for developing lasting positive and productive relationships that stand the test of time.

What destroys our relationships? The answer can be found in attitudes of self-reliance, self-righteousness, self-sufficiency, and self-centeredness. *Accountability* has become the lost word in many relationships, with devastating results. The lack of it has been the downfall of so much potential and promise. Accountability is the "ability" to be open and allow a small number of trusted, loyal, and committed friends to speak truth into us in love. We should be accountable only to those who have our best interests in mind. We all need a person from whom we can receive wise counsel and willing correction.

To whom are you accountable, and who is accountable to you?

APRIL 29

Submit, Resist, and Draw Near

Therefore submit to God. Resist the devil and he will flee from you. Draw near to God and He will draw near to you.
JAMES 4:7–8

We have an enemy. His name is Satan, and 1 Peter 5:8 describes him as a "roaring lion, seeking whom he may devour." Ever since he confronted Adam and Eve in the garden with his subtle and subversive ways, he has been about the business of deploying his forces of evil with the goal of the ultimate defeat of every believer.

We may have a persistent protagonist in the devil, but we also have a precious promise from the Lord. He promises to "draw near" to us and to cause the devil to "flee" from us. James laid out three verbs for us that are all in the imperative mood, signifying they are commands—not options—for us. We are to "submit to God." We are to "resist the devil." And we are to "draw near to God." And when we do, we have His overcoming promise that the devil will take momentary leave from us and that God Himself will come very near to enable, energize, and encourage us along our journey of life.

How can you submit to God, resist the devil, and draw near to God?

APRIL 30

JESUS IS ABLE

Now to Him who is able to keep you from stumbling.
JUDE V. 24

Our Lord's heroics are not confined to the bygone days we read about in Scripture. Jude did not say that Jesus *was* able. Our God is not powerless in the present, only offering bright hope for tomorrow. Jude did not say that He *will be* able. He wrote, "To Him who *is* able." Right now. God was able in the past, and He will be able in the future. Jesus *is* also able to meet our every need, right now in the present.

Jude bookended his letter with strong words about our eternal security in Christ. In the opening verse, he affirmed the eternal security of the believer. We are not only called and sanctified by God the Father but "preserved in Jesus Christ" (v. 1). And on the back end, he framed it this way: "To Him who is able to keep you from stumbling." Jude wanted us to know that in Jesus we are secure in the now life as well as in the next life.

How does it strengthen your faith and courage to know that Jesus is able to keep you from stumbling—now, today?

MAY

MAY 1

Famous Last Words

He said, "It is finished!" And bowing His head, He gave up His spirit.
JOHN 19:30

Arguably, no one else's dying words have been more quoted or more memorable than those of Jesus of Nazareth. Nailed fast to a Roman cross, He spoke, and we are wise to pay attention to what He said.

Jesus' first words from the cross were a prayer: "Father, forgive them, for they do not know what they do" (Luke 23:34). Jesus died praying for others. What He preached about loving enemies to a crowd in Galilee (Luke 6:27), He practiced on a cross on Golgotha.

Next came a promise to a man hanging near Him: "Today you will be with Me in Paradise" (Luke 23:43). It is never too late for a new beginning.

Then, seeing His mother in the crowd, He pronounced to John, "Behold your mother!" (John 19:27) and to His mother, "Woman, behold your son!" (v. 26). Jesus gave John the responsibility of caring for His mother because He Himself was no longer Mary's son; He was now her Savior!

Which of Jesus' words from the cross touch you most powerfully, and why?

MAY 2

The Prayer of Confession

For the eyes of the LORD are on the righteous, and His ears are open to their prayers; but the face of the LORD is against those who do evil.
1 PETER 3:12

The Bible clearly lays out a route of prayer for us, and it begins with the prayer of confession. Our sins have separated us from God "so that He will not hear" (Isaiah 59:2). King David lamented, "If I regard iniquity in my heart, the Lord will not hear" (Psalm 66:18). The place to begin in prayer is to come clean and confess our sins to Him while standing on His promise that "if we confess our sins, He is faithful and just to forgive us our sins and to cleanse us from all unrighteousness" (1 John 1:9).

Spend a moment confessing your sins to the Lord. Consider sins of the tongue, things you have said. Or sins of action, something you have done. What about sins of thought? It is not a sin to have a certain thought pass through your mind. It becomes one when you continue to harbor it in your heart. There are also sins of omission, things we did not do that we know we should have.

Why is it so important to confess your sins before praying?

MAY 3

Do You Need Wisdom?

If any of you lacks wisdom, let him ask of God, who gives to all liberally and without reproach, and it will be given to him.

JAMES 1:5

In our educated and sophisticated world, we need wisdom. The present generation is more progressive than all those before it. We travel farther and fly faster and higher. More young people have graduate degrees than ever before. Knowledge is exploding. We accumulate data in a way that would have been unfathomable to my father's generation. Technology advances so quickly that the latest and greatest computers are out-of-date a few months after their release.

Yes, knowledge is exploding, and tools for obtaining knowledge have become more advanced, but wisdom is clearly lacking. Families are broken. Lives are in shambles. Suicide rates seem higher than ever. Evidence of Christian morality is at a record low. Our world is dark and violent, constantly on the brink of one chaotic episode after another.

To whom does God give divine discernment? To those who *ask*. We don't get wisdom in school or from practical experience. Wisdom is God's gift to us. And His desire is to give it "liberally" when we ask.

When have you asked God for wisdom and clearly received an answer to your prayer?

MAY 4

Be a Light in the Darkness

If the foundations are destroyed, what can the righteous do?

PSALM 11:3

A reporter once asked someone, "What are the two greatest problems facing America?" The man replied, "I really don't know—and I really don't care!" Those are the two greatest problems facing our nation: ignorance ("I don't know") and apathy ("I don't care"). No two single factors are working harder to destroy the very foundation of our nation than ignorance and apathy.

Three thousand years ago King David asked the question posed in Psalm 11:3, which is all too relevant today. We are living in a time when many of the moral and ethical values that once formed the infrastructure of our great nation are crumbling before our eyes.

What shall we do? First, look at the root cause of our problems. Then stop trying to apply political solutions to what are essentially spiritual problems. Instead of saying, "I don't care," begin to pray. We are to be light in this dark world and take a stand for truth. Don't give up. Start saying, "I know!" and declaring, "I care!"

How can you be a light in this dark world
and take a stand for truth today?

MAY 5

Come, Lord Jesus

I am the Alpha and the Omega, the Beginning and the End, the First and the Last.
REVELATION 22:13

Alpha is the first letter of the Greek alphabet, and omega is the last letter. When Jesus declared Himself to be "the Alpha and the Omega," He declared that He is the beginning and the ending of all things. He has always existed, and He always will exist.

The Bible speaks of three major "comings" related to God. It mentions Jesus' first coming (John 1:14). It also speaks of the coming of the Holy Spirit, as was prophesied in Joel 2:28. This took place on the day of Pentecost when the Holy Spirit came to indwell the believers (Acts 2:4).

The only major coming yet to be fulfilled is the promised return, the second coming of Christ. For just as He came the first time, He will come again: "Surely I am coming quickly" (Revelation 22:20).

The Lord Jesus is the First and the Last of all things, the Author and the Finisher of our faith, the Beginning and the End of everything. Let's join John in praying, "Even so, come, Lord Jesus!" (Revelation 22:20).

What does it mean to you personally that Jesus is "the First and the Last," the Beginning and the End of everything?

MAY 6

God Works Things Together for Good

It is good for me that I have been afflicted, that I may learn Your statutes.
PSALM 119:71

How could King David believe it was good for him to have been afflicted? This reminds me of Romans 8:28: "We know that all things work together for good to those who love God, to those who are the called according to His purpose." This is one of the most comforting thoughts in all Scripture; things that happen in our lives have a supernatural way of working together for our good.

In the language of the New Testament, one Greek word is translated into this entire phrase: "things work together." The word is *synergia*, and we derive our English word *synergy* from it. This certainly does not mean that everything that comes our way is good. In fact, many of us are confronted with issues that are downright bad and painful. You may be faced with financial setbacks, sickness, disappointment, and so on. However, this verse assures us that God can take our mistakes, messes, and misfortunes and work them together for our good and His glory.

When has God used situations to work together for your good?

MAY 7

Types of Prayer

I exhort first of all that supplications, prayers, intercessions, and giving of thanks be made for all men, for kings and all who are in authority, that we may lead a quiet and peaceable life in all godliness and reverence.
1 TIMOTHY 2:1-2

Prayer brings with it an *urgent priority*. When Paul says, "I exhort," it is not a simple suggestion. Nor is it a command being forced on us. The word *exhort* means to call alongside, to plead, to encourage.

When the apostle says, "First of all," he is saying prayer should be in the forefront of everything we do. Before the church is the house of Bible teaching, fellowship, evangelism, missions, or anything else, it is the "house of prayer" (Matthew 21:13).

Paul reminds us that our prayers should consist of "supplications, prayers, intercessions, and giving of thanks." "Supplications" describes an intense, special, personal need. Then we are to pray "prayers," a word that describes the reverence with which we come before royalty. And then, the apostle adds "intercessions"—standing before God on someone else's behalf. Finally, Paul adds the "giving of thanks." This is a beautiful expression of prayer on an ascending scale.

How could understanding different types of prayer help you pray more effectively?

MAY 8

DOVE, WIND, AND FIRE

The wind blows where it wishes, and you hear the sound of it, but cannot tell where it comes from and where it goes. So is everyone who is born of the Spirit.

JOHN 3:8

There is something within most of us that likes to identify with certain brands. We wear clothing that proudly displays particular logos. Our key rings proclaim the logos of the cars we drive. And with loyalty to our colleges, we display bumper stickers, hats, and shirts.

The Holy Spirit has some unique logos that describe who He is and what He does. Fire speaks of the Spirit's consuming power in the life of the believer. John the Baptist told his followers that Jesus would "baptize [them] with the Holy Spirit and fire" (Matthew 3:11).

While the dove is perhaps the most prominent logo describing the Holy Spirit, another is wind. Wind speaks of the incredible depth of His mighty power to regenerate us.

We may not be able to see the wind, but we can see its power blowing the leaves in the trees. So it is with the Spirit. We may not be able to see Him, but we can see the powerful effect of His presence all around us.

Which characteristics of the Holy Spirit have you experienced in your life, and how did they manifest?

MAY 9

The Power of Submission

Yes, all of you be submissive to one another, and be clothed with humility, for "God resists the proud, but gives grace to the humble."
1 PETER 5:5

The words *submit* and *submission* have become anathema to many in our modern culture, due in large part to the way the concept is often presented and the connotation it has earned in some circles. But *submission* is a beautiful word when understood in its biblical context. It has nothing to do with inferiority. We see it in the military. Soldiers live in submission to their commanding officers. When people join a branch of the military, they relinquish some control over their lives. They do not get out of bed in the morning whenever they feel like it. They can't just take a few days off when they want to. They become people under authority.

In the eyes of God, we are all equal. Submission means one places himself or herself in submission to another. First we submit to God, then we submit to others in healthy, appropriate ways. Those who are being filled with God's Spirit do voluntarily what the soldier does by command.

What does submission to God look like in your life?

MAY 10

Backing Off and Stepping Up

For all have sinned and fall short of the glory of God.
ROMANS 3:23

Before we knew Him as Savior and Lord, you and I were in conflict with Jesus. We had gone our own way, we had "all" sinned and fallen short of His plan for us. So what did He do? He backed off. In His darkest hour, see Him beneath those old, gnarled olive trees in Gethsemane's garden. In serious thought, He backed off and took counsel with His own heart. Then He stood up. See Him before Caiaphas, the high priest; Herod, the puppet king; and Pilate, the Roman governor. When asked if He was the Son of God, Jesus boldly replied, "You rightly say that I am" (Luke 22:70). Next, He gave in. He was not pushed, shoved, and kicked up the Via Dolorosa. He gave in and willingly went, "led as a lamb to the slaughter" (Isaiah 53:7). Finally, Jesus reached out. Suspended between heaven and earth on a cross, with arms outstretched, Jesus reached out, imploring us all to be "reconciled to God" (Romans 5:10).

What does Jesus' backing off and stepping up mean to you in terms of being saved from sin and reconciled to God?

MAY 11

DON'T BE DECEIVED

Do not be deceived, my beloved brethren.
JAMES 1:16

The song "Tie a Yellow Ribbon Round the Ole Oak Tree" tells of a young man going home from prison and wondering if his love wanted him back. If he was welcome, he asked her to tie a single yellow ribbon on the oak tree in the front yard. To his surprise, he saw "a hundred yellow ribbons" on the tree.

If you've wandered off course and want to go home and begin again, know that God has tied His own red ribbon around Calvary's tree and that the blood of His Son cleanses us from all sin.

We should not be deceived about sin by minimizing or dismissing it. And we should not be deceived about our salvation. We are saved not because of our own good works, but by God's grace when we put our faith in Christ (Ephesians 2:8–9). Finally, we should not be deceived about our Savior. Jesus was not merely another prophet, teacher, or religious leader. He was God who came in human flesh, died for our sin, and rose again!

What types of deceptions have you encountered about sin, salvation, and our Savior, and how have you responded?

MAY 12

Love Cements Relationships

God is love.
1 JOHN 4:16

Agape love epitomizes Jesus of Nazareth. He could have pulled our strings like a puppeteer to force us to fall in step and love Him. But what did He do? What does He still do? He appeals to us in love. In fact, in the Bible's attempt to define Him, it simply says, "God is love." This type of love breaks down barriers and cements relationships. There can be no long-term, constructive, interpersonal relationships without their being based on the appeal of love.

Think about it: Which motivates you and appeals to you the most—an order or a loving appeal? What real motivation do you think commands or orders have on most people? How much better is it when we approach people in love? Those who are sensitive and appeal on the basis of love with a submissive spirit are the ones who build lasting, positive relationships.

Why is love necessary for long-term, constructive interpersonal relationships?

MAY 13

Make the Ask

At Gibeon the Lord *appeared to Solomon in a dream by night; and God said, "Ask! What shall I give you?"*
1 KINGS 3:5

Not yet twenty years old, Solomon was about to be crowned king, following one of the greatest leaders in human history, King David. At this time in his life, his heart was pure and virtually empty of pride. He journeyed to Gibeon to seek God's direction. And God said, "Ask! What shall I give you?"

What do you want? It may not be what you need, but it is often a good indication of where your heart is. A greater danger than not getting what you want is getting it and realizing it is not what you needed after all.

With his priorities in proper order, Solomon had the right answer: "Give to Your servant an understanding heart to judge Your people, that I may discern between good and evil" (1 Kings 3:9). Solomon asked for three things. He wanted God to work with him, not with others; to work in him, not around him; and to work through him, not for him.

Ask! This simple word is a key to prayer.

When you think about what you want in this season of your life, how does it indicate where your heart is?

MAY 14

Active Waiting

Wait for the Promise of the Father, "which . . . you have heard from Me; . . . you shall be baptized with the Holy Spirit."

ACTS 1:4–5

Waiting is something many of us are not very good at. But waiting on the Lord is an essential element of Christian growth. Christ's final words to His followers before "He was parted from them and carried up into heaven" (Luke 24:51) were, "Behold, I send the Promise of My Father upon you; but tarry in the city of Jerusalem until you are endued with power from on high" (Luke 24:49).

Reading this in the original Greek, we discover an amazing truth. The word *endued* is in the middle voice. The subject is not acted upon by another but acts upon itself for its own benefit. What happened in the upper room before the Holy Spirit fell on the believers? Jesus' followers were getting themselves right with God and then with each other. They were not passively sitting around waiting. They were taking action. When we get right with God ourselves—and get right with others in the process—we, too, can expect God to manifest His awesome presence in our lives.

How can you apply active waiting as you walk with God in a certain situation right now?

MAY 15

The Promise of Forgiveness

If we confess our sins, He is faithful and just to forgive us our sins and to cleanse us from all unrighteousness.
1 JOHN 1:9

Today's scripture is one of the most prominent conditional promises in God's Word. It contains the big "if." God gives His word that *if* we do a certain thing, *then* He will respond in a certain way. In this case, *if* we "confess our sins," *then* He will "forgive us our sins." Forgiveness doesn't just happen. It is preceded by true confession. The writer of this promise from God was the same John who found his place in the Lord's inner circle along with his brother James and Simon Peter (Mark 14:33; Matthew 17:1). He is the same John who leaned on the Lord's breast in the upper room (John 13:23). He is the same faithful follower who, when all the others had forsaken the Lord and fled, stood by Mary's side at the foot of the cross (John 19:26–27). He was there. He witnessed it all. He had seen forgiveness and known the One who forgives. We can trust this promise that if we confess our sins, we are forgiven and cleansed.

How does the promise of forgiveness strengthen and encourage you?

MAY 16

The Faith vs. Works Debate

You see then that a man is justified by works, and not by faith only.
JAMES 2:24

The debate between faith and works hinges on the failure to make a distinction between the *requirement* for true salvation and the *result* of true salvation. Good works are never a requirement for salvation, but they are certainly the result of it.

Paul and James have been viewed as sparring about faith versus works. But they say the same thing (Ephesians 2:10; James 1:18). They complement, not contradict, each other. Paul emphasized faith because he wrote primarily to the Judaizers, people of the Jewish faith who had proclaimed to the early church the false teaching that new Christ-followers had to add works to faith. James wrote to people at the other extreme, who understood faith as being the key to salvation but didn't care about the fruit of that faith. So Paul and James leave the ring arm in arm: faith and works. And that's the way it should be, because salvation is about a strong faith that leads to good works.

How do your actions reflect your faith to a watching world?

Don't Let Resentment Damage You

When you stand praying, if you hold anything against anyone, forgive them, so that your Father in heaven may forgive you your sins.

MARK 11:25 NIV

The most devastating effect of resentment is not what it does to someone else but what it does to us. It can damage us *physically and mentally.* Harboring resentment can have an adverse effect on blood pressure and sleep quality and to contribute to ulcers and other health problems. It can warp our capacity to think straight on matters of importance. Many people suffer from mental and emotional problems simply because they have harbored deep resentment toward others for an extended period of time, refusing to forgive—even though the offending party has returned in genuine repentance, asking for forgiveness.

Resentment also has a debilitating effect on us *spiritually.* It is not possible to have an effective prayer and Bible study life when harboring resentment. This is one reason Jesus teaches us to not hold anything against anyone when we pray (Mark 11:25). One of the most damaging results of broken relationships is that resentment can harm the offended party when they simply cannot bring themselves to forgive.

In your own words, how would you describe the potential negative impact of resentment?

MAY 18

Believe on Jesus

He brought them out and said, "Sirs, what must I do to be saved?"
ACTS 16:30

When the Philippian jailer wondered what he had to do to be saved, Paul and Silas wasted no time in pointing out the answer: "Believe on the Lord Jesus Christ" (Acts 16:31). Note that the instruction was to believe "on" the Lord. Prepositions in Greek are powerful and expressive. The apostles did not use the Greek preposition we translate "in" (*en*), nor the Greek preposition *eis*, which describes "into," describing a movement toward something that had not necessarily reached its destination. They used the Greek preposition *epi*, meaning "upon." The promise is for those who believe "on," who lay their trust on, the Lord Jesus. And the word *believe* is recorded here in the aorist tense, meaning it is punctiliar—at a set moment of time he believed, he transferred his trust to Christ alone to save him. Salvation is not something we grow into. It is a crisis moment, experienced in a moment of time when we believe on the Lord and transfer our trust from ourselves to Him alone for our salvation.

How does believing on Jesus make a difference in your life?

MAY 19

The Path to Purity

How can a young man cleanse his way? By taking heed according to Your word.
PSALM 119:9

How can one keep pure in a world of perversion? "By taking heed according to Your word." It is virtually impossible, however, for the Bible to impact our lives if we know little about it. So the first step in overcoming a corrupting culture is to know what the Bible says.

Every believer should be able to give an answer to three vital matters in Scripture, beginning with *the inerrancy of the Word of God*: "All Scripture is given by inspiration of God, and is profitable for doctrine, for reproof, for correction, for instruction in righteousness, that the man of God may be complete, thoroughly equipped for every good work" (2 Timothy 3:16–17). Second, *the deity of Christ* is an essential and basic truth: "In the beginning was the Word, and the Word was with God, and the Word *was* God" (John 1:1). Third, believers should be able to explain *the means of salvation*: "For by grace you have been saved through faith, and that not of yourselves; it is the gift of God" (Ephesians 2:8).

In what ways does knowing the Bible help you stay pure?

MAY 20

Pointing People to God's Word

Ezra . . . was a skilled scribe in the Law of Moses, which the Lord God of Israel had given. . . . For Ezra had prepared his heart to seek the Law of the Lord, and to do it.

EZRA 7:6, 10

Following the Babylonian exile, three prominent Jewish leaders returned to the devastated city of Jerusalem. Zerubbabel was assigned the task of leading in the rebuilding of the temple, which had been plundered and left in ruins. Nehemiah mobilized and motivated the Jewish exiles to rebuild the city's broken walls and burned gates that left it vulnerable to enemies. But it was the faithful scribe Ezra's task to accomplish the most important of the rebuilding assignments. Ezra pointed the people to God's Word and led in the crucial rebuilding of the spiritual integrity of God's people. And, like all great leaders, he led by example: "Ezra had prepared his heart to seek the Law of the Lord, and to do it."

While we never read of a direct mention of the Messiah in Ezra, it is impossible to miss Jesus walking through these verses, manifesting Himself in the life of this faithful scribe.

Who in your life needs to be pointed to the Word of God, and how might you do that?

Always in All Things

In everything give thanks; for this is the will of God in Christ Jesus for you.
1 THESSALONIANS 5:18

There is an *upward* evidence of the Spirit filling our lives. "Giving thanks always for all things to God the Father in the name of our Lord Jesus Christ" (Ephesians 5:20). When we realize that the Father is the source of everything and we allow His Spirit to fill us, our hearts will be full of thanksgiving to Him "always" and "in all things."

I can imagine some saying, "But you don't know my problem." Some of us give thanks only when we get a blessing, but the evidence that God's Spirit is filling us is that we give thanks "always for all things" even in the midst of less-than-desirable circumstances.

Jonah, from inside the fish's belly, said, "I will sacrifice to You with the voice of thanksgiving. . . . Salvation is of the LORD" (Jonah 2:9). The next verse says, "So the LORD spoke to the fish, and it vomited Jonah onto dry land." Thanksgiving will set you free. It is the upward evidence of the filling of the Spirit.

When have you experienced the power of giving thanks to God in the midst of problems?

MAY 22

YOUR PRAYER PERSPECTIVE

The Lord is in His holy temple.
HABAKKUK 2:20

Some people place their prayer focus *on* their present circumstances. This is Habakkuk's consuming prayer focus when he asks, "O Lord, how long shall I cry, and You will not hear?" (Habakkuk 1:2).

When unfair circumstances surround us and we focus our prayers on them, it leads us to ask questions that have no satisfactory answers. There is a better way to focus in prayer than by placing all our attention *on* our circumstances and situations.

We can place our prayer focus *through* our present circumstances. The prophet changes his focus in chapter 2 when he climbs up on a watchtower to "watch to see what He will say to me" (Habakkuk 2:1). He begins to focus his prayers *through* his present challenges instead of *on* them.

Perspective is vital in our prayer life. Habakkuk began to look at the issue from God's perspective and not his own. His focus led him to understand that God had not abdicated His throne, that in and through it all, He was still in charge.

How could a change of perspective help you when it seems God is not answering your prayers?

MAY 23

Wisdom from Above

But the wisdom that is from above is first pure, then peaceable, gentle, willing to yield, full of mercy and good fruits, without partiality and without hypocrisy.
JAMES 3:17

When we apply heaven's wisdom in our lives, purity—or spiritual integrity—results. We don't become pure through our own efforts but through the blood of Jesus and His finished work on the cross. A pure person will be "peaceable," a promoter of peace. Jesus didn't pronounce a blessing on the peace lovers in the Beatitudes but on the peacemakers (Matthew 5:9).

Another benefit that comes when we apply the wisdom of God is patience—or "gentleness," a willingness to yield and show consideration for others.

Next, God's wisdom is characterized by an abundance of mercy and forgiveness and being "full of good fruits." Jesus' true followers will be known "by their fruits" (Matthew 7:20).

Finally, heaven's wisdom results in our being "without partiality and without hypocrisy." We aren't "hypocrites"—two-faced individuals hiding behind the mask of a false life.

Each of us must choose between the wisdom of the world and the wisdom of the Word. The wisest decision is to line up on God's side.

Why is regular Bible study so important in seeking and maintaining the "wisdom that is from above"?

MAY 24

God Receives Us with Open Arms

But now, O Lord, You are our Father; we are the clay, and You our potter; and all we are the work of Your hand.

ISAIAH 64:8

Father is a difficult word for some of us to get our minds around. In fact, for many people, this very word is at the root of many unresolved problems in relationships with others. It is an all-too-common reality that some of us have difficulty relating to others due to feelings of inadequate self-confidence and self-worth that are rooted in unpleasant relationships with our earthly fathers. But God is not an earthly father. He is a perfect, loving heavenly Father.

When we are ready to connect, or reconnect, with God, He receives us with open arms and gives us a brand-new beginning. He will become a source of strength and power to any and all of us who come to Him—especially those of us who may not have had positive relationships with our earthly fathers. This eternal connection, touching our source of being, begins when we see Him as our Father and view ourselves as His beloved sons and daughters.

How do you view your personal connection to God the Father?

MAY 25

God's Sustaining Word

So Ezra the priest brought the Law before the assembly. . . . Then he read from it in the open square . . . and the ears of all the people were attentive to the Book of the Law.

NEHEMIAH 8:2–3

Ezra, like Jesus, gave the people of God something that would endure through the centuries to come. He organized the chosen people around the Torah, the Word of God. To this very day, this is the distinguishing mark of the Jewish people—not geography or national origin but adherence to God's Word, the sacred Torah. This is what sustained them through Roman persecution, worldwide dispersion, the Spanish Inquisition, the Russian pogroms, the Polish ghettos, and the Nazi death camps. God's Word, both living in the person of Christ and written in the holy Scriptures, is alive and well. When we see Ezra, there is a real sense in which we see our own faithful Scribe, the Lord Jesus Christ, for "in the beginning was the Word, and the Word was with God, and the Word was God. . . . And the Word became flesh and dwelt among us, and we beheld His glory, the glory as of the only begotten of the Father, full of grace and truth" (John 1:1, 14).

In what situations in your life has God's Word sustained you?

MAY 26

Don't Delay in Seeking the Lord

Seek the Lord *while He may be found, call upon Him while He is near.*
ISAIAH 55:6

The wisest people I have known are not those with degrees from esteemed institutions of higher learning but those whose lives are characterized by seeking the Lord continually.

The Bible admonishes us to seek Him "while He may be found." This brings the element of urgency into the equation. There will not always be adequate time to call on Him. We derive our word *callous* from the Greek word found in Ephesians 4:19 where Paul described someone who is "past feeling." I have a callus on the bottom of my foot. I can stick a pin in it and not feel it. There comes a time, after one repeatedly rejects Christ, that his heart "hardens" toward spiritual things like a callus and he becomes "past feeling." It is not that the Lord ceases to call but that we can reach a point where we cease to hear and feel. Seek the Lord while He may be found. Remember, there will not always be adequate time.

In what ways do you need to seek God without delay?

MAY 27

The Spirit Knows What We Need

But the Helper, the Holy Spirit, whom the Father will send in My name, He will teach you all things, and bring to your remembrance all things that I said to you.
JOHN 14:26

The Holy Spirit helps us in our "weaknesses" (Romans 8:26). It's no surprise we are weak at times and need help with our prayer life. Remember our Lord's words to His disciples in Gethsemane's prayer garden, "Could you not watch one hour?" (Mark 14:37). Jesus knew our weakness, so He sent us a prayer partner to help us.

We "do not know what we should pray for as we ought" (Romans 8:26). Even the great apostle Paul unsuccessfully prayed three times about a "thorn in the flesh." And then he heard from his prayer partner, "My grace is sufficient for you, for My strength is made perfect in weakness" (2 Corinthians 12:9).

We often confuse our needs with our wants and do not know what is in our best interests or "do not know what we should pray." The something or somcone we think we want is often not what we really need. But the Spirit knows exactly what we need—and He lovingly intercedes on our behalf with the Father.

When have you prayed for something and later realized it was not what you really needed after all?

MAY 28

Transparency in Friendship

Faithful are the wounds of a friend, but the kisses of an enemy are deceitful.
PROVERBS 27:6

Accountability calls us to be transparent with our friends. Everyone needs someone with whom they can be genuinely open, honest, and candid. This vulnerability carries with it the risk of being wounded. But transparency is imperative if we are ever to be truly accountable to one another.

Those who live in accountable relationships must also be touchable. That is, we must be accessible and approachable, especially toward those with whom we entrust our transparency. To his friends in Rome, Paul wrote, "I myself am confident concerning you . . . that you also are full of goodness . . . able also to admonish one another" (Romans 15:14). Earlier he stated in a letter to his friends in the region of Galatia, "Let us not become conceited, provoking one another, envying one another" (Galatians 5:26). To be in an accountability relationship demands transparency but also that we be touchable, accessible, and approachable.

In a specific relationship, what steps could you take to become more accountable and more accessible?

MAY 29

Establish Your Heart

You also be patient. Establish your hearts, for the coming of the Lord is at hand. Do not grumble against one another, brethren, lest you be condemned. Behold, the Judge is standing at the door!

JAMES 5:8–9

When we find ourselves in a holding pattern—such as waiting for the Lord to return—it's easy to become irritated and frustrated, to hold grudges and be bitter and resentful. Since Christ could return any day and at any time, we should keep our hearts clean and be ready to meet Him at any moment.

"Establishing your heart" is something only you can do. No one can do it for you. As the voice and tense of this Greek phrase indicates, the subject has to take action. Until the Lord returns, therefore, we should not just look up to Him and be calm. We should also look in and be clean.

James called upon us to cease grumbling against one another. This refers to resentment buried deep within our hearts that manifests itself in negative and sometimes harsh words. Why cease to grumble? Because "the Judge is standing at the door!" And this Judge knows the secrets of every heart.

Why doesn't God want us to hold bitterness and resentment toward others?

MAY 30

The Who and What Questions

But the manifestation of the Spirit is given to each one for the profit of all.
1 CORINTHIANS 12:7

In Acts 9:6, after his dramatic conversion, Paul's first question to Jesus was, "Lord, what do You want me to do?" Notice who He asked. Many of us pray something like this: "Lord, here are my marching orders for You today." But a day will dawn on your Christian experience when you put Christ first and begin by praying, "Lord, what do *You* want *me* to do today?" It is not what you want to do but what God wants you to do that matters most.

Next comes the question "what?" Just as God "ordained" Jeremiah and Paul to a specific task, He has uniquely assigned you a specific assignment. *Ordained* is from the Old Testament word meaning "to assign; to designate." The same word is used in Genesis 1:17 when God "set [the stars] in the firmament." Just as God has set and assigned each star, He has assigned each of us a job to do.

Make Paul's question your daily prayer: "Lord, what do You want me to do?"

How often do you tell God what you want to do instead of asking Him what *He* wants *you* to do?

MAY 31

The Power of Submitting to God's Will

Not My will, but Yours, be done.
LUKE 22:42

Many well-meaning believers rush into the promise of James 4:7–8, which says we are to "resist the devil and he will flee," attempting to resist the devil and draw near to God. But they completely ignore the first phrase of the verse, which calls us to "submit to God." Our ability to resist satanic influences and overcome in life has a prerequisite. First and foremost, it calls on us to live a life of submission to God's will and way and not to insist on our own. To submit literally means to "line up under." The first step in overcoming our setbacks and sins is to place ourselves under the lordship of Jesus Christ. This is accomplished by a single act of our will, which precludes having our own way. Our life becomes characterized by "His will, not our will" and "His way, not our way." It is closely akin to the prayer Jesus Himself prayed on the eve of the crucifixion in Gethsemane's garden: "Not My will, but Yours, be done."

Are you facing a situation in which you need to submit to God's will? What is it, and how can you submit?

JUNE

JUNE 1

The Acid Tests of True Discipleship

We know that we have passed from death to life, because we love the brethren. . . . If someone says, "I love God," and hates his brother, he is a liar.

1 JOHN 3:14; 4:20

A good percentage of Americans indicate they still believe in some type of relationship with God and believe Him to be the source of all being. But the two tests of authentic discipleship are found in Paul's words in Philemon verse 5, where he speaks of hearing of Philemon's "love and faith" that he has "toward the Lord Jesus and toward all the saints"—a personal belief followed by a positive behavior. Loyalty to Christ and love for others. These are two wings on the same airplane, two sides of the same coin. Like ham and eggs, and steak and potatoes, they appear together. In our increasingly secular age, we are constantly being told it does not matter what we believe as long as we love others and tolerate their aberrant lifestyles. But what we truly believe has its own way of determining how we behave. Paul's own leader, Jesus of Nazareth, when asked which was the greatest of all the commandments, said that it was loving others out of a genuine love for God (Matthew 22:36–40).

How do faith and love work together?

JUNE 2

The Pastor's Crown

Shepherd the flock of God which is among you, serving as overseers, not by compulsion but willingly, not for dishonest gain but eagerly; nor as being lords over those entrusted to you, but being examples to the flock; and when the Chief Shepherd appears, you will receive the crown of glory that does not fade away.

1 PETER 5:2–4

As the Chief Shepherd, it is Jesus' responsibility to mend broken relationships, to save our country and appoint godly leaders when we deserve such, and to meet our needs. Pastors and ministers are simply His representatives who are called to feed, lead, protect, and provide for His sheep.

The faithful pastor has a special prize awaiting him, the "crown of glory" mentioned in today's scripture. At Jesus' glorious appearing, when He comes again, He will set the faithful pastor, His under-shepherd, apart from everyone else for an unusual recognition and reward. Just think of it—the Chief Shepherd, the Lord Himself, will say, "Well done, good and faithful servant" (Matthew 25:21). Then upon the pastor's head He will place the "crown of glory." All those times of being misunderstood, misrepresented, unappreciated, or unwelcome will pale into nothingness on that glorious day. It will all be worth it.

Which faithful pastors have influenced you in godly ways?

JUNE 3

Flee Sexual Immorality

Flee sexual immorality. Every sin that a man does is outside the body, but he who commits sexual immorality sins against his own body.
1 CORINTHIANS 6:18

Notice the force and urgency of Paul's admonition in today's scripture. He was not exhorting us to flee sex. Within the marriage relationship, where it is intended, sex is pure and beautiful. He was addressing sexual immorality, encounters and acts that fall outside biblical boundaries. The Greek word from which we get *immorality* is the same root word from which the English word *pornography* comes.

Paul admonished believers to flee, to run, to get out of there. While a slave in Egypt, Joseph did exactly that—he immediately resisted Potiphar's wife's seductive advances and fled (Genesis 39:12). Like Joseph, we are to consciously, purposefully, and even perpetually run away from sexual immorality whenever we notice it lurking.

Some try to fight rather than flee. Overconfident, they think they can resist the temptation and handle the situation. To this Paul said, "Let him who thinks he stands take heed lest he fall" (1 Corinthians 10:12).

Sexual immorality can devastate three types of relationships—with others, with our own selves, and with God. So "flee sexual immorality."

Why is it so important to "flee sexual immorality" immediately?

JUNE 4

Always Present

Where can I go from Your Spirit? Or where can I flee from Your presence?
PSALM 139:7

No matter where we are, God is there. Jonah attempted to flee from God's presence. But to no avail. Adam and Eve tried to hide from God in the cool of the garden. But, again, to no avail. Isaiah's prophecy that the coming Messiah would be called "Immanuel," meaning "God with us," underscores this wonderful truth that He is always with us (Isaiah 7:14). Where can we go from God's presence? There is not a corner of this big world where He is not present.

Because God is always present, we are never alone. And this assurance of His presence brought comfort and hope to the apostle Paul in some of his darkest hours. On more than one occasion Paul described how the Lord stood by him or with him (Acts 23:11; 2 Timothy 4:16–18). God's constant presence with us is indeed a wonder. He knows you, and He is always near.

Our God of wonder is everywhere always. He knows the number of hairs on your head, and there is nowhere you can go from His Spirit (Matthew 10:30).

How does knowing that God is always with you bring you comfort?

JUNE 5

OUR KINSMAN-REDEEMER

Then Naomi said to her daughter-in-law, "Blessed be he of the LORD, who has not forsaken His kindness to the living and the dead!" And Naomi said to her, "This man is a relation of ours, one of our close relatives."

RUTH 2:20

Ruth, the previously pagan widow who chose to worship the God of Israel, married Boaz, the lord of the harvest, her kinsman-redeemer. They had a son, Obed, who had a son named Jesse, who had a son named David, the shepherd, psalmist, king. Ruth, this former godless Moabite, became the great-grandmother of Israel's greatest king. She lived a beautiful life and left a lasting legacy, totally separated from her old life in Moab. The entire course of her life was determined by another person, Boaz. What a wonderful picture of you and me when we truly say to our Redeemer what Ruth said to her mother-in-law, Naomi: "Wherever you go, I will go; and wherever you lodge, I will lodge; your people shall be my people, and your God, my God" (Ruth 1:16). Today, Ruth lives on in history and in heaven, an example for us all, because of her very own kinsman-redeemer, Boaz. Jesus is our Boaz, our very own Kinsman-Redeemer.

How have you seen Jesus as a Kinsman-Redeemer in your life or in someone else's life?

JUNE 6

All Things

And we know that all things work together for good to those who love God, to those who are the called according to His purpose.
ROMANS 8:28

Thinking of today's scripture, I am prone to ask myself if I can really believe it. Had Paul said "some things" or "many things" or even "most things," it would be a bit more palatable. But "all things"? *All things* can include unfair things. This was certainly true for Joseph, who was sold into slavery, taken to a foreign land, falsely accused of a crime, and thrown into an Egyptian dungeon. Also, consider the one from whom these words flowed. Paul was shipwrecked at Malta, stoned at Lystra and left for dead, and repeatedly beaten and berated during the years of his missionary journeys. For Paul, these words were not simply trite platitudes but came out of his personal experience as the Holy Spirit led him to record this promise.

Yes, *all things* are what? *Working together.* For what? *Our good.* All things—not in isolation, not necessarily in and of themselves, but when worked together in the tapestry of the cross—have a way of coming out on the other end for our good.

When have you seen God work all things together for good?

JUNE 7

Don't Stop Praying

I say to you, though he will not rise and give to him because he is his friend, yet because of his persistence he will rise and give him as many as he needs.

LUKE 11:8

The highest level of prayer is *persisting in a petition*. "Knock, and it will be opened to you" (Matthew 7:7). Knocking implies perseverance. We see this in Jesus' story of the man who came to his friend's home at midnight and continued knocking on his door until the friend opened it (Luke 11:5–8). We persist in prayer when we are confident of God's will in a matter but have not yet seen the answer. The verb tense indicates a continuous action. We are to keep on knocking.

Those of us with children know that when they are small, we teach them to "ask." As they grow, we teach them to "seek." We teach them to show real earnestness until doors open for them. Some children are given everything they ask for and are never taught to seek . . . much less knock.

If you are confident of God's will in the matter for which you are praying but have not yet seen the answer, keep on knocking "and it will be opened to you."

Why can you be encouraged to keep "knocking" even if you don't get an answer right away?

Are You a Good Friend?

A man who has friends must himself be friendly, but there is a friend who sticks closer than a brother.
PROVERBS 18:24

You know you have a true friend when they are not simply sensitive to your feelings but are supportive of you in front of others. Think about your own relationships. Do your friends see you as one who is as sensitive to their needs as you are to your own? Or would they say you too often think only of yourself and how the relationship can benefit you? Do those in your inner circle of relationships think of you as being submissive? Or do you generally insist on getting your own way in order to relate and be happy? Do they have the assurance that you will be supportive of them when issues might arise? Do they know, without a shadow of a doubt, that you would rise to their defense if the situation called for it? These are valuable questions to ask yourself, and even to ask of a true and trusted friend, as you grow and mature in your ability to be a good friend and build strong, long-term relationships.

How do you think your true friends view you?

JUNE 9

The Fear of the Lord

And now, Israel, what does the Lord *your God require of you, but to fear the* Lord *your God, to walk in all His ways and to love Him, to serve the* Lord *your God with all your heart and with all your soul.*

DEUTERONOMY 10:12

The oft-forgotten idea of living in the fear of the Lord is woven like a thread through the pages of Scripture.

What does it really mean to live in the fear of the Lord? Are we to live our lives in constant fright or flight, concerned that if we do or say something wrong, God will zap us with His hand of retribution? Nothing could be further from biblical truth.

Living in the fear of God is not living with the fear that God might put His hand of retribution upon us in discipline. It is the fear that God might take His hand *off* us—His hand of protection, His hand of blessing, His hand of anointing. Living the Spirit-filled life means we have a conscious awareness of His continual presence, and we do not want to do anything that would cause God to take His hand of anointing off us. This makes a difference in where we go, what we watch, what we say, and how we live.

How could living in greater fear of the Lord make a difference in your life?

THE POWERFUL BLOOD OF CHRIST

And as they were eating, Jesus took bread, blessed and broke it, and gave it to the disciples and said, "Take, eat; this is My body." Then He took the cup, and gave thanks, and gave it to them, saying, "Drink from it, all of you. For this is My blood of the new covenant, which is shed for many for the remission of sins."

MATTHEW 26:26–28

Fifteen hundred years following the first Passover, Jesus gathered His disciples in an upper room on Mount Zion in Jerusalem to commemorate the Passover with those nearest and dearest to Him. He knew when He passed the bread and lifted the cup that in a few hours His own body would be broken for us and His own blood would be poured out to make a way to heaven for us. Applying the blood to the doorposts of those Israelite homes back in Egypt meant two things: freedom from slavery and deliverance from death. Applying the blood of Christ to our own lives means the same two things: freedom from slavery to sin, which has its way of binding us and enslaving us, and deliverance from spiritual death. It's no wonder Paul said, "The wages of sin is death, but the gift of God is eternal life in Christ Jesus our Lord" (Romans 6:23).

How has Jesus set you free from slavery to sin and delivered you from spiritual death?

JUNE 11

Salvation Begins with God

Of His own will He brought us forth by the word of truth, that we might be a kind of firstfruits of His creatures.
JAMES 1:18

Biblical salvation does not and cannot result from any human effort or good works. Salvation begins with God, not with us. Had God not chosen us, we never would have chosen Him.

Without Christ, we are *unresponsive* to the offer of salvation. We are "dead in trespasses and sins" (Ephesians 2:1). We are also *unperceptive*: The gospel "is veiled to those who are perishing . . . who do not believe" (2 Corinthians 4:3–4). We are *unteachable* as well: "The natural man does not receive the things of the Spirit of God, for they are foolishness to him; nor can he know them, because they are spiritually discerned" (1 Corinthians 2:14). Finally, we are *unrighteous.* King David reminded us all of this fact: "I was brought forth in iniquity, and in sin my mother conceived me" (Psalm 51:5).

But here's the good news. Since we can do nothing to reach our holy God, He must be the initiator of our salvation—and He is! As Jesus said, "You did not choose Me, but I chose you" (John 15:16).

How did God initiate your journey to faith in Christ?

The Importance of an Understanding Heart

Give to Your servant an understanding heart to judge Your people, that I may discern between good and evil.
1 KINGS 3:9

Some people feel that all their problems are someone else's fault. Not Solomon. He asked that God would work with him, not someone else. He asked God for "an understanding heart," meaning wisdom. Too often we go about trying to change the world with external forces. We are prone to think social activism or shouting a little louder will effect change, when what we really need is an internal change of heart.

Solomon asked for something he lacked inside himself—wisdom and understanding. He had the greatest education money could buy, but there's a difference between knowledge and wisdom. Knowledge is the accumulation of facts; wisdom is the ability to take those facts, discern them, and make the right decisions from them.

Solomon could have asked for anything. But he knew his greatest need was for God to work in him and not just outside him, to give him wisdom. If we have a heart that can hear from God, understanding His will and way for us, what else would we ever need to live life well?

How could wisdom and an understanding heart help you change the world around you?

JUNE 13

God in Us

They were all filled with the Holy Spirit.
ACTS 2:4

The streets of Jerusalem were jammed with Jews who had descended upon the city for the celebration of Pentecost, fifty days after the Passover. Jesus had ascended to heaven and, obedient to His instructions, the disciples had gathered in the upper room. On the day of Pentecost, suddenly there came the sound of a mighty rushing wind followed by the sight of tongues of fire resting on each one's head. Then the disciples began to speak in languages and dialects they did not know, and people heard these utterances—each in his own language.

This was a onetime event when the Holy Spirit came to dwell in every believer with the promise never to leave. Pentecost can never be repeated any more than Bethlehem or Calvary. Bethlehem was a onetime event when God came to be *with* us. Calvary was a onetime event when we see God *for* us on the cross. In like manner, Pentecost was a onetime event when we see God *in* us.

How does the disciples' experience on Pentecost give you hope about the power within you to serve the Lord?

JUNE 14

Call Sin, "Sin"

And many who had believed came confessing and telling their deeds.
ACTS 19:18

We are adept at having all sorts of ways to avoid personal responsibility for our sins. We say, "Oh, that is not worry; it's simply concern." Or, "That is not anger; it's righteous indignation." We say, "That is not lust, simply an appreciative glance." But confession does not say such things. Confession agrees with God about our sin. What we may try to camouflage as concern, God calls the sin of worry. What we like to call righteous indignation, God, who knows our hearts, calls the sin of anger. What we like to think is just an admiring glance, God calls the sin of lust and even says, "Whoever looks at a woman to lust for her has already committed adultery with her in his heart" (Matthew 5:28). Confession gets open and honest in agreement with God, and without it there is no forgiveness of our sins.

When you sin, are you easily tempted to call it something other than "sin"? If so, how can you become more open and honest with God about it?

JUNE 15

Faith That Works

Was not Abraham our father justified by works when he offered Isaac his son on the altar? Do you see that faith was working together with his works, and by works faith was made perfect?
JAMES 2:21–22

In the faith-versus-works debate, people tend to gravitate toward the extremes. Some overemphasize the faith aspect while completely neglecting the fact that it should result in good works. According to this "faith, not works" school of thought, people can pray a simple "sinner's prayer," have no change of lifestyle, develop no desire to pray, never open a Bible, exhibit zero desire for spiritual things, yet still be saved because they "believed." I call this an easy believism.

Other believers argue for "faith or works." If you say you have faith, that's fine with them. Or if you do good works around the community, that's also fine. This universalist mentality trusts that ultimately everyone will arrive at some type of utopian existence.

There are also those who start arguing for "faith and works." This mindset overemphasizes works and de-emphasizes faith. They think there's a way to earn our way into eternal life.

Here is the code we need to understand the relationship of faith and works: Salvation is not about faith and works; it is about a faith that works!

If someone asked you about the relationship between a Christian's faith and works, how would you explain it?

JUNE 16

Forgiveness Requires Strength

Then Peter came to Him and said, "Lord, how often shall my brother sin against me, and I forgive him? Up to seven times?" Jesus said to him, "I do not say to you, up to seven times, but up to seventy times seven."

MATTHEW 18:21–22

Relationally speaking, the way forward is always back—back to forgive and find a place of new beginnings. It was on this very point that Paul said, "Let all bitterness, wrath, anger, clamor, and evil speaking be put away from you, with all malice. And be kind to one another, tenderhearted, forgiving one another, even as God in Christ forgave you" (Ephesians 4:31–32). In our self-centered world, some people have a warped and wrong image of someone who forgives and begins again in a relationship. One who forgives is caricatured in the minds of some as one who is weak and wimpy. However, just the opposite is true. Forgiveness is not only a positive force but a powerful one as well. It takes someone with inner strength to forgive. Anyone can wallow around, harboring resentment with an unforgiving spirit. It takes no strength to do that. But it takes a person of strength and depth to be able to say and mean, "I forgive you. Let's start all over with a new slate and begin again."

Why is forgiveness an act of strength, not a demonstration of weakness?

JUNE 17

GOD IS WITH YOU

And the LORD, He is the One who goes before you. He will be with you, He will not leave you nor forsake you; do not fear nor be dismayed.

DEUTERONOMY 31:8

God's promise to be with us always is woven like a thread throughout the entire Bible, showing up time and again throughout the Scriptures. Let's think today about how we see it in the Old Testament. Moses heard it from a burning bush in Exodus 3:12. God spoke it to His people, Israel, in the words of today's scripture. Joshua clung to it as he led the people into their promised possession (Joshua 1:9).

When Gideon needed a word from God, the Lord promised to be with him (Judges 6:16). And when things looked bleak for King Jehoshaphat, the prophet told him not to fear or be dismayed because the Lord was with him (2 Chronicles 20:17).

In moments of great need, God promised Isaiah and Jeremiah that He would be with them (Isaiah 43:2; Jeremiah 42:11). The prophets Haggai and Zechariah received the same assurance (Haggai 1:13; Zephaniah 3:17). When God repeats something throughout Scripture, we know it's important and we can count on it. We can count on Him to be with us.

How does the knowledge that God is with you make a difference in your life?

JUNE 18

SHIFT YOUR FOCUS

Though the fig tree may not blossom, nor fruit be on the vines . . . the olive may fail . . . the fields yield no food . . . the flock may be cut off . . . no herd in the stalls . . . yet I will rejoice in the LORD, I will joy in the God of my salvation.

HABAKKUK 3:17–18

Habakkuk 1 shows us the prophet placing his prayer focus *on* his present circumstances. In chapter 2 he shifts his perspective to focus *through* his circumstances. Finally, in chapter 3 verse 18 he is able to place his focus *beyond* his circumstances. "*Yet I will rejoice* in the LORD, I will joy in the God of my salvation."

This is the same man who, three brief chapters earlier, was shaking his fist in the face of God and blaming Him for his desperate dilemma. What changed? In a word, *focus*; his prayer focus. The same thing can happen to you when you are tempted to question, accuse, and even blame God for what may feel like His coldness to you. Stop focusing your prayers *on* your circumstances and put your prayer focus *through* them. If you will do this, you will begin to focus your prayers *beyond* your present problems. Then you, like Habakkuk, can find the comfort only God can bring to your heart.

How can you look beyond your circumstances when praying?

Anger Hurts Us

Then the Lord said, "Is it right for you to be angry?"
JONAH 4:4

One would think that after all the prophet Jonah had been through, he would be praising God for sending revival to the people of Nineveh. Instead, we read that God's mercy "displeased Jonah exceedingly, and he became angry" (Jonah 4:1). The Greek word we translate as *angry* means "to burn." Jonah was fuming. This is the first by-product of harboring resentment and anger: It takes away our own peace of heart and mind.

Anger has a far more debilitating effect on us than the object of our anger. It not only destroys our peace but it diverts us from our God-given purpose. Jonah's anger caused him to make decisions on a what's-best-for-me basis. No longer was he concerned about God's purposes in his life or in the lives of the Ninevites.

Anger eats at us like a cancer while almost never affecting the one to whom it is directed. So deal with anger just as you would any other sin: Confess it and forsake it. And let God's grace and pardon transform your perspective through new eyes.

Have you confessed any anger you may feel toward anyone for any reason and received God's forgiveness?

JUNE 20

The Passover Lamb

Now the blood shall be a sign for you on the houses where you are. And when I see the blood, I will pass over you; and the plague shall not be on you to destroy you when I strike the land of Egypt.
EXODUS 12:13

The last plague God sent upon Egypt was the most devastating: the death of all the firstborn throughout the entire land. To be spared the plague, the Jews were instructed to take a young lamb—perfect and without blemish—slay it, and spread its blood over the lintels and doorposts of their homes so that on the fateful night the Lord passed through, He would "see the blood" and "pass over." Every home where the blood was applied was spared the death of their firstborn.

The sacrificial lamb is a perfect picture of the coming Deliverer, the Lord Jesus Christ. Just as Christ was in the prime of life when He went to the cross, the lamb had to be a male of the first year. Just as Christ was perfect and without sin, the lamb was to be "without blemish." It's no wonder that when Simon Peter spoke of Christ's sacrifice, he declared that we are saved by "the precious blood of Christ, as of a lamb without blemish and without spot" (1 Peter 1:19).

What qualities come to mind when you think of a lamb, and how is Jesus the perfect representation of them?

JUNE 21

VISIBLE FRUIT

The fruit of the Spirit is love, joy, peace, longsuffering, kindness, goodness, faithfulness, gentleness, self-control.
GALATIANS 5:22–23

The sentence structure in today's Scripture verses appears to include a grammatical error—"The fruit of the Spirit *is* love, joy, peace" and so on. But the apostle is correct. This ninefold fruit of the Spirit is the outward evidence of the presence of the One living within us. It is beyond our natural ability to produce. The Holy Spirit is the Author of these attributes and the Source from which they flow. The fruit is *what we are*, and it is wrought in us by *whose we are*—not by anything *we do* in our own strength.

This fruit produced by the Spirit-controlled life manifests itself in three areas. First, in your *countenance*—that is, your personal relationship with God, the expression of which is love, joy, and peace. Second, in your *conduct*, in your relationship with others, the outward expression of which is long-suffering, kindness, and goodness. Finally, by your *character*—who you are in your relationship with yourself—the expression of which is faithfulness, gentleness, and self-control.

What type of fruit do you see manifesting in your life?

JUNE 22

The War Within

Where do wars and fights come from among you? Do they not come from your desires for pleasure that war in your members? You lust and do not have. You murder and covet and cannot obtain. You fight and war. Yet you do not have because you do not ask. You ask and do not receive, because you ask amiss, that you may spend it on your pleasures.

JAMES 4:1–3

War of any kind and on every scale always finds its origin in selfish desire. It doesn't matter whether it is a global war, a gang war, a family feud, or a war of words between friends or acquaintances.

In the fleshly realm there is a part of us that wants what we do not have—someone else's job, opportunity, even their spouse. This war within ourselves drives us to desires that are outside God's boundaries. Ask those consumed by money or lust or popularity, "How much is enough?" The reply will be, "Just a little more." Worldly things will never permanently satisfy the void in the human heart.

Selfishness is what causes wars among us. But the wars are simply external symptoms, not the source. Many interpersonal relationships are never healed because we focus on the externals—the fight—rather than the real issues. All the outward manifestations of conflict are symptoms of a problem that has its source in the selfishness within us.

How have you experienced pain or trouble because of selfish desires outside of God's boundaries?

JUNE 23

Purchased and Secured

The next day John saw Jesus coming toward him, and said, "Behold! The Lamb of God who takes away the sin of the world!"

JOHN 1:29

Paul, a learned and aristocratic Jew, found his source of strength in the long-awaited and promised Messiah, to whom the world had been looking and for whom the world had been waiting for centuries.

Throughout his life in the synagogue and as a member of the Jewish Sanhedrin, Paul had celebrated that high and holy Day of Atonement, Yom Kippur. In Hebrew, *Yom Kippur* means "the day of covering." It was on this holy day that the sins of the previous year were "covered" by the blood of animal sacrifice.

The old covenant between God and man with its sacrificial system "covered" the faults and failures and the sins of those who believed in the Promised One who was coming. And He came! He made the final payment for our covering with the sacrifice of His own life and the shedding of His own blood on a Roman cross of execution outside the city walls of Jerusalem. Consequently, through Christ, our relationship with the Father has been purchased and secured.

How does Christ's sacrifice make a difference in your personal life?

JUNE 24

JESUS UNDERSTANDS

Surely He has borne our griefs and carried our sorrows; yet we esteemed Him stricken, smitten by God, and afflicted.

ISAIAH 53:4

Talk about heartbreak, sorrow, misery, and grief—all these are woven through the fabric of our Lord's family tree. Can you feel their grief behind the words? The grief of Abraham leaving all he had known to go to a land where he had never been. The grief of letting go of his firstborn, Ishmael, whom he loved. And what about King David? He had a son who died in infancy because of David's own sin. Later, his son Absalom killed his brother Amnon, and if that were not enough to break a father's heart, Absalom led a revolt against his own dad.

But all these names in Christ's family tree don't hold a candle to the grief that many of us feel. Jesus understands the grief in His ancestors and His descendants. Perhaps your own heart is heavy. Perhaps you have been misunderstood. Jesus was. He says, "I understand." Perhaps you are lonely. Jesus says, "I know the loneliness of Gethsemane's garden." He will bear your griefs and carry your sorrows . . . if you will let Him.

How does the fact that Jesus experienced grief help you cope with the grief you may feel at times?

JUNE 25

Celebrate Christmas Today

Then the shepherds returned, glorifying and praising God for all the things that they had heard and seen, as it was told them.

LUKE 2:20

Whatever the date, resolve to make room for Christmas today. Because when Christmas does roll around at the end of every year, we get so caught up in the season—decorating the house and tree, getting that special gift, seeing relatives, and getting invited to that certain someone's party—but then the season ends, and we leave it all behind until next year. It shouldn't be that way.

Today—in the heat of summer—join the shepherds in "glorifying and praising God." Make this day a time of celebration. God "inhabitest the praises" of His people (Psalm 22:3 KJV). This is where and when God feels at home—in the midst of your praise. So welcome Him today.

And note this: The shepherds "returned." Where? To their homes and businesses, to their daily lives. What an impact this must have had on those who knew them best. May God give you the grace to follow these shepherds and make Christmas a part of every day of the year.

What are some ways you can keep Christmas in your heart all year?

JUNE 26

THE RIGHTEOUS WILL FLOURISH

The righteous shall flourish like a palm tree.
PSALM 92:12

The promise that the righteous person shall flourish and grow "like a palm tree" is not known by many but is fully descriptive of God's faithfulness to those who live righteous lives. It is imperative to note the *person described* in this promise. It is addressed to that one who is "righteous." But we meet an apparent dilemma. The Bible tells us, "There is none righteous." And to add emphasis, the verse continues, "no, not one" (Romans 3:10). The Bible is also clear in saying that "all our righteousnesses are like filthy rags" (Isaiah 64:6). While it is true in and of ourselves that we are unrighteous, it is also true that in Christ Jesus the Lord is our righteousness (Jeremiah 33:16). When we put our faith in Christ, we can say with Isaiah, "He has clothed me with the garments of salvation, He has covered me with the robe of righteousness" (Isaiah 61:10).

What does it mean to be righteous? And if you are a believer in Jesus Christ, why can you consider yourself righteous?

JUNE 27

Teachability and Truthfulness

Instead, speaking the truth in love, we will grow to become in every respect the mature body of him who is the head, that is, Christ.
EPHESIANS 4:15 NIV

Relationships profiting from genuine accountability also have the element of teachability. We should never stop learning. It is a dangerous time in a relationship when one of the parties begins to feel as if he or she has all the right answers and no longer possesses a teachable spirit. This insight requires a spirit of humility. We should never get to the point at which we feel we can no longer learn from one another, or teach one another, for that matter.

Those accountable to one another must also be truthful. Many of us cannot be held accountable because of a spirit of deception. We become so deceived in our thinking processes that we are convinced that any issue that arises in relationships is always someone else's fault. Some of us have left dozens of relationships in our wake across the years, and in our minds, we are convinced that we were not responsible for the breakup of any of them. We are deceived. Without total truthfulness in relationships, there can never be accountability.

When have you benefited from being teachable and from being truthful in your relationships?

JUNE 28

The Patience of the Prophets

My brethren, take the prophets, who spoke in the name of the Lord, as an example of suffering and patience. Indeed we count them blessed who endure.

JAMES 5:10–11

Being aware of both the patience of the prophets and the price they paid for their faith challenges me in this day of grace to keep moving forward in my own faith. This time of waiting and being encouraged by those who have waited before me builds up my anticipation for Jesus' return.

So why did James call us to "be patient" (James 5:7)? One reason is that impatience is at the root of many failures. Simon Peter came close to committing murder in the garden of Gethsemane (John 18:10). Moses' impatience caused him to strike the rock instead of speaking to it as God commanded (Numbers 20:1–13). Abraham's impatience, while waiting for God's promise to be fulfilled, led to the birth of Ishmael (Genesis 16:1–16). Paul affirmed the importance of patience when he wrote, "Whatever things were written before were written for our learning, that we through the patience and comfort of the Scriptures might have hope" (Romans 15:4).

How can the example of the patience of people mentioned in the Bible help you endure in your spiritual walk?

JUNE 29

God Sees You

She gave this name to the Lord who spoke to her: "You are the God who sees me," for she said, "I have now seen the One who sees me."

GENESIS 16:13 NIV

Have you ever not known what to do and felt that hope was almost gone? This happened to the early believers mentioned in Acts 12. John the Baptist had been beheaded, Jesus had been crucified, James had been martyred, and now Herod had thrown Peter in prison.

We, too, often face our own obstacles and feel that hope is almost gone. We wonder if God is even aware of our need. But remember that God is always looking: "The eyes of the Lord run to and fro throughout the whole earth, to show Himself strong on behalf of those whose heart is loyal to Him" (2 Chronicles 16:9). If He sees a sparrow when it falls (Matthew 10:29), how much more is He aware of your every need?

Sometimes we think no one sees us, that no one cares. But God does. Later Peter would quote King David and write, "The eyes of the Lord are on the righteous, and His ears are open to their prayers" (1 Peter 3:12). God sees you.

When have you wondered if God knew about a problem or a need in your life, then realized that He did?

JUNE 30

Stand Against the Devil

And the God of peace will crush Satan under your feet shortly.
The grace of our Lord Jesus Christ be with you. Amen.
ROMANS 16:20

Today's scripture reminds us that God will ultimately crush our enemy, Satan. In the meantime, the Enemy is determined "to steal, and to kill, and to destroy" (John 10:10), so we need to learn to resist him. James 4:7–8 challenges us, once we have submitted to God's will, to oppose evil, to "resist the devil." This Greek verb literally means "to stand against." This is a military phrase ordering us to take a stand against someone or something. It entails the defensive aspect of our struggle against the devil. Paul had this in mind when he wrote from his first Roman incarceration. He was most likely looking at the Roman guard standing over him as he wrote, "Take up the whole armor of God, that you may be able to withstand in the evil day, and having done all, to stand. Stand therefore, having girded your waist with truth, having put on the breastplate of righteousness" (Ephesians 6:13–14).

In what practical and spiritual ways can you take a stand against the Enemy?

JULY

Healing Broken Relationships

Bearing with one another, and forgiving one another, if anyone has a complaint against another; even as Christ forgave you, so you also must do.
COLOSSIANS 3:13

The problem with many of us who find ourselves in estranged relationships is that it seems easier to just walk away, resigned to the belief that we will go forward without any resolution leading to a reconciliation. But this is not the biblical model we see in the broken relationship between Philemon and Onesimus. You, like Onesimus, may be the one who has hurt or offended someone. You, like Philemon, may be the one who is hurt or offended. Or you may be like Paul, the one helping to bring restoration between two friends who need to mend a relationship. If you are the offending party in a broken relationship, first, get right in your relationship with yourself by getting right in your relationship with God. Then begin to anticipate the possibility of reconciliation through your own repentance and possibly even restitution. If you are the offended party, receive and forgive the one who offended you when, and if, they return in genuine remorse and repentance.

If you are dealing with a broken relationship, who are you most like: Onesimus, Philemon, or Paul, and why?

JULY 2

Three Steps to Repentance

Search me, O God, and know my heart . . . see if there is any wicked way in me, and lead me in the way everlasting.

PSALM 139:23–24

The essence of biblical repentance is embedded beautifully in the story of the prodigal son, who found himself not only broke—having left his family home and spent his inheritance—but broken. While feeding swine, he longed for the husks they were eating, and he "came to himself" (Luke 15:17). This first step in the repentance process, this change of mind, brought about the second step, a change in his will, his volition. In the next verse he exclaimed, "I will arise and go to my father." Once his mind and will were changed, his actions were sure to follow. Thus we read, "He arose and came to his father" (v. 20). Repentance is a change of mind. If we have truly changed our minds, our volition will be changed as well, and our changed actions—resulting in a new life direction—will follow as naturally as water running downhill.

Repentance and faith are inseparable, born at the same time. Repentance alone will not get you to heaven, but you can't get there without it.

In what situation is God showing you that you need to repent and change your mind?

JULY 3

Heavenly Equality

Let the lowly brother glory in his exaltation, but the rich in his humiliation, because as a flower of the field he will pass away. . . . So the rich man also will fade away in his pursuits.

JAMES 1:9–11

It has been said that Christians are like tea bags: They are not worth much until they have been through some hot water. And hot water—stressful trials—can be profitable to the believer. Trials have a way of bringing all of us to the same level of need.

Take the person in poverty. While the world might think little of that person, God thinks much of them. Here is one of the mysteries of God's economy: The last shall be first, and the low shall be made high in God's sight.

People blessed with material possessions may take pride in them, but Christians know that earthly treasures will one day rust, rot, or be devoured by moths. Poverty and plenty are temporary, and neither makes for happiness in the Christian life. As Jesus taught, "One's life does not consist in the abundance of the things he possesses" (Luke 12:15). Those with plenty as well as those with little should rejoice in the spiritual things they cannot lose.

Why is it important to see both those who are rich materially speaking and those who have few resources as equally important to God?

JULY 4

MERCY IN ACTION

He has shown you, O man, what is good; and what does the LORD require of you but to do justly, to love mercy, and to walk humbly with your God?

MICAH 6:8

God requires us Christ-followers to "love mercy," and the emphasis is on action, not thought. We are not simply to show mercy to others but to passionately "love mercy." *Mercy* is best defined as "not getting what we deserve," whereas *grace* is "getting what we don't deserve." This means we are required to give people what they don't always deserve—to cut them some slack and show them some mercy.

When we see someone in a difficult situation, though, we sometimes take the seat of the judge when our love for mercy should be compelling us to be Christ's hand extended to someone in need, whether or not they deserve it.

The apostle John wrote, "Beloved, let us love one another, for love is of God; and everyone who loves is born of God and knows God. He who does not love does not know God, for God is love" (1 John 4:7–8). For the one who truly loves God, doing justly and loving mercy are as natural as water running downhill.

When has someone shown you mercy when you didn't deserve it?

FATHER AND SON

Then He said, "Take now your son, your only son Isaac, whom you love, and go to the land of Moriah, and offer him there as a burnt offering on one of the mountains of which I shall tell you."
GENESIS 22:2

Abraham and Isaac's trek up Mount Moriah reminds us of a journey that would be taken some two thousand years later to the same mountain by our heavenly Father and His only begotten Son, Jesus Christ. Upon arriving at the foot of the mount, Abraham instructed his servant to stay there, saying, "The lad and I will go yonder and worship, and we will come back to you" (Genesis 22:5). On that summit a transaction took place between father and son alone. The same would be true at Mount Calvary (the northern extension of Mount Moriah). During the three hours of darkness while Jesus hung on the cross, God the Father and God the Son did business alone (Matthew 27:45). The agony of those hours was indescribable. While the final sacrifice for the sins of the world was being made, God closed the door to human eyes and turned out the lights of heaven. For three hours, the eternal transaction for your sin and mine was between the Father and the Son alone.

How has the transaction that took place between God the Father and Jesus Christ changed your life?

JULY 6

A Divine Deposit

And the Scripture was fulfilled which says, "Abraham believed God, and it was accounted to him for righteousness." And he was called the friend of God.
JAMES 2:23

Abraham was not saved by his good works or by keeping the Jewish law. Abraham was saved in the same way we are today: by faith. The only difference is that Abraham was looking forward to God's promise of redemption in the coming Messiah, and we are looking backward to the same event.

Abraham had a genuine faith that resulted in good works. He was put to the test when God instructed him to take Isaac, his only son, and sacrifice him on Mount Moriah. Abraham's faith was "accounted to him for righteousness." In some translations we read that it was "credited" for righteousness. In Greek this is an accountant's term meaning that we take a payment from someone but enter it into someone else's accounts received ledger. Like yours—like mine—Abraham's spiritual bank account was empty. We were all spiritually bankrupt. When Abraham trusted in God, God made a deposit in his account. Abraham didn't work for it; he couldn't earn it. That deposit of Jesus' righteousness was a gift in response to Abraham's faith.

When you trusted in God, what deposit did God make in your account, spiritually speaking?

JULY 7

Our Prayer Helper

In the same way, the Spirit helps us in our weakness.
ROMANS 8:26 NIV

What does the Holy Spirit do for us? He helps us. In John 14:26, Jesus actually referred to Him as "the Helper." And where does He help us? In our "weakness." This word is at times translated "crippled" or "invalid" in Scripture. The truth is, many of us are not very healthy when it comes to having an effective prayer life. Jesus knew this. After all, His own disciples could not even watch and pray with Him for an hour in His greatest time of need. So He sent each believer a prayer partner, the Holy Spirit, to help us where we are weak.

However, just because someone is there to help us does not mean we let them. Some of us are too proud to admit we are weak, much less in need of help. Unfortunately, some "resist the Holy Spirit" (Acts 7:51); others "grieve the Holy Spirit" (Ephesians 4:30) by never acknowledging their need of His help; and some "quench the Spirit" (1 Thessalonians 5:19) when they continue to live with unconfessed sin.

When have you failed to realize or acknowledge that you need the Holy Spirit's help and either resisted, grieved, or quenched Him?

JULY 8

His Perfect Promise

For God so loved the world that He gave His only begotten Son, that whoever believes in Him should not perish but have everlasting life.
JOHN 3:16

If you have ever memorized a verse of Scripture, most likely it is John 3:16. It is the entire gospel in a nutshell.

John 3:16 speaks of the *cause* of this great salvation: "For God so loved . . ." The single motivating factor behind God's entire redemptive plan is His love for you and me. This beloved verse also speaks of the *cost* of this salvation: "He gave His only begotten Son." Jesus paid a high price to redeem us to Himself—death on a Roman cross outside the city gates of Jerusalem. And salvation's *condition*? "Whoever believes in Him . . ." That speaks of me. It speaks of you. And any and all may come, placing their faith in Him alone. Finally, this verse speaks of salvation's *consequence*: We "should not perish but have everlasting life." Those without Christ are perishing . . . a little more each day.

Let God love you today as you meditate on this old and oft-repeated promise.

What new insights have you gained about God, Jesus, and yourself from today's meditation?

JULY 9

A Fruitful Vine

Abide in Me, and I in you. As the branch cannot bear fruit of itself, unless it abides in the vine, neither can you, unless you abide in Me.

JOHN 15:4

People judge the worth of a gardener by his or her fruit. Similarly, the fruit of the Spirit is a by-product of God's presence in us. First, abiding believers know *who they are.* Jesus, as the Vine, is the channel though which the life-producing sap flows into the branches to produce the fruit. We are the branches—an extension of the Vine for the purpose of bearing fruit to bless others. We must stay connected to produce fruit, or we wither and die.

Abiding believers also know *where they are.* When a branch is grafted into a vine, it becomes one with the vine. True fruit bearers abide in the living Word, the Lord Jesus, and have the written Word, the Scriptures, abiding in them. Then we can "ask what [we] desire, and it shall be done" (John 15:7).

Third, abiding believers know *why they are.* Our primary purpose is to bring glory not to our ourselves but to our heavenly Father (John 15:8).

How well is the fruit from your vine feeding others?

JULY 10

Jesus Is the Bread of Life

And Jesus said to them, "I am the bread of life. He who comes to Me shall never hunger, and he who believes in Me shall never thirst."

JOHN 6:35

There is so much behind Christ's words, "I am the bread of life." He is the true manna that came down from the Father to sustain us and give us life. The manna God provided to His people as they wandered in the wilderness demonstrated to the world that we have a God who cares and provides for us. Just as the manna arrived supernaturally, so did Jesus Christ. He miraculously came down from heaven; was planted into the womb of a young Jewish virgin; and appeared in a Middle Eastern stable one star-filled night. Just as the manna had to be gathered and eaten by each individual, so each of us individually must receive Jesus by faith through being born again. Just as this manna was needed day by day, our Lord prayed, "Give us this day our *daily* bread" (Matthew 6:11). With Jesus, God's mercies are "new every morning" (Lamentations 3:23). And just as the manna never ran out, in Christ there is an inexhaustible supply of love, joy, peace, and all the remaining fruit of the Spirit.

In what ways is knowing Jesus life-giving to you?

JULY 11

Faith Comes by Hearing

Having been born again, not of corruptible seed but incorruptible, through the word of God which lives and abides forever.

1 PETER 1:23

No one has ever been converted apart from God's Word. As Paul stated, "Faith comes by hearing, and hearing by the word of God" (Romans 10:17).

Conviction always precedes conversion in a Christian's life. God's Word cuts us "to the heart" (Acts 2:37). The Word of God reveals to us that we are sinners in need of salvation. God's Word also makes plain to us the way to eternal life.

The Word of God, living and written, is God's instrument of salvation. True faith involves knowing Christ as Savior and Lord, knowing that salvation has its very origin in the sovereignty of God, and knowing that salvation operates through the Bible, God's Word to us.

The outcome of our salvation is "that we might be a kind of firstfruits of His creatures" (James 1:18). The Word of God is the seed that brings forth fruit in our lives. Once we become a part of God's family, we, too, will bear fruit; and Jesus said that people will know His people "by their fruits" (Matthew 7:16).

What role has God's Word played in your conversion experience?

Relationships, Not Religion

And may the Lord make you increase and abound in love to one another and to all, just as we do to you.
1 THESSALONIANS 3:12

There are a lot of people who think that when we put on the uniform of the Christian faith, we start playing on a losing team. There are a lot of people who go through life thinking that Christianity is about religion without ever discovering that it is all about relationships. Religion has a history of playing win-lose. It has coerced, controlled, oppressed, obsessed, and virtually enslaved people through the centuries. It has been at the root of world conflicts and today is the cause of so much tension and unrest in the Middle East.

Paul was not about religion. He was all about relationships. And there is a world of difference. For Paul all meaningful relationships began by getting connected through faith to the Lord Jesus Christ. Jesus was never about religion. In fact, He openly and often rebuked its excesses and perversions of God's original intent. He was, and still is, about relationships.

How does knowing Christ make a difference in your relationships?

JULY 13

Choose the Best

I have done according to your words; see, I have given you a wise and understanding heart. . . . And I have also given you what you have not asked: both riches and honor, so that there shall not be anyone like you among the kings all your days.

1 KINGS 3:12–13

Too often we ask God to bless us instead of asking Him to work through us to bless others. Solomon asked God to work through him. He chose the best, and God threw in the rest.

However, there is a sad postscript. When you start to hold your blessings closer than the Blesser, you can cease hearing from God. Solomon, blessed with great power and wisdom, allowed his focus to shift. As an old man he concluded, "Vanity of vanities . . . all is vanity" (Ecclesiastes 12:8). This is someone whose heart can no longer hear from God. But listen to the hard-won wisdom of Solomon's last words: "Remember now your Creator in the days of your youth. . . . Hear the conclusion of the whole matter: Fear God and keep His commandments, for this is man's all" (Ecclesiastes 12:1, 13).

When God asks you, "What do you want?" choose the best—and God will more than bless.

When you consider all God offers you,
how can you choose the best?

JULY 14

EXPECT THE SUDDENLY!

When the Day of Pentecost had fully come, they were all with one accord in one place. And suddenly there came a sound from heaven, as of a rushing mighty wind, and it filled the whole house where they were sitting.

ACTS 2:1–2

As I have read and reread the Bible, I have been captured by the word *suddenly.* We find it again on the day of Pentecost. What took place that day was not the result of some process of growth and development. No one was taught how to do what happened. It was the work of God, and it came *suddenly.* The disciples were surprised by God!

One of the problems with our modern, sophisticated church is that some of us have lost our expectancy, the wonder of it all in the work of it all. Remember the shepherds of Bethlehem? They were out tending their sheep, just like any other night, when *suddenly* a great angelic choir announced the Savior's birth (Luke 2:13). Paul was en route to Damascus when *suddenly* he saw a light from heaven (Acts 9:3). He and Silas were once in jail when *suddenly* a violent earthquake opened the prison doors (Acts 16:26).

Oh, the possibilities for us if we would only live in the realm of expecting the unexpected—the *suddenly*—today!

What are the possibilities for you if you expect the unexpected—the *suddenly*—today?

JULY 15

Forgiveness Is Conditional

He who covers his sins will not prosper, but whoever confesses and forsakes them will have mercy.
PROVERBS 28:13

Many of God's promises to us are conditional on certain requirements being met by us first. The forgiveness John talked about is conditional upon the confession of our sins.

The word *confession* is a compound word in Koine Greek, the language of the New Testament. It comes from the combination of a verb meaning "to say" and a word meaning "the same." Literally, *confession* means "to say the same" as God says about our sin. It means that we come into agreement with God about our sin. Sin is not some little vice that we can laugh off as no big deal. It is not something we can minimize by saying it is not as bad as a lot of other people's sins we know about. Your sin—my sin—is so serious that it alone necessitated the cross. The twinge of guilt we often feel in the aftermath of committing sin is in essence the voice of God saying to our hearts, "You have sinned." Confession is our way of "agreeing with God" and responding, "I agree with You, Lord; I have sinned."

What do you need to confess today so you can be forgiven and cleansed?

JULY 16

False Faith

What does it profit, my brethren, if someone says he has faith but does not have works? Can faith save him?
JAMES 2:14

In today's scripture James was not referring to a man who has faith but to someone who "says he has faith." James was addressing a false claim to faith, not the nature of genuine faith. The mere claim that one is a believer does not make him such. Many people say they are people of faith but have never placed their faith in Christ alone and experienced what Jesus called "the new birth."

Much unnecessary confusion in the faith-works debate stems from how the King James Version and the New King James Version ask, "Can faith save him?" The Greek text has an article in front of the word *faith*, indicating that this faith is the same faith just mentioned in the first question of verse 14—a false faith. Properly translated, the question reads, "Can such a faith, can that kind of a faith, save him?" James was not saying that faith cannot save a person but that a faith characterized only by intellectual assent but that exhibits no fruit is a false faith.

What are some examples of "false faith" you have witnessed?

JULY 17

Forgiveness Makes an Impact

Blessed is he whose transgression is forgiven, whose sin is covered.
PSALM 32:1

Think for just a moment about the individuals who have had the greatest impact on your life. If you are like me, a few people will surface to mind, likely with a common characteristic. It wasn't simply that they surrounded you with love, were always there for you, believed in you, did things for you, or encouraged you. But each in their own ways forgave you of your faults. There were more times than I can remember when I disobeyed my dad. But he always forgave me and never brought it up again. As many times as I haven't measured up to being the husband I should be to Susie, she has always forgiven me and forgotten it. Forgiveness has a dynamic power in our lives. It helps bring out the best in all of us, regardless of whether we are on the giving or receiving end of the equation.

Who has made an impact on your life because they have forgiven you, and why?

JULY 18

CHRIST'S ABIDING PRESENCE

Go therefore and make disciples of all the nations, baptizing them in the name of the Father and of the Son and of the Holy Spirit, teaching them to observe all things that I have commanded you; and lo, I am with you always, even to the end of the age.

MATTHEW 28:19–20

In the New Testament, we find the promise of Christ's abiding presence with us laced throughout its pages. In the upper room, Jesus told the disciples that He would "pray the Father, and He will give you another Helper, that He may abide with you forever" (John 14:16). Jesus ascended back to heaven with these words from today's scripture: "I am with you always" (Matthew 28:20). And the final verse in the Bible leaves us with this promise of Christ's presence through His grace: "The grace of our Lord Jesus Christ be with you all" (Revelation 22:21). There is no promise in the entire Bible repeated so many times, to so many different people, in so many different circumstances, as this one: "I am with you always."

Promises made are appreciated. But, as I have noted previously, promises kept are what mean the most. Jesus promised, "I am with you always." Believe it. Hold to this promise. And when, like Isaiah, you pass through the waters of difficulty, remember: He is with you—always!

What have you experienced that caused you to know Jesus is with you—always?

JULY 19

The Blessings of Giving

"Bring all the tithes into the storehouse, that there may be food in My house, and try Me now in this," says the Lord *of hosts, "if I will not open for you the windows of heaven and pour out for you such blessing that there will not be room enough to receive it."*

MALACHI 3:10

Our finances generally mark the condition of our spiritual pilgrimage. We are often no further along in our walk with God than the point where we have learned to trust Him with our tithes and offerings. God never emphasizes our giving; He always focuses on our receiving. God desires to open for us "the windows of heaven" and pour out His blessings on us.

So God presents us with a proposition: "Bring all the tithes . . . and try Me now in this." God is saying, "Put Me on trial! Test Me! Try Me in this." If there is any doubt as to God's desire to bless us, here is a way to prove Him. This is amazing condescension.

Don't rob God. Pray about your stewardship and ask God to guide, provide, and embolden you. Make your tithe your top financial commitment; let it take priority over everything else. Be as systematic with your tithing as you are in your business matters. Rest in the fact that you can trust Him.

What blessings do you believe God has poured out on you because of your giving?

JULY 20

RAHAB'S LIFE REDEEMED

Salmon begot Boaz by Rahab, Boaz begot Obed by Ruth, Obed begot Jesse, and Jesse begot David the king.

MATTHEW 1:5–6

When Rahab said yes to the God of Israel and, by faith, hung the scarlet cord out her window, it set in motion her deliverance.

Rahab was saved when judgment came to Jericho (Joshua 6:22–25). She then took her place among the Israelites in the family of God's people. The old things had passed, and all became new for her. God redeemed her life in a powerful way. She lived among the children of Israel and married a man named Salmon. They had a son and named him Boaz. Yes, the same Boaz who became the husband of Ruth and the father of Obed, who later gave birth to Jesse the father of David, who became the king. And as though this were not honor enough for Rahab, she is listed in the lineage of Jesus Himself in Matthew 1:5–16. She is the incarnate truth of 2 Corinthians 5:17: "If anyone is in Christ, he is a new creation; old things have passed away; behold, all things have become new."

Whose life have you seen God redeem in a powerful way, and how?

JULY 21

Humble Submission

Submitting to one another in the fear of God.
EPHESIANS 5:21

There is an inward and upward evidence to the filling of God's Spirit—overflowing thanksgiving—and there is an *outward* evidence as well. How will people know we are being controlled by God's Spirit? We are to esteem others as better than ourselves and put them before us. It's not the things we say that let them know we are filled with God's Spirit; it is how we act in our personal relationships that reveals the Spirit at work within us.

Christ washed the disciples' feet. The greatest among them became the servant of them all, and He is our example.

Submission to one another is to be done "in the fear of God." This is not a fear that God might put His hand *on* us in retribution but a fear that He might take His hand of blessing and anointing *away* from us. We should live each day being careful not to say or do anything that might cause God to remove His hand of blessing from our lives.

In what ways do you esteem others as better than yourself and put them first?

JULY 22

Therefore Pray

Therefore pray the Lord of the harvest.
MATTHEW 9:38

So here we are, like the disciples, often just content in our snug little comfort zones. The multitudes are all around us; they are weary and without spiritual direction; they are ripe to be harvested (Matthew 9:36–37). But few are willing to go into the fields and bring them in. What do we do? Human reasoning says get a plan, enlist the workers, beg, plead, coerce if necessary, strategize, find a catchy theme, use all your best motivational techniques, and, if needed, even try guilt for motivation.

But God has a better way. Jesus says, "Therefore *pray.*" Jesus moves prayer to the very top of the priority list when it comes to evangelism and the harvest. We should not lose sight of the fact that this was always Jesus' priority. Before He chose the Twelve, He spent the entire night in prayer (Luke 6:12–13). If time and space permitted, this could be illustrated again and again. Prayer was the priority of our Lord . . . always.

How often do you make prayer your first priority in your efforts to share Christ with others?

JULY 23

Do You Love God or the World?

Adulterers and adulteresses! Do you not know that friendship with the world is enmity with God? Whoever therefore wants to be a friend of the world makes himself an enemy of God.

JAMES 4:4

The real source of our personal and private conflicts lies not in the relationships we have with others or even in the relationship we have with ourselves but in our relationship with God. Rebellion against God in the human heart is the root cause of every war.

When we choose to be a "friend of the world," we are choosing to be an enemy of God. The prevailing world system of thought is utterly anti-God and anti-Christ. When we aren't on our spiritual guard, we can develop an affection for the things of the world that God says we should avoid.

Are any of us guilty of this charge of spiritual adultery? Perhaps we once came to an altar and made a pledge to Christ. But in becoming "friends with the world," we have sought the affection of other gods such as materialism or popularity. Start doing what you once did.

What are some obvious signs that a Christian has become a "friend of the world," and how can you guard against this in your life?

JULY 24

Our Sin, His Account

He is the atoning sacrifice for our sins, and not only for ours but also for the sins of the whole world.

1 JOHN 2:2 NIV

The Bible refers to what we owe as a sin debt. We cannot pay it. Just as Paul had nothing to do with Philemon's runaway servant, Onesimus's, sin and guilt, neither did Christ have anything to do with ours. And yet as Paul assumed this debt of Onesimus's that Paul did not himself owe, so the Lord Jesus paid the debt for our sin on the cross of Calvary. In essence, Jesus was saying to His Father what Paul was saying to Philemon, "If he has wronged you or owes anything, put that on my account. . . . I will repay" (Philemon vv. 18–19). No wonder seven hundred years earlier Isaiah said, "All we like sheep have gone astray; we have turned, every one, to his own way; and the Lord has laid on Him the iniquity of us all" (Isaiah 53:6). Those of us who are in relationship with Jesus Christ can go to the computer in heaven, pull up our accounts, and beside our names are the words *Paid in full.*

How do you feel when you think about the fact that Jesus paid your sin debt in full?

JULY 25

JESUS, YOUR STRONGHOLD

The LORD is a stronghold for the oppressed, a stronghold in times of trouble. And those who know your name put their trust in you, for you, O LORD, have not forsaken those who seek you.

PSALM 9:9–10 ESV

Where do you flee for refuge? Time and again, King David fled to one of his strongholds. He writes in today's scripture that the Lord is our stronghold when trouble comes. We can take refuge in Him. The night before the crucifixion, Jesus said, "At that day you will know that I am in My Father, and you in Me, and I in you" (John 14:20). Your stronghold is not in what you are, or who you are, or why you are, but *where* you are.

Jesus is positioned "in My Father." He is your stronghold, and you are "in Him"—a very safe place to be. If you are *in* Christ and He is *in* the Father, nothing can get to you that doesn't first have to pass through God the Father and God the Son. And if it penetrates that fortress, you can rest assured there is a purpose for it in your life.

Where do you flee when you need a place of refuge?

JULY 26

Joy Comes in the Morning

For His anger is but for a moment, His favor is for life; weeping may endure for a night, but joy comes in the morning.

PSALM 30:5

Weeping endures through the night. But you can cry your eyes out for all kinds of reasons, and when all is said and done none of that worldly sorrow can bring about life, much less the kind of joy that comes in the morning. This promise of joy in the morning does not simply mean that we can get everything all cried out during the nighttime hours and when we wake up in the morning everything will be fixed. Of course it doesn't. Only one type of weeping brings the promise of joy in the morning. This is the point of Paul's words to the Corinthians, and to us: "For godly sorrow produces repentance leading to salvation, not to be regretted; but the sorrow of the world produces death" (2 Corinthians 7:10). The only kind of weeping that brings real joy is godly sorrow that leads to repentance. When we weep over our own sin, we will understand the truth of this promise, and we can embrace the joy of being forgiven.

When has weeping given way to joy in your life?

God's Seal of Approval

In Him you also trusted, after you heard the word of truth, the gospel of your salvation; in whom also, having believed, you were sealed with the Holy Spirit of promise.
EPHESIANS 1:13

When you become a believer, God stamps you with His seal of approval. In the ancient world a seal was used to authenticate a document. A letter would be secured with hot wax and then sealed with the imprint of a signet ring to show it was real. The Holy Spirit is our seal to prove we are saved and secure: "The Spirit Himself bears witness with our spirit that we are children of God" (Romans 8:16).

A seal also shows ownership. Cowboys brand their cattle with hot irons to forever show others who the owner is. God seals us with His Spirit to let the world know we are His.

The seal of the Holy Spirit also shows that we are secure—no one can snatch us away from God (John 10:28). The same power that raised Jesus from the grave secures you in Him.

God has placed His own seal on you. It proves you are authentic, that you belong to Him, and that He will keep you secure forever.

How does your knowledge of God's seal of ownership give you assurance of your salvation?

JULY 28

Confronting a Friend in Love

Then the Lord *sent Nathan to David.*

2 SAMUEL 12:1

It is extremely therapeutic to have a faithful friend in whom we trust and with whom we can be truthful, even when the truth hurts. We never have to be afraid of the truth. It always wins in the end, and Jesus said in John 8:32 that this attribute has a liberating effect on us.

Take the well-known case of King David and Bathsheba, recorded in 2 Samuel 11. Like so many today, David tried his best to cover up his sin. He did not want any of his family or friends to know about it. But he was fortunate to have a true and trusted friend, Nathan, who held him accountable. Nathan cared enough to confront David when he saw he was on a collision course. And when he did so in confidence and love, David came clean. It hurt. But it also eventually healed. Nathan kept his friend from greater hurt and heartache. It worked because their relationship with one another was transparent, touchable, teachable, and truthful.

When has someone cared enough about you to confront you, and how did it help you?

JULY 29

SHARED SHAME

I gave My back to those who struck Me, and My cheeks to those who plucked out the beard; I did not hide My face from shame and spitting.
ISAIAH 50:6

It is impossible to imagine the pain, the grief, the sorrow Christ endured as He died such a slow, agonizing death. Hebrews 12:2 reminds us that it was "for the joy that was set before Him" that Jesus "endured the cross, despising the shame."

Shame is a dreadful emotion. Our Lord was stripped naked . . . *naked* . . . before all the onlookers. He was then beaten like a common criminal and finally nailed to a cross. He endured the physical shame, the emotional shame, and what was worse, the spiritual shame as the Father turned away His face from all the vile sinfulness Jesus was bearing in His own body on the cross. Jesus, the heaven-sent Messenger of love, the beloved and only begotten Son of the Father, had to suffer not only the guilt but the shame of the sin of the entire world . . . murderers, molesters, racists, and oppressors of the poor.

Think about the cross today. Stay there for a while. Jesus' death deserves our serious reflection.

When you suffer shame and embarrassment, how does it encourage you to know that Jesus understands?

Four Ways God Answers Prayer

Peter was therefore kept in prison, but constant prayer was offered to God for him by the church.
ACTS 12:5

How wonderful to know that God truly hears us. While Peter was incarcerated under heavy guard, the church was praying, and God heard them. Two words—*influence* and *power*—are useful as we try to understand what happened in this situation. The early believers did not have enough influence to keep Peter out of prison, but they had enough power to pray him out because they were convinced that God was listening.

God is listening and always answers your prayers in some way. Sometimes His answer is *direct*—an immediate answer. Sometimes His answer is *delayed*—He puts us in a holding pattern. Sometimes the answer is *different*. He answers in a different and better way than we anticipated. Finally, sometimes our requests are *denied*. I am grateful God has not answered all my prayers with a yes when certain things are not best for me. When we pray, we can be sure God is listening and will answer.

When have you experienced each of the four ways God answers prayers?

JULY 31

Our Foe Is Defeated

For this purpose the Son of God was manifested, that
He might destroy the works of the devil.
1 JOHN 3:8

Many of us live defeated Christian lives because we are fooled by the demonic deceiver. But, for the most part, the devil is not the problem—we are. Consider this promise: "Resist the devil and he will flee from you" (James 4:7). Do we really believe this? We would if we realized he is already a defeated foe and that, as today's scripture teaches, Jesus came to destroy his evil works. John attested to this fact when he acknowledged, "He who is in you is greater than he who is in the world" (1 John 4:4).

Satan's doom is already sealed. When Jesus said, "All authority has been given to Me in heaven and on earth" (Matthew 28:18), it was an indication that if He has "all" authority, then Satan, in actuality, has *none*. The only authority he can exert over you is that which you allow him to have when you fail to "submit to God" and "resist the devil."

In your own words, how does Jesus destroy the works of the devil?

AUGUST

Love That Refreshes

We have great joy and consolation in your love, because the hearts of the saints have been refreshed by you, brother.
PHILEMON V. 7

Philemon's letter from Paul included some of the most beautiful words of admiration he could have received. It was not just Philemon's love for Paul that brought him so much encouragement, but it was the fact that this love spread to "all the saints" (v. 5). It was Philemon's heart of love that was so admirable to the great apostle. This love that originated in his faith toward the Lord Jesus (v. 5), his eternal connection. This was what inspired his love for others. His genuine love for other people was what cheered and challenged, motivated and moved others to greater service and what brightened Paul's day miles across the Aegean Sea and all the way into the damp and dark prison cell where Paul was incarcerated. This warm and wonderful character trait of Philemon was what led Paul to declare that it was Philemon's love that gave Paul great hope and encouragement, for it refreshed the hearts of the saints everywhere.

Who has a heart of love that you admire,
and how does this love refresh you?

AUGUST 2

Take His Hand

Or do you despise the riches of His goodness, forbearance, and longsuffering, not knowing that the goodness of God leads you to repentance?
ROMANS 2:4

Once, when our daughters were small, my wife and I rented a vacation home deep in the Smoky Mountains. I was awakened in the middle of the night by the cries of our little seven-year-old. I bounded up the stairs to find her disoriented and scared in the darkness. I reassured her that she was safe, comforted her, and brought her to our room, where she slept soundly the rest of the night.

Our dear Lord finds us in the night, often disoriented by the issues of life. He takes us by the hand, and His own goodness "leads [us] to repentance."

When all is said and done, what difference will it make if we drive luxury cars, eat vitamin-enriched foods, live in palatial homes, and are buried in mahogany caskets if we rise up in judgment to meet a God we do not know? Let His goodness take you by the hand today and lead you to repentance.

Why would God's goodness be more likely to lead you to repentance than His wrath?

AUGUST 3

DON'T FORFEIT YOUR CROWN

Blessed is the man who endures temptation; for when he has been approved, he will receive the crown of life which the Lord has promised to those who love Him.
JAMES 1:12

Satan attempts to use our stressful trials to cause us to stumble, but the Lord allows them in order to strengthen our faith muscles so we can stand strong. James chose the word *endures* to indicate staying power. Here is a man who holds his ground and stands up under life's stressful trials: He endures.

"Blessed"—happy—is the person who endures under stressful trials. Why? Because we know that after the trial we will receive the "crown of life." In the ancient Grecian games, a wreath was placed on the head of the victor as a sign of honor and triumph. This is the very crown the apostle Paul had in mind when, in some of the last words he wrote before being martyred, he said, "I have fought the good fight, I have finished the race, I have kept the faith. Finally, there is laid up for me the crown of righteousness" (2 Timothy 4:7–8).

God has a special reward for those patient sufferers who endure their stressful trials. They win in the end.

When you think of people who have endured a stressful trial, which one or ones do you most admire, and why?

AUGUST 4

FLAVOR YOUR WORLD

You are the salt of the earth; but if the salt loses its flavor, how shall it be seasoned? It is then good for nothing but to be thrown out and trampled underfoot by men.

MATTHEW 5:13

There should be an ingredient in our lives that makes people thirsty for what we have in Christ—salt. Jesus attracted all sorts of needy people. Why? Because He made them thirsty for what only He could give.

Tragically, in our world today, the salt seems to be losing its flavor. We need to begin to see ourselves as salt. *We* "are the salt of the earth." Little does our world system realize that the presence of God's people is preventing the final collapse of our civilization and ultimate judgment. We are the only ones who can truly flavor the lives of those around us.

As more and more Christians retreat within the comforts and convenience of the church, their salt will lose its flavor. We are commissioned to go out and be the salt of the *earth*, and not just salt for the church. The lost are waiting for each of us to get out among them, truly being the kind of salt that preserves, flavors, stings, and makes them thirsty for Christ.

How can you be flavoring for the people you meet each day?

AUGUST 5

The Plumb Line

And the Lord *said to me, "Amos, what do you see?" And I said, "A plumb line." Then the Lord said: "Behold, I am setting a plumb line in the midst of My people Israel; I will not pass by them anymore."*

AMOS 7:8

Like Amos's plumb line, the Lord Jesus came down and by His life set the standard of holiness for us. And since none of us can meet that standard, we must run to Jesus, put our trust in Him, and claim Him as our substitute. Christ alone is our plumb line. It is no wonder the Bible says, "For He made Him who knew no sin to be sin for us, that we might become the righteousness of God in Him" (2 Corinthians 5:21).

Into our moral failures and shortcomings, Christ comes to show us God's plumb line, not weighted by the law but weighted by grace. He says to us today, "I am the plumb line. I alone measured up to its perfect standard. But by grace, through faith in Me alone, you can stand in My own righteousness so that when God tests you with His plumb line, instead of condemning you, He will receive you faultless before His throne."

What happens when you try to measure up to God's standards on your own merit?

AUGUST 6

There's Purpose in Our Pain

Lest I should be exalted above measure by the abundance of the revelations, a thorn in the flesh was given to me.
2 CORINTHIANS 12:7

None of us is immune to disappointments and defeats, heartaches and heartbreaks, struggles and setbacks. Even the apostle Paul had a "thorn in the flesh." What this "thorn" actually was no one knows for sure. He had asked the Lord not once, not twice, but three times to remove it from him. But God did not remove it, for He had a greater purpose in it. Paul knew that this problem was "given" to him by God. God had big plans for Paul. He later went from this experience to take the gospel to the entire Mediterranean world and ended up giving us half our New Testament through his own pen.

Haven't most of us been there, having something, or someone, who becomes a "thorn" in our own flesh? Perhaps, like Paul, we have asked the Lord repeatedly to free us from the problem only to find that it had been "given to [us]" by the Lord Himself to keep us humble and to fulfill His purpose in our lives.

How have you seen God's purpose unfold in a painful situation in your life?

Praying as We Ought

But when the Helper comes, whom I shall send to you from the Father, the Spirit of truth who proceeds from the Father, He will testify of Me.

JOHN 15:26

One reason the Holy Spirit helps us in our weaknesses is that "we do not know what we should pray for as we ought" (Romans 8:26). The Greek word translated *ought* appears more than one hundred times in the New Testament, usually translated *must*. We see this in John 3:7: "You must be born again." God brings His plans into being through the prayers of His people. It is not just that you and I ought to pray; we must pray!

It is true that we do not always know how we ought to pray. In the New Testament, there is a definite article before "what" in Romans 8:26 as if to convey that we do not know "the what" for which to pray. This refers not to general praying but to a specific need for which we need help praying. We have a prayer partner who helps us in our weaknesses because we do not know "the what" for which to pray as we ought.

What prayer requests can you enlist the Holy Spirit's help in knowing how to pray about today?

AUGUST 8

The Most Meaningful Relationship

But as many as received Him, to them He gave the right to become children of God, to those who believe in His name.
JOHN 1:12

The consensus of sociology confirms that the number one quest in life for most men and women is a search for a meaningful relationship. Many have never known even one. Truly meaningful relationships are few and far between.

Paul reminds us that "in Him [Christ] we have redemption through His blood, the forgiveness of sins, according to the riches of His grace" (Ephesians 1:7). Note those first two words: "in Him." What Christ has to offer is not a religion or a ritual but a vibrant and meaningful relationship in Him.

There are only three types of relationships in life: outward (your relationships with others), inward (your relationship with yourself), and upward (your relationship with God through Jesus Christ). And the bottom line? We will never be properly related to others until we are properly related to ourselves, and this will never happen until we discover how valuable we are to God and come into a relationship with Him by placing our trust in Christ alone.

In what ways have you noticed that your relationship with God impacts your relationships with yourself or others?

AUGUST 9

WE ARE ALL "CHARISMATIC"

Now concerning spiritual gifts, brethren, I do not want you to be ignorant.
1 CORINTHIANS 12:1

There is some concern today over the word *charisma*. Someone might be said to have charisma or a charismatic presence—a winsome charm that is attractive to other people. In the New Testament this word is most often used to describe the supernatural gifts that God bestows upon His children. The word *charisma* (plural *charismata*) is derived from the Greek word for grace, *charis*. Charismata, in the language of the Bible, means "a gift of grace."

Today, however, some have exchanged the word *charisma* for what I will call *charisphobia*. They seem to fear these gifts of grace and avoid the mention of them altogether. Others suffer from what might be called *charismania*. They've become so consumed with the supernatural and certain gifts that manifest themselves in miracles that in some cases the *gift Himself* is overtaken. The truth is, every believer in Christ is a charismatic, meaning they have a spiritual gift, sovereignly bestowed upon them from God for the edification and the building up of the body of Christ.

How does a biblical understanding of *charismata* clear up misconceptions about the word *charismatic*?

AUGUST 10

Clean Hands, Pure Heart

Who may ascend into the hill of the Lord? Or who may stand in His holy place?
PSALM 24:3

No sooner did the psalmist ask the question in today's scripture than he provided the answer: "He who has clean hands and a pure heart" (Psalm 24:4). None of us meets this standard—not on our own. Our hands are dirty with sin, and our hearts are far from pure.

The hill referred to in Psalm 24 is Mount Calvary. Only one person in human history met the righteous demands of the law accompanied by the two qualifications of clean hands and a pure heart: the Lord Jesus Christ. His hands were clean, uncontaminated by sin. His heart was pure. Knowing I was without hope, He descended from heaven to make a way for me to one day ascend to Him there. His clean hands became dirty with my sin and yours so our dirty hands could become clean. Jesus' pure heart became filled with our sin so our sinful hearts could become pure in God's eyes. So, who now shall ascend into the hill of the Lord? You can. I can.

When you think of Jesus' sacrifice to make you clean, how does it inspire you to praise Him today?

AUGUST 11

Consistency

So then, my beloved brethren, let every man be swift to hear, slow to speak, slow to wrath; for the wrath of man does not produce the righteousness of God. Therefore lay aside all filthiness and overflow of wickedness, and receive with meekness the implanted word, which is able to save your souls.

JAMES 1:19–21

One obvious mark of genuine Christianity is having one's conversation consistent with biblical standards and Christian beliefs. James emphasized how important it is to say the right thing in the right way and to be "swift to hear" as well. Credible Christian living demands we be cautious in our conversation and that our words are consistent with God's Word and character.

James also admonished us to be "slow to wrath," to "lay aside all filthiness and overflow of wickedness." Although God chooses us and calls us to Himself, there is something for us to do: We are to take off our old coats of sin and strip away all filth. This is not a requirement for salvation, since only the blood of Christ can cleanse us of sin. James was writing to believers like you and me who already know Christ. Knowing and therefore representing Jesus, we need to be consistent in our conversation as well as our conduct.

How does your speech and conduct reveal to people that you are a Christian?

AUGUST 12

A Family Affair

Behold what manner of love the Father has bestowed on us, that we should be called children of God!
1 JOHN 3:1

As believers who know God as our Father, we need to see each other as family. The apostle Paul did. And this was one of the secrets to his success. He built a family consciousness and cohesiveness with those in his inner circle. He spoke of Timothy as his "brother" (1 Thessalonians 3:2) and in many translations referred to Apphia, most probably Philemon's wife, as our "sister" (Philemon v. 2 NIV). Paul thought of these individuals not merely as friends but as close members of his family of faith. His repeated use of the plural pronoun *our* was no accident. He said, "our brother . . . our dear friend and fellow worker . . . our sister . . . our fellow soldier" (Philemon v. 1 NIV). It is of vital importance in the building of positive relationships that we create a spirit of camaraderie and community. True friendships among believers become family affairs. There is a sense in which we are more closely related to each other through the blood of Christ than to our own blood relatives who do not know Him.

Among your friends, who has become family to you?

AUGUST 13

SEND ME!

Also I heard the voice of the Lord, saying: "Whom shall I send, and who will go for Us?" Then I said, "Here am I! Send me."

ISAIAH 6:8

What a different world we would live in if every believer answered the Lord's question, "Whom shall I send, and who will go for Us?" as Isaiah did in today's scripture. We, like Isaiah, will respond this way only when we begin to see God, ourselves, and others in new and powerful ways.

We need to *see God in His holiness*. Isaiah was given a glimpse of the Lord "sitting on a throne, high and lifted up" (Isaiah 6:1). This incredible vision that awaits all believers led him to exclaim, "My eyes have seen the King, the LORD of hosts" (v. 5).

Worship is not about us—what we do, sing, or say. It is about almighty God and His glory. The first step in a desire to be used by God is when we see God in His own holiness and recognize and realize, no matter what our earthly situation may be, He is in total control.

If God asked you to go somewhere for Him, how would you answer?

AUGUST 14

MIRACLE LANGUAGE

Though I speak with the tongues of men and of angels, but have not love, I have become sounding brass or a clanging cymbal.

1 CORINTHIANS 13:1

One of the miracles on Pentecost was the believers speaking in other "tongues." Perhaps no other subject in Scripture has been as misunderstood as this phenomenon that took place when the Holy Spirit fell on that band of early believers.

The Bible records that they "began to speak with other tongues, as the Spirit gave them utterance" (Acts 2:4). The Greek word for "tongue" here is *glossa*. We get our English word *glossary* from this word. It is linguistic. These were known languages. They were languages foreign to the speaker—ones he or she had never heard—but that they were supernaturally empowered to speak. The actual miracle was in the hearing: "Everyone heard them speak in his own language" (v. 6). The word for "language" here is *dialectos*, from which we get our word *dialect*.

God performed a miracle. Everyone heard the gospel message in his own language and dialect. Three thousand Jews became followers of the Messiah that day and scattered back across the Mediterranean world to their homes sharing this good news.

How does the fact that people heard the gospel in their own language comfort and encourage you as you think about people in your life who need to know God's saving power?

AUGUST 15

Temptation Is Not Sin

No temptation has overtaken you except such as is common to man; but God is faithful, who will not allow you to be tempted beyond what you are able, but with the temptation will also make the way of escape, that you may be able to bear it.

1 CORINTHIANS 10:13

It is not a sin to be tempted. Temptation is a reality. It comes our way daily in all sorts of forms and sizes. Your mind is like a hotel. The manager cannot keep someone from entering the lobby. However, he or she can certainly keep that person from getting a room. In a similar way, it is not a sin when some temptation passes through your mind. After all, Jesus was in all points "tempted as we are, yet without sin" (Hebrews 4:15). The sin takes root when we give that thought a room in our mind and let it dwell and get comfortable there. Quite the contrary to the old adage "The devil made me do it!"—he never made us do anything. He simply dangles his bait in front of us. Then, we are tempted, "drawn away by [our] own desires and enticed" (James 1:14) by that which is outside the boundaries laid out clearly for us in God's Word.

In your own words, what is the difference between temptation and sin?

AUGUST 16

Is Your Faith Breathing?

If a brother or sister is naked and destitute of daily food, and one of you says to them, "Depart in peace, be warmed and filled," but you do not give them the things which are needed for the body, what does it profit? Thus also faith by itself, if it does not have works, is dead.

JAMES 2:15–17

James paints the picture of someone in need of food and clothing, the basic necessities of life. This person is not a professional con artist or streetwise person with a slothful lifestyle, but someone with a legitimate and immediate need. A person who claims to have faith goes to him, puts his hand on his shoulder, pats him on the back, and says, "Have a good day. Be careful out there and try to stay warm. I hope you find something to eat. Bless you."

Then came the rhetorical question: "What good does that response do for the hungry and cold man?" James was shining the spotlight on those of us who seem to prefer words over works, who know how to talk a good faith game yet have no impact on the world around us because our faith does not produce fruit.

If James took the mirror of God's Word and held it under our noses, would we see our faith breathing? A faith without works is dead.

When have you seen someone's faith in action, and how did you recognize it?

AUGUST 17

White as Snow

Purge me with hyssop, and I shall be clean; wash me, and I shall be whiter than snow.

PSALM 51:7

I stood one cold winter day at the spot outside what we call Skull Hill, Golgotha. Snow covered the landscape of the Holy City in a blanket of white and was nestled into the crevices of the face of Calvary. The holes, which appeared like eye sockets, were filled with snow. The words of the ancient prophet Isaiah came quickly to mind: "'Come now, and let us reason together,' says the Lord, 'though your sins are like scarlet, they shall be as white as snow; though they are red like crimson, they shall be as wool'" (Isaiah 1:18). When we come home to Him in humility and repentance, God receives us with open arms, no clenched fists, no crossed arms, just open arms of love and forgiveness. Then we can begin the great journey for which we were created in the first place, to know Him whom to know is life, abundant in the here and now and eternal in the then and there. It takes two! And He has already done His part.

How will you thank God today for cleansing you of all your sin?

AUGUST 18

GOD'S WORD ENDURES FOREVER

The grass withers and the flowers fall, but the word of our God endures forever.
ISAIAH 40:8 NIV

One spring my wife, Susie, planted a beautiful array of colorful spring flowers. It was not long before they withered and faded away as the months gave in to the hot Texas heat. As I watched their demise, this verse from Isaiah came to my mind with its promise that God's Word will never fade away but will stand as long as God lives.

Most of the books of centuries past are lost in the darkness of antiquity. But the Bible is different from any other book ever written. It is actually a library in itself of sixty-six different books written over a period of more than fourteen hundred years by at least forty different authors. Some were callus-handed fishermen, others were kings, prophets, doctors, shepherds, and rabbis. Yet the Bible has one theology, one plan of redemption, and one theme woven through its pages, leaving no explanation for its unique and lasting nature other than the fact that behind the pen of each writer was the hand of God Himself.

Why is the Bible unlike any other book ever written?

AUGUST 19

THE FUTILITY OF WORRY

Which of you by worrying can add one cubit to his stature?
MATTHEW 6:27

At first reading, the question Jesus posed in Matthew 6:27 sounds like a reference to physical height. But a cubit equals eighteen inches, far more physical height than the context of this rhetorical question suggests. *Cubit*, however, can also mean "duration of life." Worrying will not increase your physical size, elevate your standing in the community, improve your reputation, or add any length to your life. So what will worry do for you? Absolutely nothing. Worrying is futile.

One of my own biggest challenges when trying not to worry about a problem is to hurry toward the solution. But no matter how bleak a situation looked, Jesus never hurried to solve it. Not once in the Gospels do we find Him saying, "Let's go! We have to hurry or we'll be late for the miracle!" Waiting rather than hurrying—learning to wait on the Lord—is essential to overcoming worry.

Worrying has never solved a single problem. In fact, it has complicated and compounded many of them. Worrying accomplishes nothing.

If worry accomplishes nothing, why do so many people waste their time doing it?

Whoever Calls

And it shall come to pass that whoever calls on the name of the Lord shall be saved.
ACTS 2:21

The truth is often stated that the church was a mystery, a hidden secret unrevealed to the Old Testament writers and saints. But for a moment, God drew back the curtain and let Joel see what was to come. And Joel took pen in hand and wrote it down. There was coming a day that would usher in the "last days" when God would pour out His Spirit on all flesh. From that day forward, until Christ's glorious second coming, the Spirit would baptize each believer into the body of Christ. And the result? In Joel's words, "And it shall come to pass that whoever calls on the name of the Lord shall be saved" (Joel 2:32). And true to his words, it has come to pass! In one of the most often quoted verses in the New Testament, the apostle Paul would borrow these words from Joel when writing to the believers in Rome, and to us, saying, "For 'whoever calls on the name of the Lord shall be saved'" (Romans 10:13).

Who in your life needs to call on the name of the Lord today, and how can you pray for them?

AUGUST 21

Come to Jesus

If anyone desires to come after Me, let him deny himself, and take up his cross daily, and follow Me.
LUKE 9:23

Jesus' invitation to those of us who are thirsty is, "Let [them] come to Me and drink" (John 7:37). *Come* is one of the simplest words in our entire vocabulary. A little child understands the word. But in our more mature "wisdom," many of us hear Jesus' invitation to come to Him and seem to think He is saying, "Go." So we *go* and try to do more. We somehow think the busier we get with His work, the more we will please Him. When all along He is whispering, "Come to Me."

Come to Jesus, not to some new devotional program or some formula or even some spiritual gift. When we come to Jesus, we do with our hearts what little children learning to walk do with their feet. We simply come . . . to Jesus.

But it is not enough to thirst for Him or even to come to Him. His instructions are to "drink." To drink of this water of life means to ask God to fill us with His Spirit.

How can you prioritize coming to Jesus instead of being busier with His work?

AUGUST 22

THE URGENCY OF EVANGELISM

Do you not say, "There are still four months and then comes the harvest"? Behold, I say to you, lift up your eyes and look at the fields, for they are already white for harvest!
JOHN 4:35

My first pastorate was in the wheat-farming community of Hobart, Oklahoma. Being a city boy, I was enthralled by the wheat harvest that consumed the area in late May and early June. For miles you could see nothing but a vast bronze ocean.

I asked a farmer about today's verse. Jesus said the fields were "white" to harvest, yet all I could see were "amber waves of grain." He quickly explained that when the wheat starts turning white, it's almost too late to get it out. You have to move with urgency before it rots in the field.

Yes, the harvest fields around us today are "white for harvest." This is a time for us to leave our comfort zones and put our priority where Jesus did—*pray* . . . to the Lord . . . to send out laborers . . . into His field. In all our talk of evangelism and the need to reach the lost, remember that prayer is always our priority.

What does the image of the wheat harvest bring to mind when you think of the lost people around you?

AUGUST 23

Grace for the Humble

Or do you think that the Scripture says in vain, "The Spirit who dwells in us yearns jealously"? But He gives more grace. Therefore He says: "God resists the proud, but gives grace to the humble."

JAMES 4:5–6

I don't believe James was speaking softly in today's verses. I think he was shouting when he said, "Do you think that the Scripture says in vain, 'The Spirit who dwells in us yearns jealously?'" He was expressing shock and surprise at those who had embraced Christ, known His love, and now were flirting with the world around them. He was saying, "What are you thinking? Have you left behind your moral compass? Don't you know that your God is a jealous God?"

But James didn't leave us there. Remembering the words of wise King Solomon, James added, "God resists the proud, but gives grace to the humble." (See Proverbs 3:34.) Our God is the God of the second chance. Our own internal wars can come to an end once we humble ourselves before God. We have this promise from Christ's own lips: "He who humbles himself will be exalted" (Matthew 23:12).

When you think of God as being jealous for your love, how does it make you feel?

Stick Up for Your Friends

Defend the poor and fatherless; do justice to the afflicted and needy.
PSALM 82:3

Many in our world today simply bounce from one relationship to another to another while always placing the blame for failure on the attitudes and actions of someone else. When it comes time to make a commitment in a relationship, it is easier for some people to just move on.

Relationships endure through the years when those involved stick up for one another. I recall a time in years gone by when I was falsely accused, and a friend rose to my defense and passionately spoke up for me. Although today we are separated by hundreds of miles and decades of years, I will never forget his loyalty and the deeper bond that developed because of it. In the book of Philemon, Paul defended the runaway servant, Onesimus. How much more do you imagine Onesimus became committed to Paul when he got wind of the fact that Paul had risen so strongly to his defense (Philemon vv. 17–18)? And how much more would your friends be committed to you if you proved beyond any doubt your unconditional defense of them?

In your friendships, who needs you to stick up for them?

AUGUST 25

THE BODY OF CHRIST

And He is the head of the body, the church.
COLOSSIANS 1:18

For thirty-three years the world looked upon the physical body of Christ. With His feet He walked among us, sometimes among great throngs of people, other times in the solitude of a single searching soul. From His lips emerged the most tender and penetrating words ever spoken. Through His piercing eyes He looked deep into the hidden recesses of hearts. Through His ears He listened patiently to pleas for mercy. Through His hands He touched at the point of greatest need.

Today, you and I are the visible "body of Christ" being watched by a seeking world so desperately in need of His touch. We each occupy a special place in His body. Like our own bodies, when one member suffers, it affects the whole body. You are vitally important to God, and His body will never be complete without you serving in that part of the body to which you are assigned. There is something for you to do in the body of Christ that no one else can do quite like you can.

What can you do to serve the church that
no one else can in the same way?

AUGUST 26

Repentance Leads to Joy

Very truly I tell you, you will weep and mourn while the world rejoices. You will grieve, but your grief will turn to joy.

JOHN 16:20 NIV

Jesus spoke the words of today's scripture to His disciples, preparing them for what was to come. Most of us can relate to having our grief turned to joy, and that is what God desires for us. The one who truly knows what it is to be so burdened by their sinful state without Christ is the one who can know true and lasting joy. Why? Because the tears of true godly sorrow lead to repentance (2 Corinthians 7:10). When we begin to weep over our own sin and get right with God, joy is on the way. The world tells us in the words of the old Broadway song by George Henry Powell and his brother, Felix, to "pack up your troubles in an old kit-bag and smile, smile, smile." But it never works. Everything we try to cover God has a way of uncovering. And everything we uncover before Him in godly sorrow and repentance, He covers over with His blood, and a shout of joy then follows in the morning.

Why is it necessary for us to feel sorrow over our sin?

What Is Your Gift?

When He ascended on high, He . . . gave gifts to men.
EPHESIANS 4:8

The church, born on the day of Pentecost, is supernatural in its origin and in its operation. Every believer has been given a spiritual gift "for the equipping of the saints for the work of ministry, for the edifying of the body of Christ" (Ephesians 4:12). These gifts are given by God; they are not sought, caught, bought, or taught. In Romans 12, there are gifts of prophecy, ministry, teaching, exhortation, giving, leadership, and the like. In 1 Corinthians 12, there are gifts of the word of knowledge, faith, and other supernatural strengths.

These sovereignly bestowed gifts are not rewards or natural abilities. No one has every gift, and no one gift is given to every believer. The gifts are distributed in God's perfect wisdom.

You will learn to recognize your own gift—it's the thing you love to do, the thing that energizes you. Your gift will also be publicly recognized. The body of Christ will use it—and God will be glorified by it.

How can you use the spiritual gift(s) God has given you?

AUGUST 28

STAY AWAY FROM GOSSIP AND JUDGMENT

A perverse person stirs up conflict, and a gossip separates close friends.

PROVERBS 16:28 NIV

Too many of us have had personal friends we observed heading in the wrong direction on a road that led to a dead end. But we let them go. Some of us simply do not care enough to confront others with compassion. Real friends are those who hold real friends accountable.

The subject of accountability comes with a warning. Being accountable does not suggest open season. The Bible does not advocate for us to open up our lives to anyone and everyone. And in particular, it does not mean becoming accountable to those who have the decidedly unspiritual gifts of gossip and judgment and who perform them with frequency. Stay away from those types of folks. They do not have your best interests at heart. They usually end up hurting you instead of helping you. Accountability exists with a very small number of loyal, affirmative, forgiving, and committed friends who have earned the right to ask the hard questions.

How have you personally witnessed the dangers of gossip and judgment?

The Healing Power of Confession

Confess your trespasses to one another, and pray for one another, that you may be healed.
JAMES 5:16

When James said we should confess our sins to others, he was not advocating going from one person to another, filling them in on all the sordid details. We don't have to go through anyone or to anyone with our sin. We are privileged to be able to go straight to God, through the Lord Jesus Christ. However, at times, in order to be right with God, we need to be right with each other. To be right vertically, we must be right horizontally.

When we sin against God alone, we are to go to Him privately in prayer and ask Him to forgive us. This *private* confession is for those sins that no one needs to know about.

Sometimes, however, we have sinned against another person. Then we are to go to him or her personally and ask forgiveness. This is *personal* confession.

And if your sin is public, you may need an honest confession and a public apology from a truly repentant heart.

Healing comes when we confess our trespasses to one another.

Is there anyone from whom you need to ask forgiveness?

AUGUST 30

Together Forever

Keep through Your name those whom You have given Me, that they may be one as We are. . . . I do not pray that You should take them out of the world, but that You should keep them from the evil one. . . . I do not pray for these alone, but also for those who will believe in Me through their word; that they all may be one.

JOHN 17:11, 15, 20–21

In John 17 Jesus prayed for His disciples, beseeching the Father to "keep [them] through Your name." He was focused not only on their security but their purity: "Keep them from the evil one." He concluded with a plea that they would be "sanctified by the truth" (v. 19).

The night before He was crucified, we were in His prayers. Jesus wanted us to be together, forever. His heart's desire is that believers become "one." Why? The result of believers living in love and unity together is that others might be drawn to Christ.

Jesus concluded by asking that "the love with which You loved Me may be in them, and I in them" (v. 26). What amazing love is in each of us who believe. Jesus Himself is alive in everyone who believes and is still praying that we will be one with Him and with each other, forever.

Why do you think the unity of believers is so important to Jesus?

AUGUST 31

Prayer for a New Beginning

Have mercy upon me, O God . . . blot out my transgressions. Wash me . . . cleanse me. . . . I acknowledge my transgressions, and my sin is always before me. Against You, You only, have I sinned. . . . Restore to me the joy of Your salvation.

PSALM 51:1–4, 12

One is prone to wonder how King David, in light of such failings in life, not the least of which was his notorious adulterous affair with Bathsheba, could end up being such a spiritual giant, producing inspiring and God-honoring psalms. But in reading his prayer of repentance in Psalm 51, all wonder soon vanishes. In these words he bared his heart to God, and to us. He was sin sick. He realized that sin is at the very heart of so many wrecked and ruined lives, and he learned how to deal with it and put it away.

Psalm 51 is a paradigm for the type of prayer that leads to forgiveness—one that issues from true repentance. Repentance is not remorse, regret, or reform, turning over a new leaf. Repentance is a true change of mind leading to a change of action.

This psalm has comforted believers through the centuries with the fact that if King David could find forgiveness and a new beginning, so can we.

How can you take a step toward forgiveness and a new beginning today?

SEPTEMBER

SEPTEMBER 1

Speak an Encouraging Word

Let no corrupt word proceed out of your mouth, but what is good for necessary edification, that it may impart grace to the hearers.
EPHESIANS 4:29

Try giving someone a positive word of encouragement next time you are standing in an office elevator, delayed at an airline counter, or conversing with a favorite server at your local restaurant. We will touch the lives of people today, many of whom have not heard a positive word of affirmation or admiration from anyone in years. Perhaps some for a lifetime. Some people go months, maybe years, without a personal word of admiration directed to their spouse and then wonder why the relationship has lost its spark. Some parents allow their teenagers to graduate from high school and move away without any remembrance of a word of affirmation or encouragement from a mom or a dad. A simple verbal pat on the back can change someone's entire day and, in some cases, even the way they think about themselves. It can make work more productive, make the home more respectful and loving, and move your friends to enjoy your company and look forward to being in your presence.

How has a specific word of encouragement or affirmation made a difference in your life?

SEPTEMBER 2

The Humility of God

And being found in appearance as a man, He humbled Himself and became obedient to the point of death, even the death of the cross.
PHILIPPIANS 2:8

John 1:14 says, "And the Word became flesh and dwelt among us." Who is this "Word"? John leaves no doubt concerning this identity: "In the beginning was the Word, and the Word was with God, and *the Word was God*" (John 1:1).

Jesus came down to where we are so that we could one day go to where He is! He came not clinging to the brightness of His glory, not shunning us for our sinful condition, but humbling Himself and taking on a garment of flesh. No matter our emotional condition, temptations, or pain, He understands.

He "dwelt among us . . . full of grace and truth" (John 1:14). Jesus is full of grace. Because of His sacrifice, we don't get what we deserve. And He is full of truth. It is only when His grace leads us to know the truth that we are truly free.

But that is not all. "We beheld His glory" (John 1:14). Paul said it like this: "Christ in you, the hope of glory" (Colossians 1:27).

How have you personally experienced Jesus' grace and truth?

SEPTEMBER 3

What Is Truth?

Pilate therefore said to Him, "Are You a king then?" Jesus answered, "You say rightly that I am a king. For this cause I was born, and for this cause I have come into the world, that I should bear witness to the truth. Everyone who is of the truth hears My voice." Pilate said to Him, "What is truth?"

JOHN 18:37–38

The prophets of relativism preach that morality exists only in relation to the present culture within its historical and societal context. There is no room for anything as archaic as long-standing moral absolutes. All truth claims are valid regardless of their origin or outcome. This philosophy creates a world in which nothing is necessarily wrong and where there are no right or wrong answers to any issues of life. In the mind of the relativist, the end result is that evil does not exist.

Morality is a forgotten concept in our culture today. Relativism, this religion of modern man that offers a life with no moral absolutes, is our culture's chosen altar of worship. Consequently, as the news headlines attest, there are basically no restraints on words, actions, or relationships in the twenty-first century.

Don't believe the false religion of relativism. There are and always have been moral absolutes in life. We need these boundaries. After all, when is a train most free—when it is running on or off its tracks?

What are some signs that relativism has infiltrated our culture and even the church?

SEPTEMBER 4

Who Is Jesus to You?

He said to them, "But who do you say that I am?" Simon Peter answered and said, "You are the Christ, the Son of the living God."

MATTHEW 16:15–16

Jesus asked His disciples, "Who do men say that I, the Son of Man, am?" (Matthew 16:13). This is a question about public opinion. Jesus wanted them to know what people were thinking and saying about Him. Our world today is still more interested in what people say than what God says.

Jesus' next question was personal and direct: "Who do you say that I am?" The "you" is emphatic: Its placement at the front of the sentence gives it significance and weight. Had we been there, it would have sounded like this: "What about you, you and you only, you and no one else, you and you alone—who do *you* say that I am?"

How someone answers this question has eternal implications, and each person must ultimately answer it. Is Jesus who He said He was when He declared, "I am the way, the truth, and the life. No one comes to the Father except through Me" (John 14:6)? He is still asking, "Who do *you* say that I am?

Who do you say Jesus is?

SEPTEMBER 5

Your Purchase Price

So I bought her for myself for fifteen shekels of silver,
and one and one-half homers of barley.
HOSEA 3:2

Just as Hosea purchased his runaway wife, Gomer, out of the marketplace when she was prostituting herself, Christ stepped into the marketplace where we were slaves to our own sin. We, too, played the harlot by turning our backs on the One who loves us like no one else ever has or will. The price He paid to free us from our slavery to sin was the most valuable purchase price ever paid for anyone or anything: His life's blood.

Peter framed it perfectly:

> If you call on the Father, who without partiality judges according to each one's work, conduct yourselves throughout the time of your stay here in fear; knowing that you were not redeemed with corruptible things, like silver or gold, from your aimless conduct received by tradition from your fathers, but with the precious blood of Christ, as of a lamb without blemish and without spot. (1 Peter 1:17–19)

He took you and me, clothed us with His own righteousness, and one day will robe us in gowns of spotless white and present us faultless before His Father's throne.

When you think about how much Christ paid to redeem you, how does it make you feel toward Him?

Finding the Direction You Should Go

I delight to do Your will, O my God, and Your law is within my heart.
PSALM 40:8

God has His own purpose and His own plan for each of His children. Jesus' passion during His own earthly pilgrimage was to do His Father's will. Once, in the middle of the day at a Samaritan well in Sychar, He testified that the thing that sustained Him on the path of life's journey was being where the Father wanted Him to be and doing what the Father wanted Him to do. He said, "My food is to do the will of Him who sent Me, and to finish His work" (John 4:34). For our Lord, nothing was more important than finding the direction in which He should go and following it. At the end of His life, as the shadows began to fall from the ancient olive trees over Gethsemane's garden, He knelt and prayed, "Not My will, but Yours, be done" (Luke 22:42). Earlier, He had pointedly addressed this passion with His disciples by saying, "I have come down from heaven, not to do My own will, but the will of Him who sent Me" (John 6:38).

In what ways are you seeking God to discover God's direction for your life?

SEPTEMBER 7

The Sword of the Spirit

Therefore He is also able to save to the uttermost those who come to God through Him, since He always lives to make intercession for them.
HEBREWS 7:25

How does the Holy Spirit help us pray? He "makes intercession" for us. He pleads on our behalf before the Father's throne. Think about the Good Samaritan, who happened upon a beaten man on the road. He got involved, interceded on the man's behalf, took him to an inn, paid his bill, and met his needs (Luke 10:25–37). This is how the Holy Spirit moves in our prayer lives. We are weak. We do not know how to pray as we ought. So, He comes alongside to help us, pleading on our behalf.

The Spirit "helps" us because He knows the mind of God and always prays "according to the will of God" (Romans 8:27). In areas of uncertainty, we find God's will for our lives through Scripture and the Spirit. We need both. This is why the Bible is called the "sword of the Spirit" (Ephesians 6:17). To find God's will, we trust in His revealed Word to us as we yield to the Holy Spirit.

In what ways do you use the "sword of the Spirit" (the Bible) when praying to know God's will?

SEPTEMBER 8

A Fragrant Faith

The house was filled with the fragrance of the oil.
JOHN 12:3

Have you noticed how a particular smell can bring instant memory recall of a particular place or a particular person from the past—even decades later? One of my high school teachers wore a fragrance called Jungle Gardenia. To this day when I get a whiff of it, my mind immediately races back to her.

Fragrance takes center stage in the story of Mary of Bethany. Along with her siblings, Martha and Lazarus, she was a devoted follower of Jesus of Nazareth. On one occasion Jesus, along with other invited guests, joined them in their home for a dinner party. After dinner Mary brought some very expensive and precious oil and poured it out on Jesus' feet. While some rebuked her for not selling it and giving the money to the poor, Jesus blessed her for this extravagant act of worship.

Mary's gift became a blessing to everyone that night who got caught up in its sweet fragrance. A life fully devoted to the Lord will have a lingering effect of His own sweet fragrance.

How does the fragrance of your faith in
Christ affect those around you?

SEPTEMBER 9

Spiritual Gifts Produce Spiritual Maturity

There are diversities of gifts, but the same Spirit.
1 CORINTHIANS 12:4

Spiritual gifts should produce maturity in the believer—first, maturity in *character.* You are an important part of His body, and your gifts are given to help build it up. We will grow in maturity as we use our gifts and become more like Christ.

Second, spiritual gifts should produce maturity in *conduct.* We all began as babies, just "born again" by the Spirit. We started like little children. Then we grew and matured in the faith. While Scripture exhorts us to be childlike in our faith, it abhors our being childish (Ephesians 4:14).

Third, your spiritual gifts should produce maturity in *conversation*—speaking the truth in love (Ephesians 4:15). Some speak the truth but not in the environment of love. Others speak in love but sacrifice the hard truth.

Fourth, your spiritual gifts should produce maturity in *cooperation.* Christ as the head desires His whole body to be "joined and knit together" (Ephesians 4:16). Every part of the body is intended to work together in cooperation and harmony.

How do you see yourself maturing in character, conduct, conversation, and cooperation as you use your spiritual gift(s)?

SEPTEMBER 10

Three, Four, Three

Blessed be the God of Shadrach, Meshach, and Abed-Nego, who sent His Angel and delivered His servants who trusted in Him.

DANIEL 3:28

Deliverance *from* the furnace experiences of life is not nearly as significant as deliverance *in* the fiery furnace. God delivered the three young Hebrew men from the fiery furnace without a hair of their heads singed. This caused the king himself to declare the words of today's scripture.

These men would not bow to any god except the one true God of Israel. Consequently, they would not burn in the furnace. The king looked into the furnace and was astonished. "Look! . . . I see four men loose, walking in the midst of the fire; and they are not hurt, and the form of the fourth is like the Son of God" (Daniel 3:25). Three men went into the fiery furnace, yet the king saw four. Then three came out of the furnace. What does this tell us? Our Lord Jesus is always with us. When we find ourselves in our own furnace experiences of life, if we look closely, we will find Jesus walking in the flames with us.

When have you sensed Jesus with you in your own fiery furnace experiences?

SEPTEMBER 11

Look in the Mirror

But be doers of the word, and not hearers only, deceiving yourselves. For if anyone is a hearer of the word and not a doer, he is like a man observing his natural face in a mirror; for he observes himself, goes away, and immediately forgets what kind of man he was. But he who looks into the perfect law of liberty and continues in it, and is not a forgetful hearer but a doer of the work, this one will be blessed in what he does.

JAMES 1:22–25

As a pastor for several years, I would rather see my people live one sermon than hear a hundred of them. James likened the one who only hears God's Word but does not do it to "a man observing his natural face in a mirror; for he observes himself, goes away, and immediately forgets what kind of man he was." His message is all too clear. A mirror doesn't lie; it tells the truth. The Bible is like a mirror. When we look into it, we see ourselves as we really are in God's eyes, not who we say we are or who others might think we are.

Have you looked at yourself in the mirror of the Bible lately? Oh, I don't mean a passing glance. Stand there before it. Look at yourself in the mirror of Psalm 51 or Psalm 139. James spoke of one who—every day—opens the Word and looks intently into it. As a result, this person stays on the Lord's course and is "blessed in what he does."

What do you see when you look at yourself in the mirror of God's Word?

SEPTEMBER 12

Give and Receive Forgiveness

And be kind to one another, tenderhearted, forgiving one another, even as God in Christ forgave you.
EPHESIANS 4:32

Any relationship that is lasting and worthwhile will have its moments of stress and disappointment, even brokenness, at times. The ability to forgive a wrong is always found in the most lasting relationships. In fact, the most secure ones are usually those in which people have weathered the storms and buried the hatchets.

Unfortunately, many interpersonal relationships with so much potential are destroyed by a lack of forgiveness. When some cannot swallow their pride and bury the hatchet with another, they are building barriers in place of bridges to better relationships. Forgiveness, accompanied by the desire to move forward, is key to successful marriages, productive business ventures, continued local church health and growth, and lasting friendships.

In broken relationships, there is an offending party and an offended party. And if we are honest, each of us has been both the offender and the offended. This means we need to practice both extending and receiving forgiveness.

Why is it important to be able to both extend and receive forgiveness?

Our Helplessness and God's Holiness

Woe is me, for I am undone! Because I am a man of unclean lips, and I dwell in the midst of a people of unclean lips; for my eyes have seen the King, the LORD of hosts.

ISAIAH 6:5

Isaiah's prayer, "Here am I! Send me" (Isaiah 6:8), becomes a reality for us not only when we see God in His holiness but when we see ourselves in our helplessness as Isaiah did. Too often we don't allow ourselves to be used by God because we measure ourselves by the wrong standard—comparing ourselves to others instead of to God's righteousness. As soon as Isaiah saw the Lord, he realized the hard truth about himself.

Isaiah did not try to sweep his sinfulness under the rug, nor did Job in Job 42:5–6, Peter in Luke 5:8, and John in Revelation 1:17 when they saw the Lord's holiness.

When we see the Lord in His glory, we see ourselves differently. And when we confess our own helplessness to Him, we hear the same pronouncement Isaiah heard: "Your iniquity is taken away, and your sin purged" (Isaiah 6:7).

How would you respond if God were to appear to you in all His glory?

SEALED FOR ETERNITY

You were sealed with the Holy Spirit of promise, who is the guarantee of our inheritance until the redemption of the purchased possession, to the praise of His glory.
EPHESIANS 1:13–14

On Pentecost, not only were the believers "*all* with one accord in one place" but they were "*all* filled with the Holy Spirit" (Acts 2:1, 4). Not some of them . . . all of them. They had been baptized into the body of Christ and sealed by the Holy Spirit, and now they were filled with all His fullness. While the baptism of the Holy Spirit is a once-and-for-all-time experience at conversion, the filling is to be repeated over and over in the Christian's experience. At conversion we have the Holy Spirit; when we are filled, He has us.

The Holy Spirit's work in our lives involves many factors. Among them is the baptism of the Holy Spirit: "For by one Spirit we were all baptized into one body" (1 Corinthians 12:13). This brings about the indwelling of the Holy Spirit: "The Spirit of God dwells in you" (Romans 8:9). Then we are sealed with the Holy Spirit: "Having believed, you were sealed with the Holy Spirit" (Ephesians 1:13).

If you are a believer, God the Holy Spirit has come to live in you. He is the guarantee, the seal, that secures your eternal destiny.

How does it make you feel to know you have a guarantee that secures your eternal destiny?

SEPTEMBER 15

No One Escapes Temptation

For we do not have a High Priest who cannot sympathize with our weaknesses, but was in all points tempted as we are, yet without sin.
HEBREWS 4:15

Temptation is *unavoidable*. First Corinthians 10:13 says, "No temptation has overtaken you except such as is common to man," and today's scripture says that even Jesus was tempted. Make no mistake about it: As long as we are encased in this human flesh, we will be tempted to sin. It is unavoidable. Think about it. We never have to teach our children to disobey. They pick right up on that due to their nature. We have to teach them to obey. The same is true with God the Father and His children, you and me. Some of us live with the false concept that the longer we walk the Christian pathway and the deeper we go in devotion to God, the less we will be tempted. Untrue. Most of our great heroes in the Bible faced their greatest temptations near the end of their pilgrimages, not at the beginning. This was certainly true of Moses, Elijah, and David. Do not be surprised when you are tempted. Simply stand strong against it.

What is your greatest temptation, and how can you stand against it?

What Is Saving Faith?

You believe that there is one God. You do well.
Even the demons believe—and tremble!
JAMES 2:19

It may surprise some to discover that demons have faith. They believe in the one true God. As the possessed man in the synagogue in Capernaum asked, "What have we to do with You, Jesus of Nazareth? Did You come to destroy us? I know who You are—the Holy One of God!" (Mark 1:24).

The devil and his demons recognize the holiness of God and the deity of Christ, but they do not possess saving faith. Their faith is an intellectual assent that goes no further than mere head knowledge, yet they tremble about the coming judgment.

Many professing believers today are further from God than the demons, going through the motions of a lifeless faith with no real fear of God. Many acknowledge that Jesus existed as a real person but do not trust their lives and eternal destiny to Him.

But as Paul put it, "If you confess with your mouth the Lord Jesus and believe in your heart that God has raised [Christ] from the dead, you will be saved" (Romans 10:9). Stop trying. Start trusting.

How would someone move from mere head knowledge about Jesus to saving faith in Him?

Forgiveness Leads to Freedom

In Him we have redemption through His blood, the forgiveness of sins, according to the riches of His grace.
EPHESIANS 1:7

Along with the Lord's command to forgive others, He imparts the love we need to do so.

Remember, forgiveness involves a repentant heart on the part of the offending party, and there must be a receptive heart on the part of the offended party. Which party are you?

Are you the offending party? Be honest. Is there something you may have done in the past that brought about the breach in a relationship? Is there anything you may have left undone? You will never stand taller than when you go to that someone and voice those two liberating words, "I'm sorry." And accompany them with "I wronged you; please forgive me." Do it for your own sake.

Are you Philemon, the offended party? Be willing to forgive. Let God help you forgive, and you will find it liberating. Pass along the forgiveness you have found in Christ yourself to someone else in your life. It will set you free.

How does forgiveness lead to freedom?

The Bible Is a Gift from God

Forever, O Lord, Your word is settled in heaven.
PSALM 119:89

We can rest in the Bible's promise of its abiding forever due to its *supernatural origin.* Writing to young Timothy in his last pastoral letter before his own execution, Paul said that "all Scripture is given by inspiration of God" (2 Timothy 3:16). The Scripture you hold in your hands and read each day has been "given" to you. Unlike all other books, it is supernatural in its origin. It originates with God, not with man. The phrase "given by inspiration" means "God-breathed." God used men in the process of giving us His Word. But He did not breathe on them. He breathed out of them His abiding Word. Just as a skilled musical composer creates a score utilizing flutes and trumpets, strings and percussion as his instruments, so God chose His own instruments, some as different as common laborers and powerful kings, and breathed out His words through them. Your Bible is "given" to you by God Himself.

Gifts are intended to bless and to benefit. How does the Bible bless and benefit you?

SEPTEMBER 19

Who Is This?

And when He had come into Jerusalem, all the city was moved, saying, "Who is this?" So the multitudes said, "This is Jesus, the prophet from Nazareth of Galilee."

MATTHEW 21:10–11

Those faithful followers lining the street on that original Palm Sunday did not only praise Jesus; they began to extend Him to others. They wanted others to meet their Savior and Lord. Nothing could keep them from sharing the good news that Jesus was their long-awaited Messiah and that they had found in Him their hope.

When we do the same—when we praise Jesus for what He has done in our lives and share our stories with others—the people around us will also ask, "Who is this?" Who is this . . . who transformed your life? Who is this . . . who put your family back together? Who is this . . . who brought you peace in the midst of such tragedy? Who is this . . . who enabled you to be victorious over your addiction? Who is this . . . who gave you hope in the darkness of your circumstances? "This is Jesus!" You have experienced Him, so now extol Him and extend Him to others.

What has Jesus done for you that you can share with others?

SEPTEMBER 20

God's Glory Dwells in You

Do you not know that you are the temple of God
and that the Spirit of God dwells in you?
1 CORINTHIANS 3:16

In the language of the New Testament, there are two distinct Greek words translated into our English word *temple.* One describes the entire Temple Mount, even including the portico of the temple where Jesus drove out the money changers (Mark 11:15). The other describes only the inner sanctuary itself, the holy of holies, the holiest of all places where the shekinah glory of God filled the room as He visited with His people.

When the Bible speaks of our bodies being the "temple" of the Holy Spirit today, it is this latter word that is used to describe it. This is not just an awesome thought but an awesome reality. You are God's holy of holies. You are His place of worship. You are where His glory dwells. Right now. Christ in you. Jesus is the manifestation of the glory of God. No wonder the Scriptures remind us that we "were bought at a price; therefore glorify God in your body and in your spirit, which are God's" (1 Corinthians 6:20).

What thoughts come to mind when you realize that your body is the temple of God?

SEPTEMBER 21

Drink the Living Water

The Lord will guide you continually . . . you shall be like a watered garden, and like a spring of water, whose waters do not fail.
ISAIAH 58:11

In the midst of the Lord's invitation to us to come and drink, He inserted these words: "He who believes in Me, as the Scripture has said, out of his heart will flow rivers of living water" (John 7:38). God's blessings always turn on the hinge of faith. It is "he who believes in Me." Faith is the way we drink of this living water that satisfies our souls.

Jesus backed up this amazing promise by establishing a biblical basis for it from the Hebrew Bible: "as the Scripture has said." What scripture? Jesus, no doubt, had in mind the words of the ancient prophet Isaiah—chapter 58, verse 11.

When speaking to the Samaritan woman at the well, Jesus referred to living water (John 4:13–14). This indicates that we are never to be stagnant; we are to be like a fountain or a river, always flowing to bless others. Drinking of the water that Christ gives is less about *getting* a blessing and more about *being* a blessing.

What are some specific ways you can be a blessing to someone who might not otherwise feel blessed this week?

SEPTEMBER 22

Listen to Him

While he was still speaking, behold, a bright cloud overshadowed them; and suddenly a voice came out of the cloud, saying, "This is My beloved Son, in whom I am well pleased. Hear Him!"

MATTHEW 17:5

Many of us share a common fault in our conversations with others. We fail to listen. We're so immersed in preparing our next brilliant comment that we don't hear what the other person is saying. How many times have we been introduced to someone and immediately forgotten his or her name? On the Mount of Transfiguration, the Father gave us good advice. He introduced His Son, affirmed His pleasure in Him, and then admonished us to "listen to him" (Matthew 17:5 ESV).

One thing we often forget about prayer is that it is communication with the Lord. And communication is a two-way street. We talk . . . and, if we are smart, we listen even more than we speak. Perhaps one of the most overlooked and forgotten elements of prayer is taking the time to listen to Him. He still speaks to us through His Word and by His Spirit. God is essentially saying to us here, "This is My Son; I love Him; I am pleased with Him. Stop talking so much and listen to Him."

How often do you stop to listen to the Lord when praying, and why would it be important to do it more regularly?

SEPTEMBER 23

Foolish Presumptions

Come now, you who say, "Today or tomorrow we will go to such and such a city, spend a year there, buy and sell, and make a profit.". . . . Instead you ought to say, "If the Lord wills, we shall live and do this or that." But now you boast in your arrogance. All such boasting is evil.

JAMES 4:13, 15–16

What motivates you? There is nothing wrong with making a profit. But profits made without any desire to honor the Lord with our possessions often bring misery.

The individual of whom James spoke complicated his predicament by arrogantly "boasting and bragging" about his plans. The warning for us is plain: Don't make presumptions about the future without consulting God. This warning doesn't mean that we should be passive. We ought to do more detailed planning than anyone else. We should be goal-oriented and profit-motivated because we have Someone on our side guiding us and leading us, and He always knows best. He is also "able to do exceedingly abundantly above all that we ask or think" (Ephesians 3:20). And, as Christians, we need to include this in all our plans: "If the Lord wills."

Perhaps you're experiencing a recession of the soul, a period of reduced spiritual activity. Be watchful. Recessions—whether economic or spiritual—are often rooted in foolish presumptions.

In what ways do you consider the Lord in your plans when setting goals and making decisions?

Relationships Are Like a Seesaw

And just as you want men to do to you, you also do to them likewise.
LUKE 6:31

One of the major reasons for the trend of short-term relationships we see today is a lack of objectivity. Some are overly focused on being on the receiving end of every relationship. Few seem to be objective enough to realize that reciprocity, the returning of favors, and giving of themselves are key for building lasting relationships.

When our daughters were little, they loved going to the local neighborhood park. They especially loved to ride the seesaw. In my mind's eye, I can still see those two little toddlers now on it . . . up and down . . . up and down . . . up and down. Relationships can be like that . . . up and down. We might call it the seesaw effect. There are times in a relationship when one of the parties does most of the giving and the other does most of the receiving. Then circumstances change, the tables are turned, and the roles are reversed.

In an important relationship in your life, how are you giving, and how are you receiving?

SEPTEMBER 25

VOLUNTARY, VICARIOUS, AND VITAL

He was oppressed and He was afflicted, yet He opened not His mouth; He was led as a lamb to the slaughter, and as a sheep before its shearers is silent, so He opened not His mouth.

ISAIAH 53:7

Let's make three observations about Christ's death on the cross. First, it was *voluntary*: Jesus said in John 10:17–18, "I lay down My life. . . . No one takes it from Me, but I lay it down of Myself."

Christ's death was also *vicarious.* All our iniquity was laid on Him (Isaiah 53:6). He died our death—yours and mine—then and there so we could live His life in the here and now. He took our sin so we could take His righteousness.

The death of Christ was also *vital.* It was necessary to take away our sin. In fact, Isaiah concluded by saying, "It pleased the LORD to bruise Him" (Isaiah 53:10). God was not taking pleasure in watching the agony, suffering, and death of His only begotten Son. No. What pleased the Father was—when the suffering and sacrifice were complete—there was the possibility of relationship with all who would come to Him by faith in His Son to receive the gift of eternal and abundant life.

How much love must the Father and Jesus have for us to pay such a costly price to redeem us?

SEPTEMBER 26

Following and Fishing

Follow Me, and I will make you become fishers of men.
MARK 1:17

Discipleship is in the very heart of the Great Commission (Matthew 28:19). The church is commissioned to "make disciples," not just add to its numbers, stand for justice, or meet the social needs of its community. Authentic disciples are "made." They don't just happen into being.

When we turn just one page in our Bibles from the Great Commission into Mark's gospel, we discover what authentic discipleship is really about. The first word Jesus ever used to describe those who would become His followers was not *Christians* or *disciples,* which we don't see in Scripture until Acts 11:26 and Matthew 10, respectively. The first term ever to escape Jesus' own lips to describe what He desired His followers to be was "fishers of men." In Jesus' mind authentic discipleship always involves two actions: following and fishing. We follow Jesus, and we "fish" for others who need to follow Him too.

How well are you following, and how well are you fishing?

Forgiveness and Accountability

Barnabas wanted to bring John called Mark along with them too, but Paul insisted that they should not take along this one who had left them in Pamphylia and had not accompanied them in the work.

ACTS 15:37–38 NET

Paul mentioned a man named Mark in Philemon verse 24, as he urged Philemon to receive Onesimus back in total forgiveness. Philemon would remember that Mark stood as a testimony of Paul's ability to forgive. Young Mark had accompanied Paul on his first missionary journey but quit along the way. He went AWOL when the going got tough. Twelve years had since passed, and Philemon verse 24 was Paul's first mention of Mark in any of his writings. Obviously, Paul had extended his forgiveness to him. And in case anyone might doubt that their new relationship was flourishing, Paul mentioned him in his last recorded letter to Timothy, saying, "Only Luke is with me. Get Mark and bring him with you, for he is useful to me for ministry" (2 Timothy 4:11). Mark knew what it meant to be forgiven and, thus, to be accountable.

When have you received forgiveness and responded with accountability?

SEPTEMBER 28

Prayer's Ultimate Purpose

For this is good and acceptable in the sight of God our Savior, who desires all men to be saved and to come to the knowledge of the truth.
1 TIMOTHY 2:3–4

Prayer brings with it an *ultimate purpose*: to glorify God through the salvation of souls whom Jesus came to save. Our nation once believed that prayer could really change things in our lives and world. But prayer has been relegated to the ranks below pickets and protests and politics. The early church never tried to change their world from without—with plans and programs—but from within, keeping their priority on prayer. And they saw God's ultimate purpose fulfilled in ways that no generation has seen since.

This is no guarantee that all will be saved. They won't. We are not puppets; we are people with the ability to make choices in life. God made us this way because the love we can voluntarily return to Him is indescribably valuable to Him. He sends the Holy Spirit to convict us; He draws us to Himself; His love constrains us; His kindness leads us to repentance. But ultimately, the choice is ours.

How could you follow the example of the early church in prioritizing prayer?

SEPTEMBER 29

Your Position in Christ

At that day you will know that I am in My Father, and you in Me, and I in you.
JOHN 14:20

Have you awakened to the reality that Christ is really alive in you in the person of His Holy Spirit at this very moment? Today, fix your thoughts not on who you are, or what you are, or why you are, but on *where* you are.

Jesus revealed that He is positioned in the Father. Then He said, "You [are] in Me"! No matter what may come your way, you are in a good place. You are in Christ, and Christ is in the Father. Nothing can get to you that does not first have to pass through the Father and the Son to reach you. And if it penetrates that shield and gets that far, you can rest in the fact that there is a purpose for it in your life.

But that is not all. Jesus continued, "And I [am] in you." Christ is taking care of the outside of you (you are in Him), and He is also taking care of the inside of you (He is in you).

Why is *where* you are more important than who, what, and why you are?

SEPTEMBER 30

Grace Is Essential to Healthy Relationships

All who are with me greet you. Greet those who love us in the faith. Grace be with you all. Amen.
TITUS 3:15

Paul concluded many of his epistles by expressing his desire for his readers to experience grace. In so doing, he was indicating that we need grace and that without it, there is little hope of authentic accountability in our relationships. Many of us equate accountability with judgment, while Paul equated it with grace. Accountability is not about judging one another's faults; it issues from God's mercy and grace and results in a mutual love and respect among friends.

Grace is lacking in many relationships. *Grace* can be defined as unmerited favor extended toward someone. If grace is good enough for us to receive it from God, it is also good enough to extend to others in our relationships. We all need to see that extending grace to others is essential for building healthy relationships. If you make a mistake in one of your relationships, err on the side of mercy and grace, not on the side of judgment.

Who has extended grace to you, and what did it mean to you?

OCTOBER

OCTOBER 1

Words Are Powerful

Death and life are in the power of the tongue,
and those who love it will eat its fruit.
PROVERBS 18:21

How would you feel if you got a letter today saying, "Your love has given me great joy and encouragement, because you . . . have refreshed the hearts of the Lord's people," as Paul wrote to Philemon in Philemon verse 7 (NIV)? You would sit up, eager to read what was coming next. In stark contrast, when we receive letters with words of caustic criticism in the first paragraph, we don't want to read further. One day after I had recently preached on this very subject from Philemon, I received several letters in the mail. I opened the first one, and it blasted and blistered me and did so extremely unjustly. It wounded me greatly. The next several letters were filled with encouragement and affirmation. Others told of miracles that had taken place in relationships when they put in place these principles of affirmation. Needless to say, words of affirmation go a long way in refreshing the hearts of those who receive them. We can keep going and keep doing what is right on the wings of one great compliment.

Who in your life needs a compliment, whose heart needs to be refreshed, and how can you use your words to do it?

Finding Our First Love

So when they did not find Him, they returned to Jerusalem, seeking Him.
LUKE 2:45

One of the most misquoted verses in all the Bible is Revelation 2:4: "You have left your first love." Ask a hundred people who may have heard of this verse and the majority will remember it as saying, "You have lost your first love." But there is a world of difference in admitting that we left something and having to admit we lost something.

Mary and Joseph could relate to leaving something. They had gone on an annual pilgrimage with twelve-year-old Jesus to Jerusalem and were returning home. Since Jesus was still a child, He could have traveled in the men's caravan or the women's. As Jesus' parents came to the end of the first day's journey, they realized He was not with either of them. It was not until they admitted they had not *lost* Him but *left* Him back in Jerusalem that they found Him—right there at the temple, in dialogue with the elders (Luke 2:42–49).

Have you *lost* or *left* your first love on your journey through life, and if so, are you willing to go back and find Him?

OCTOBER 3

The True Source of Temptation

Let no one say when he is tempted, "I am tempted by God"; for God cannot be tempted by evil, nor does He Himself tempt anyone. But each one is tempted when he is drawn away by his own desires and enticed.

JAMES 1:13–14

When our "own desires" attach themselves to an evil object, we are "drawn away" from our place of security. James painted a picture of us living in a secure place, only to allow a desire contrary to God's will to draw us away from that place of security into the open where we become vulnerable to sin.

Such temptation to sin is a personal matter—what tempts one person may not tempt someone else. We cannot blame God, the devil, or circumstances for our temptations. If there were no evil desire in our hearts, there would be no temptation to sin. Yet this internal source seeks to draw us away and causes us to want to play outside of God's boundaries.

The internal source of temptation is selfish desire, the external force is deception; and when these two coincide, the result is sinful behavior. We are to be alert, to watch out. The bait of temptation has a hook in it. If we look closely enough, we will see it is a trap!

If you've ever succumbed to temptation, what selfish desires and deceptive forces were at work?

OCTOBER 4

The Oxygen of God's Kingdom

Teacher, which is the great commandment in the law?
MATTHEW 22:36

Jesus commanded His followers to love one another as He loved us (John 13:34–35). We are to love one another with an unlimited, unchanging, unselfish, and unconditional love, just as He loved us then and continues to love us. How can we possibly love like this? We can't. It is impossible in our own strength. Only if we love God above and beyond all else, only if we love Him with all our soul and mind, will His love, abiding in us, overflow through us to the people around us. Only then will we be able to love one another as He loved us.

When asked, "Which is the great commandment in the law?" Jesus didn't hesitate to respond: "Love the LORD your God with all your heart, with all your soul, and with all your mind" (Matthew 22:37). Love is the oxygen of God's kingdom, the distinguishing characteristic that shows we belong to Him. You have a single, primary purpose in life—to love the Lord your God with every part of your being!

In your own words, what does it mean that "love is the oxygen of God's kingdom"?

OCTOBER 5

All We Like Sheep

We all, like sheep, have gone astray, each of us has turned to our own way.
ISAIAH 53:6 NIV

We see a poignant picture of Jesus in Isaiah 53 and a revealing picture of ourselves as well. The only way to comprehend the meaning of today's scripture is to consider how we, in fact, do resemble the woolly sheep.

Fact number one: Sheep are directionless. They tend to simply wander aimlessly along the hillsides with no sense of direction whatsoever. Likewise, many of us seem to wander through life without any sense of direction, void of any real perceived purpose.

Fact number two: Sheep are defenseless. Almost every other animal has some type of defense mechanism. Rabbits can run. Dogs can bite. Cats can scratch. Bees can sting. Porcupines can puncture. But sheep? They are not prepared for fight or flight. Men and women without Christ are helpless and hopeless against the "wiles of the devil" (Ephesians 6:11), ill-equipped to fight off or flee from an attack.

Since we all find ourselves "like sheep," and since "each of us has turned to our own way," God must come to our rescue. And He has!

How are you like a sheep, and how has God come to your rescue?

OCTOBER 6

There's Strength in Weakness

Therefore most gladly I will rather boast in my infirmities, that the power of Christ may rest upon me. . . . For when I am weak, then I am strong.

2 CORINTHIANS 12:9–10

The apostle Paul penned the words of today's Scripture verses in the context of writing about his thorn in the flesh (2 Corinthians 12:7).

There is a strange kinship between Paul's thorns and the thorns that pierced the brow of our Lord. Jesus, in weakness, with thorns in His brow and spikes nailed through His hands and feet, became strong. Could it be that every time Paul sensed the pressure of his thorn it reminded him of the power of the cross? There is nothing lovely about a crown of thorns. There may be nothing lovely about the thorn that irritates you. The cross was cruel and harsh, and your thorn may be cruel and harsh to you. But note that Paul said his thorn "was given to me" (2 Corinthians 12:7). Make sure you are not trying to rid yourself of the very thing God has given you for His purpose in your life. Then, stand on His promise: "My grace is sufficient for you" (2 Corinthians 12:9).

When have you experienced Christ's strength despite your weakness?

OCTOBER 7

Two People, Two Prayers

Two men went up to the temple to pray, one a Pharisee and the other a tax collector. The Pharisee stood and prayed thus with himself, "God, I thank You that I am not like other men—extortioners, unjust, adulterers, or even as this tax collector. I fast twice a week; I give tithes of all that I possess." And the tax collector, standing afar off, would not so much as raise his eyes to heaven, but beat his breast, saying, "God, be merciful to me a sinner!"

LUKE 18:10–13

There are five instances of the pronoun *I* in the Pharisee's two-sentence petition. Pharisees compare themselves to "other men" instead of to God's standard of Christ's perfect righteousness. This man didn't go to the temple to pray; he went to inform God and others of how wonderful he was.

Contrast this prayer with that of the tax collector. He stood "afar off" and deemed himself so unworthy he could "not so much as raise his eyes to heaven." In deep remorse and repentance, he "beat his breast" and pleaded, "God, be merciful to me a sinner!"

The message is plain. God looks on the heart. Those filled with self-pride are blinded to spiritual reality. It is more important who we are when we pray and how we pray than what we say with the words of our mouths.

Are your prayers more like the Pharisee's or the tax collector's, and why?

OCTOBER 8

It Takes Two

Take heed to yourselves. If your brother sins against you, rebuke him; and if he repents, forgive him.
LUKE 17:3

To genuinely mend a broken relationship, two things must happen, one on the part of the offending party and the other on the part of the offended party. The offending party must come to the table with a repentant heart. If not, there can be no genuine reconciliation. How many times have we seen that an offending party is not truly sorry but simply sorry they got caught? There must be a truly repentant heart on the part of the offending party.

However, it takes two to bury the hatchet. There must be a receptive heart on the part of the offended party that is void of a spirit of resentment or retaliation. Most often the biggest burden falls on those who have been deeply wronged in a relationship. Many relationships are destroyed not because the offending party lacked a repentant heart but because the offended party would not receive the other, forgive, and move on. Both parties have a major role in seeing true reconciliation become a reality.

Why is it important to be equally willing to forgive and to be forgiven?

OCTOBER 9

Surrender to the Holy Spirit

I say then: Walk in the Spirit, and you shall not fulfill the lust of the flesh.
GALATIANS 5:16

One of the most liberating discoveries in a believer's life is awakening to the importance of the personality and deity of the Holy Spirit. If He is your constant companion, living in you, you will want to have a close and abiding personal relationship with Him.

Many want to "get more" of the Holy Spirit. But He is a Person, not some mystical force or substance. If we know Christ, we have all the Holy Spirit we will ever need. When we think of Him as some external force that might empower us with various kinds of supernatural abilities, then our quest will lead us on a journey to seek more of Him—and that is a dead-end road.

But when we think of Him as He really is, then we will not try to *get more of Him* but to *give Him more of us*. The Holy Spirit is a Person. He lives in you. His desire is to get more of you. And this happens when you surrender every area of your life to Him.

How do you relate differently to the Holy Spirit knowing He is a person and not a force?

OCTOBER 10

Walking with the Lord

If we live in the Spirit, let us also walk in the Spirit.
GALATIANS 5:25

We have all known those who walked the Christian life for decades with seemingly little victory, while others journeyed only a short distance yet manifested joy and victory. For many Christians, the walk takes them through dark valleys. Others stumble over obstacles. Still others run into dead ends or detours. It is not *how far* we walk but *how* we walk this Christian journey that makes the difference.

My wife and I enjoy early morning walks together. This uninterrupted opportunity to talk about the deeper things of our hearts brings an intimacy that is not just helpful but essential in our lives. Walking in the Spirit does the same thing for our spiritual lives. The Lord longs for us to live in a relationship of intimacy with Him as Father and child.

God never intended the Christian walk to be one of discouragement, darkness, or defeat. As we walk this journey, there will be problems that hinder our progress. But there are also proofs that highlight our walk of faith.

How would you describe the intimacy in your walk with the Lord, and how would you like to grow in it?

OCTOBER 11

Do You Know That Your Redeemer Lives?

I know that my Redeemer lives.

JOB 19:25

Notice in today's scripture that Job said it is "*my* Redeemer" who lives. Can you embrace that little one-syllable, two-letter personal pronoun—*my*? If so, you will find Jesus to be your very own personal Redeemer who lives forever. In the midst of his great difficulties, Job's source of delight was seeing God in the next life. Job knew, and we can know, that heaven is a wonderful place. We will never see a hospital there, because there will be no more sickness. We will see no more funeral homes, because there will be no more death. We will never see or sense the need for any more counseling centers, because there will be no more depression, heartache, or mental illness. We will never see a police car, because there will be no more crime. Whatever it may be that takes the joy out of life will be gone forever for those who can say with Job, "I know that my Redeemer lives."

What hope does it give you today to know that your Redeemer lives?

OCTOBER 12

Taming the Tongue

If anyone among you thinks he is religious, and does not bridle his tongue but deceives his own heart, this one's religion is useless.
JAMES 1:26

Our Christian character is shown in the way we converse. James said that those who consider themselves religious but don't "bridle [their] tongue" are deceiving themselves, and their religion is "useless." In short, it's just an empty show.

The word we translate as *deceive* can also mean "cheat." People who cannot control what comes out of their mouth—whether it is vile speech or gossip or slander or lies or whatever—are cheating themselves in the process. We have all known people like this and seen how they are actually deceiving themselves about their spiritual health.

When James said this type of conversation results in being "useless," he picked a word that literally means "without achieving its intended result or goal." A futile, fruitless religion is of no value to anyone.

Our character is often revealed in our conversation before anyone has a chance to observe our conduct. In James's words, it is therefore wise to "bridle [our] tongue."

What differences do you find between the conversation of a Christian and that of a nonbeliever?

OCTOBER 13

The Harvest Is Ready

When He saw the multitudes, He was moved with compassion for them, because they were weary and scattered, like sheep having no shepherd. Then He said to His disciples, "The harvest truly is plentiful, but the laborers are few."

MATTHEW 9:36–37

Upon seeing the multitudes of people, Jesus was "moved with compassion for them." Weak and exhausted from the daily struggles under Roman oppression, they were beaten down, with no hope and no direction. They are still here, all around us. Many are holding on to life by a thread. When we begin to see them through the eyes of Jesus, we, too, will be moved with compassion and motivated to move out of our comfort zones.

Jesus notes that what He calls "the harvest" is full. It is ready. He doesn't issue a call to plow the fields, plant the crops, or prepare and cultivate. But He quickly acknowledges there is a major problem—"The laborers are few." Not the spectators. There are lots of them. God's problem today is not out there in the fields. They are plenteous. They are ripe and waiting. Things haven't changed much in two thousand years; God's problem is still with His own people.

How does knowing the harvest is plentiful encourage you to share the gospel?

OCTOBER 14

Be Filled

Do not be drunk with wine, in which is dissipation; but be filled with the Spirit.
EPHESIANS 5:18

In the Bible, we are not commanded to be baptized in the Holy Spirit—if we have trusted in Christ. As believers, we have already been baptized in Him. We are not commanded to be sealed with the Holy Spirit. This is God's own work in us. What we are commanded to do is found in today's verse: "Be filled with the Spirit."

Every verb has a number, tense, voice, and mood. When we parse this verb translated as "be filled," we discover that the number is plural. It is in the present tense, which indicates continuous action. The voice is passive, meaning that the subject doesn't act; it is acted upon by another. And the mood is imperative. That means this is not optional; it is a direct command. Putting all this together means that this verse is more correctly translated as, "All of us must always be being filled with the Holy Spirit." This is God's desire.

The biblical instruction to be filled with the Spirit is emphatic. Why do you think this is so important?

God's Faithfulness in the Face of Temptation

Every good gift and every perfect gift is from above, and comes down from the Father of lights, with whom there is no variation or shadow of turning.
JAMES 1:17

When we face temptation, as we all do at times, we should remember that God is unchangeable in His faithfulness. He "will not allow you to be tempted beyond what you are able, but with the temptation will also make the way of escape, that you may be able to bear it" (1 Corinthians 10:13). The word picture here is of a mountain pass. Imagine you are surrounded by an enemy closing in on you from all sides. Then, suddenly, you see an escape route through a narrow mountain pass. You run to it, and through it, to safety on the other side. Most who fall into sin do so willfully because they refuse to take the path of escape that God puts before them.

When temptation knocks on our door, we should not let it take us by surprise. It is "common to man." Just because temptation is *unavoidable* does not mean that the Lord Jesus is not *unchangeable*. Christ Himself is our way of escape. Run to Him. He is forever faithful.

When has God provided you with a way of escape, and what did you do with it?

OCTOBER 16

A Family Secret

And we know that all things work together for good to those who love God, to those who are the called according to His purpose.
ROMANS 8:28

Take a look at an important word of the Bible promise found in Romans 8:28. It begins with "And we know . . ." Note carefully the plural pronoun in play: "we." Yes, *we* know. This promise was never intended to be understood by the world. It is a foreign language to those outside Christ. It is, in its essence, a family secret for those of us in the family of God. The promise found in Romans 8:28 is something that *we* know, something those who are not part of God's forever family cannot comprehend. But we can. Yes, "we know that all things work together for good to those who love God, to those who are the called according to His purpose."

The next time you feel overwhelmed by situations or circumstances swirling around you that seem beyond your control, climb up on this Bible promise. Stand there. Believe it. Claim it as your own.

What can you do to personally believe Romans 8:28?

OCTOBER 17

FORGIVE YOURSELF

If we confess our sins, he is faithful and just and will forgive us our sins and purify us from all unrighteousness.
1 JOHN 1:9 NIV

What the world needs is more men and women who help bring people together in reconciliation. If you know someone who is the offending party, care enough about them to help them see their need and then support them in the process. Perhaps you know someone who is the offended party; care enough to encourage them to forgive as Christ forgave them. You could be the key in helping to mend a broken relationship with a result in which everyone wins.

It may be that before you can forgive others for an offense, you need to forgive yourself and simply allow God to love you and fill you with His power and forgiveness. The place to begin is in your own confession to Him accompanied by a plea, "Please forgive me." He is willing and waiting, and you can begin the great adventure for which you were created in the first place: fellowship with Christ, a brand-new beginning with total forgiveness.

In what ways do you need to forgive yourself?

OCTOBER 18

THE BIBLE IS GOD'S WORD

For the word of God is living and powerful, and sharper than any two-edged sword, piercing even to the division of soul and spirit, and of joints and marrow, and is a discerner of the thoughts and intents of the heart.

HEBREWS 4:12

Simon Peter helped us understand the power and blessing of God's Word when he declared that "holy men of God spoke as they were moved by the Holy Spirit" (2 Peter 1:21). The identical Greek word translated here as "moved" was used by Luke in describing Paul's shipwreck in the book of Acts. There came a fierce storm, and the sailors on board the ship lost all control, unable to guide the ship because of the strong winds. They stayed busy about their tasks, but the winds took the ship wherever it blew (Acts 27:15–17). Just as the sailors on board the ship were active yet had to relinquish control over where it would go, so it was with the Bible writers. In a very real sense, the writings were not their own. God Himself made this point clear to His prophet Jeremiah, saying, "I have put My words in your mouth" (Jeremiah 1:9).

When have you read the Bible and realized that it really is God's Word to you?

OCTOBER 19

A Sign of His Coming

Now as He sat on the Mount of Olives, the disciples came to Him privately, saying, "Tell us, when will these things be? And what will be the sign of Your coming, and of the end of the age?"
MATTHEW 24:3

Shortly before Jesus' second coming, an electrifying leader will emerge on the world scene. He is called the Antichrist (1 John 2:18). This charismatic leader will promise a world of peace. He will speak of freeing the world of war and tout solutions to the world's economic and political problems. Much of the world will follow after him.

Before this climactic event of Christ's return, a new religion will emerge that seeks to unite the world under one banner (Revelation 17:1–18). A new age of humanistic thought will seek to exalt man over Christ. This philosophy has already infiltrated the Western world through the media and much of the educational process. Pluralism is the new religion of the day.

Jesus said, "When these things begin to happen, look up and lift up your heads, because your redemption draws near" (Luke 21:28). In light of this verse and the events going on in our world today, it just might be time for Christians to stop looking for signs and start listening for a shout!

What signs today could point to Jesus' second coming?

OCTOBER 20

LOOK AND LIVE

Then the LORD said to Moses, "Make a fiery serpent, and set it on a pole. . . ." So Moses made a bronze serpent, and put it on a pole; and so it was, if a serpent had bitten anyone, when he looked at the bronze serpent, he lived.

NUMBERS 21:8–9

There was only one remedy for sin for the Israelites and only one remedy for us: "Look and live." They didn't have to work for their cure, pay for their cure, or earn their cure through their own good works.

Jesus still says, "Look at Me and live." Anyone can look. You can look. I can look. You don't need to have social standing or political power to look. It does not require an educational pedigree. It doesn't demand moral excellence. The vilest sinner can look to Jesus and live. To look to Jesus in faith seems so simple, yet it is all God requires. Jesus shows up in the book of Numbers to remind us of His sacrifice on the cross for you and me. Yes, just as Moses lifted up the serpent in the wilderness, so was the Son of God, our Savior, the Lord Jesus Christ lifted up on a Roman cross. And the good news is, everyone who looks to Him lives . . . and lives forever.

Why does God require nothing more than faith for us to look to Jesus and live?

The True Thirst-Quencher

The Spirit and the bride say, "Come!" And let him who hears say, "Come!" And let him who thirsts come. Whoever desires, let him take the water of life freely.

REVELATION 22:17

When we view the invitation to come to Jesus through the lens of the Greek text, it is passionately expressive: "If anyone thirsts, let him come to Me and drink" (John 7:37). The wording of the original text indicates this is a rather loud and deeply emotional outburst. Jesus was not speaking softly here. What amazes me is that we should even need this urging and that He should have to give it! Shouldn't it be the other way around? Shouldn't you and I be the ones pleading with Him to allow us to come? And yet it is Jesus who passionately pleads for us to come to Him!

I wonder who the thirsty ones are across the world right now. Some of us have tried so desperately to quench the thirst within our souls with the things this world offers. Yet it seems the more we have, the thirstier we become. Could it be that Jesus is opening your eyes to the reality that the something you think you need is really Someone?

How have you tried to quench the thirst in your soul with something or someone other than Jesus?

OCTOBER 22

Stop and Listen

But they constrained Him, saying, "Abide with us, for it is toward evening, and the day is far spent." And He went in to stay with them.
LUKE 24:29

After the crucifixion, two of Jesus' followers walked home to Emmaus in discouragement, saying, "We were hoping that it was He who was going to redeem Israel" (Luke 24:21). But they had buried that hope when Jesus' body was placed in the tomb.

Then, suddenly—the resurrected "Jesus Himself drew near and went with them," but they "did not know Him" (Luke 24:15–16). Later "their eyes were opened and they knew Him; and He vanished from their sight" (v. 31). And their response? "Did not our heart burn within us while He talked with us on the road?" (v. 32).

Their glowing hearts turned into "going" hearts. They "rose up that very hour and returned to Jerusalem" to exclaim to all the others, "The Lord is risen indeed!" (vv. 33–34).

Maybe your hopes have been dashed and your dreams smashed. Stop. Look. Listen to Jesus' Spirit through His Scriptures. He is still speaking. You just might walk away with your own heart burning within you.

When have you failed to recognize Jesus working in a situation and then suddenly realized He was right there with you?

OCTOBER 23

The Time Is Now

Whereas you do not know what will happen tomorrow. For what is your life? It is even a vapor that appears for a little time and then vanishes away.

JAMES 4:14

Proper views of life and death are forgotten perspectives for many of us. Some people live as though this life is all there is. We even seek to camouflage the aging process and pretend it isn't happening. Death is not a subject we want to dwell on. That's why many of us live as if we have a ninety-nine-year lease on our body with an option to renew. Death, however, is life's greatest certainty.

Nothing will keep us from this ultimate appointment already on God's calendar. The Bible says, "In Your book they all were written, the days fashioned for me, when as yet there were none of them" (Psalm 139:16).

Stop making foolish presumptions about tomorrow. Maintain a proper perspective on life and align your personal priorities with the Lord's.

If you have placed your faith and trust in Jesus Christ, the One who holds "the keys of Hades and of Death" (Revelation 1:18), your appointment can mean rejoicing, not fear. Yet we all need to heed Amos 4:12: "Prepare to meet your God!"

Do you need to change any of your personal priorities to align with the Lord's priorities? What needs to change?

OCTOBER 24

Be a Committed and Generous Friend

Let love and faithfulness never leave you; bind them around your neck, write them on the tablet of your heart.

PROVERBS 3:3 NIV

Loyal friends are objective. They get the big picture in relationships. They keep things in perspective. They can see past themselves to realize the importance of reciprocation. They are quick to return favors. *Commitment* is a lost word in many relationships today because so many of us are bent on getting what we can for ourselves, in place of a focus on giving.

Committed friends can see past themselves and their own momentary needs to the importance of reciprocation. So they give. They understand that friends need friendship the most often when they deserve it the least.

This lack of objectivity is the point of breakdown in many relationships. This need to always be on the receiving end is a key factor in the destruction of many relationships. Get the big picture. Decide to be a giver. Return a favor. Make a lot of deposits in your relationships because there will come a time when you need some withdrawals.

How can you be committed and generous in a friendship this week?

OCTOBER 25

Rahab Chooses God

"Now then, please swear to me by the Lord that you will show kindness to my family, because I have shown kindness to you. Give me a sure sign."
JOSHUA 2:12 NIV

The Israelites marched around the city of Jericho for seven days. As the residents of Jericho watched, hundreds of thousands of Israelites surrounded their city, marching around it. All of Jericho was terrified. Joshua was coming. Judgment was coming. Chaos and confusion ran rampant through the streets. Except for in one home. Rahab was in the midst of the chaos, but she felt no fear. She had heard what God had done for the Israelites on the other side of the Jordan and professed, "The Lord your God, He is God in heaven above and on earth beneath" (Joshua 2:11). It is one thing to believe He is God in heaven but another to believe He is in control of "earth beneath." As an expression of her faith, she hung the scarlet cord—the sure sign mentioned in today's scripture—out her window. She was looking for her salvation. Through the Israelites' faith and by a miracle of God, the walls of Jericho fell down flat, and the city was destroyed. But not Rahab.

In the midst of chaos and confusion around you, how can you choose God?

OCTOBER 26

Authentic Discipleship

As Jesus passed on from there, He saw a man named Matthew sitting at the tax office. And He said to him, "Follow Me." So he arose and followed Him.
MATTHEW 9:9

Perhaps no other subject is talked about more and practiced less in Christian circles than authentic discipleship, which is found in following Christ. *Follow Me*—these two simple words were used so often by Jesus. Not only on the Sea of Galilee—where He encountered a group of fishermen engrossed in their lifetime passion of the fishing business and saw them put down their nets to begin the journey of following Him—but also around the coast of the lake at Capernaum. There He saw a Jew taking up tax money from the local Jewish residents for the Roman government. Jesus looked squarely into his face and spoke those two words, "Follow Me." Matthew threw down his money pouch, walked away from his tax office—his livelihood—and took his first steps to becoming an authentic disciple. Authentic disciples are men and women who respond to Jesus as Matthew did and truly follow Christ wherever He leads them.

How has Jesus called you to follow Him recently, and how are you responding to Him?

OCTOBER 27

The Two Calls

Today, if you will hear His voice, do not harden your hearts.
HEBREWS 3:15

The Bible is filled with invitations to follow and serve God. For example, Elijah pleaded, "If the LORD is God, follow Him; but if Baal, follow him" (1 Kings 18:21). Joshua called Israel to "choose for yourselves this day whom you will serve" (Joshua 24:15).

The last invitation is in Revelation 22:17: "The Spirit and the bride say, 'Come!'" Here we see not one but two calls. There is an *outward* call from the bride of Christ, the church, through sermons and service. There is also an *inward* call of God, knocking at the door of our hearts. Lydia experienced this in Acts 16:14: "The Lord opened her heart to heed the things spoken by Paul." Paul gave the outward call, but the Holy Spirit issued the inward call to her heart.

Two people can read a devotional book. One experiences no urging to come to Christ, while another is drawn by supernatural power to faith in Christ. They both hear the outward call, but only the second also hears the inward call of the Spirit.

Using the example of the outward and inward calls,
how did God draw you to faith in Jesus?

OCTOBER 28

We Need Each Other

Epaphras, my fellow prisoner in Christ Jesus, greets you, as do Mark, Aristarchus, Demas, Luke, my fellow laborers.
PHILEMON VV. 23–24

Paul mentioned the name of Demas in his letter to Philemon to illustrate that accountability plays a prominent role in a long-term and productive interpersonal relationship. Demas's story ends on a lamentable note. Paul mentioned to Timothy that "Demas has forsaken me, having loved this present world, and has departed for Thessalonica" (2 Timothy 4:10). Demas was a sad commentary on the fact that without accountability, long-term relationships have little hope of survival. By mentioning these five mutual friends, each illustrative of a paragraph in his letter to Philemon, Paul was reminding us all that we need each other. We need to be connected to our source, the Lord Jesus, but we also need to be connected to each other, drawing from one another's support and strength.

Paul effectively and continually used the principle of accountability to develop productive and mutually beneficial relationships. Accountability is based on loyalty to one another. We would not want to make ourselves accountable to anyone who did not have our best interests at heart.

Why do long-term relationships have little hope of survival without accountability?

OCTOBER 29

The Power of Fervent Prayer

The effective, fervent prayer of a righteous man avails much.
JAMES 5:16

James was not talking about any prayer in today's Scripture passage but about "fervent" prayer. We derive our English word *energy* from the Greek wording for *fervent*. It means "to be stretched out," suggesting an athlete stretching out toward the finish line with a final burst of energy.

Prayers that get results are not long, drawn-out orations. They are pointed, powerful, asked with intensity, and approached with integrity. They are prayers like that of the publican, "God, be merciful to me a sinner!" (Luke 18:13); or Simon Peter while sinking in the sea, "Lord, save me!" (Matthew 14:30); or Jacob's, "I will not let You go unless You bless me!" (Genesis 32:26).

It is not the length but the depth of your prayers that makes them effective. It is not the prayers that come from your head but that spring from your heart that are effective. Approach God with integrity, do what He commands, then pray with passion and intensity.

When we are doing what is right (practicing righteousness)—praying in humility with energetic fervor—God answers.

When have you practiced fervent praying
and seen your prayers answered?

OCTOBER 30

The Armor of God

Finally, my brethren, be strong in the Lord and in the power of His might. Put on the whole armor of God, that you may be able to stand against the wiles of the devil. For we do not wrestle against flesh and blood, but against principalities, against powers, against the rulers of the darkness of this age, against spiritual hosts of wickedness in the heavenly places.

EPHESIANS 6:10–12

There is an unseen world all around us. In it, a great cosmic confrontation is raging between the forces of Satan and the forces of God. Satan is constantly seeking to deceive us and cause doubt.

How can we stand against him and his deceptions? Paul wrote the words of today's scripture from his Roman prison cell. Standing guard over him was a Roman soldier in full armor. The apostle saw a perfect analogy here and told us to "put on the whole armor of God": the belt of truth, the breastplate of righteousness, the shoes of peace, the shield of faith, the helmet of salvation, and the sword of the Spirit. I often begin my own private, personal prayer time in the mornings by going through these verses and making sure that I put on each piece of this gospel armor. (See Ephesians 6:14–17.) I encourage you to do the same.

How can you get into the habit of putting on your spiritual armor each day, and why would this be helpful?

OCTOBER 31

Two Kinds of Righteousness

To do righteousness and justice is more acceptable to the LORD than sacrifice.
PROVERBS 21:3

There are two kinds of righteousness: spiritual righteousness and moral righteousness. Spiritual righteousness is our standing before God. Paul was plain at this point, saying that the Lord Jesus "became for us wisdom . . . and righteousness" (1 Corinthians 1:30). Does this mean then that all believers are righteous to the extent that they can "flourish like a palm tree" (Psalm 92:12)? If you think you can disobey your parents, cheat on your spouse, steal from your employer, break fellowship with your friends, and expect to "flourish" in your faith, you are sadly mistaken.

It is moral righteousness that is in play in Psalm 92:12. John made this clear in his first recorded letter: "Little children, let no one deceive you. He who practices righteousness is righteous" (1 John 3:7). The promise of Psalm 92:12 is not for everyone. It is those who live out their faith in a righteous manner, who practice righteousness, who are pleasing to God.

In your own words, what is the difference between spiritual righteousness and moral righteousness?

NOVEMBER

NOVEMBER 1

The Power of Affirming Someone

The words of a man's mouth are deep waters; the wellspring of wisdom is a flowing brook.

PROVERBS 18:4

I will never forget the team meeting when my Little League baseball coach called me to his side and said to the group, "Did you boys see what Hawkins did last night? Instead of throwing home, where we had little chance to get the runner out, he faked the throw, threw to second, and caught the runner off guard and got us out of the inning. Now that is what I want all of us to do: to think, to anticipate the play." And then, with a pat on my back, he said, "Great job." He affirmed me in front of everyone. He believed in me and let me know it. I can't tell you what that word of affirmation did for me as a ten-year-old baseball player and for years afterward. I played that season over my head, won the batting title, and made the All-Star team. (Unfortunately, that was the apex of my entire athletic career!) Never underestimate the power of positive affirmation in your relationships.

Which of the young people in your life can you affirm today?

NOVEMBER 2

Spiritual Weeding

So when the woman saw that the tree was good for food, that it was pleasant to the eyes, and a tree desirable to make one wise, she took of its fruit and ate. She also gave to her husband with her, and he ate.
GENESIS 3:6

Temptation is like a weed growing in the midst of flowers in a garden: Left unchecked, it takes over. A weed has three distinct features. It has a root, a shoot, and a fruit. Similarly, the evil desires within us conceive (they take root), then they give birth to sin (they shoot up), and finally they become "full-grown" (they produce a dangerous fruit). The root of temptation is a selfish desire, the shoot is a sinful decision, and the resulting fruit is a sure defeat.

Adam and Eve's fall began with their selfish desire to eat the forbidden fruit. It continued with their sinful decision to take it and eat. And it ended with a sure defeat: They were expelled from the garden, which resulted in death and separation from God.

When dealing with weeds, cutting off the tops is not enough. The only effective way to deal with temptation is at its root. Let God pull out our sinful desires. He must change our desires and give us a new nature.

Why won't it work to keep saying, "I'll just stop sinning," when the root cause of the sin hasn't been addressed?

NOVEMBER 3

Miraculous Multiplication

Therefore they gathered them up, and filled twelve baskets with the fragments of the five barley loaves which were left over by those who had eaten.
JOHN 6:13

If you have seemingly inadequate resources at your disposal, you may be prone to ask what Andrew asked on a grassy hillside along the journey to Jerusalem: "What are they among so many?" (John 6:9). Throngs of people had gathered in Galilee to listen to Jesus, and hunger had set in. A small boy was found who had a couple of fish and five barley loaves. Most of us know the story. Jesus multiplied the loaves and fishes, had the disciples feed thousands of people, and then had them take up the leftovers.

Maybe you feel as Andrew did that day, comparing the *little* you have with the *big* challenge in your life. But little always becomes much when you factor Christ into the equation of your life.

That boy left home that morning with the potential to feed thousands of people and didn't even know it! I wonder, *Is the same true with you?* You have incredible potential wrapped up in you to bless so many people today, and you may not even know it!

What could you give to Jesus that He could multiply to bless others?

NOVEMBER 4

WATCH AND PRAY

Then He came to the disciples and found them sleeping, and said to Peter, "What! Could you not watch with Me one hour?"
MATTHEW 26:40

In ancient days, watchmen were posted on the city walls twenty-four hours a day, providing security to the people. God said, "I have set watchmen on your walls, O Jerusalem" (Isaiah 62:6). They were to remind the people of the promises of God and never be silent "day or night."

Peter, James, and John had the opportunity to provide Jesus with physical security as well as spiritual security during the hour He prayed before going to the cross. They could have prayed for strength, courage, and peace for their Master and Lord. But the disciples did neither; they slept.

Before we are too critical of this slumbering trio, remember that we, too, have willing spirits but weak flesh when it comes to serving Jesus (Matthew 26:41). Second, Jesus is asking us today to watch, pray, prepare the way, pave the way, and point the way for people who need to know Him and the way to eternal life He has provided. Let's be found faithful. Watch . . . and pray!

Why is it so important for Christians to continually watch and pray?

NOVEMBER 5

Good News in Judges

In those days there was no king in Israel; everyone did what was right in his own eyes.
JUDGES 21:25

More than any other book in the Bible, Judges describes the times in which we are living today. The last phrase in this book speaks volumes about their situation and ours: "Everyone did what was right in his own eyes." Like our Jewish forefathers in the faith, we are living in a world today where relativism is rampant and *everyone does what is right in his or her own eyes.*

Judges is the story of the good news. Man falls into sin. God brings judgment. Man cries out to God for pardon. God delivers him. This is how we see Jesus in Judges. Here is grace abounding more than sin. The Israelites may have forgotten their God, but God did not—will not—forget His people. In Judges, we can glimpse our own faithful Judge, the Lord Jesus Christ. This book is a living testimony of God's faithfulness: "If we are faithless, He remains faithful" (2 Timothy 2:13).

When have you been faithless and seen God remain faithful?

NOVEMBER 6

Salvation Is a Gift of Grace

For the grace of God that brings salvation has appeared to all men.
TITUS 2:11

When we give a gift, it costs us something to do so. But no gift ever cost as much as God's gift of eternal life. Paul writes that we are saved "by grace," making plain that the origin of our salvation is found in Him and not in us or any of our human efforts. Salvation is God's work, provided by His grace, and is not offered in response to any good thing we may have done. It is provided to us wholly because of His grace.

Grace is God's unmerited and undeserved favor toward us. It came at a great price. The Father did not send Jesus to die on the cross to provide the gift of salvation for us because we kept begging and pleading with Him to do so. It was by His grace alone. Grace can be defined as getting what we don't deserve. No wonder we call it "amazing." God's gift to us came at a high cost, the sacrificial and substitutionary death of His only Son on the cross.

How do you see amazing grace in Jesus' death on the cross?

NOVEMBER 7

TWO PARADOXES

I tell you, this man went down to his house justified rather than the other; for everyone who exalts himself will be humbled, and he who humbles himself will be exalted.

LUKE 18:14

Jesus said to the Pharisee who tooted his own horn, "Everyone who exalts himself will be humbled." The way down is up! He should have been seeking the applause of God, not men. God has ways of humbling the proud.

To the tax collector who threw himself on God's mercy, He said, "He who humbles himself will be exalted." The way up is down! In humility the tax collector sought only the applause of God as he prayed.

We all need to read and heed this lesson. Maybe, like the tax collector, you have made some mistakes for which you are truly sorry. One failure doesn't make a flop. You can bat again. It is a tale of two prayers. When you pray, remember that attitude and humility go a long way in pleasing God. And it is a tale of two paradoxes: "Everyone who exalts himself will be humbled." Everyone. And, "He who humbles himself will be exalted." Make this tax collector your prayer partner and you, too, will go down to your house justified.

Why is it true that the way up is down?

NOVEMBER 8

GRACE, NOT GUILT

But when he was still a great way off, his father saw him and had compassion, and ran and fell on his neck and kissed him.

LUKE 15:20

Most of us know the story well. The prodigal runs out of money and ends up with the menial task of feeding swine in a pigpen (not a desirable job for a Jewish boy!). But he comes to himself and heads for home. The boy came walking . . . but the father went running! His love that was tough enough to release his son was now tender enough to receive him. Look at their embrace . . . no crossed arms, pointed fingers, clenched fists; no cross-examination of "Where have you been?" or "Where is the money?" His open hands turn into open arms.

The Father is waiting for us with open arms. How grateful we can be that God does not deal with us "according to our sins" or mistakes or failures but according to His tender mercies (Psalm 103:10).

How have you experienced love that is tough enough to release and tender enough to receive?

THE NEVER-ENDING BATTLE

For the flesh lusts against the Spirit, and the Spirit against the flesh . . . so that you do not do the things that you wish.
GALATIANS 5:17

Since the war between the flesh and the spirit never ends, Paul provided some military intelligence to warn us about hindrances to our walk with Christ.

Many lose the battle because of *misdirected desires*: adultery, fornication, uncleanness, and lewdness (Galatians 5:19). Adultery and fornication are the height of immorality. Uncleanness reigns in our thought life. Lewdness describes someone lost in lust and ungodly desires.

Other hindrances include *misguided devotions*: idolatry and sorcery (Galatians 5:20). *Sorcery* comes from the word we derive *pharmacy* from—drug use. Idolatry is the worship of gods humans have made. Today, they could be a hobby, job, possessions, or a person.

Another hindrance is the *mismanaged disposition*: contentions, jealousies, outbursts of wrath, selfish ambitions, dissensions, heresies, envy, murders, drunkenness, and revelries (Galatians 5:20–21).

But Paul gives us hope by listing the fruit of the Spirit next (Galatians 5:22–23). The good news is, if we walk by the Spirit, we "shall not fulfill the lust of the flesh" (Galatians 5:16).

Knowing the devil will use any means to hinder your walk with Christ, how can you be more vigilant about his schemes?

NOVEMBER 10

A Time to Stand Up and a Time to Give In

After serious thought, I rebuked the nobles and rulers, and said to them, "Each of you is exacting usury from his brother." So I called a great assembly against them.
NEHEMIAH 5:7

Nehemiah knew that sometimes when dealing with conflict, *there is a time to stand up.* He boldly stood and confronted those he believed to be wrong and whose actions had initiated the conflict (vv. 7–9). Conflict resolution never means simply backing off and always giving in at any cost. Jesus, in the Sermon on the Mount, pronounced a blessing on the "peacemakers," not the "peace lovers" (Matthew 5:9). There are times we must stand up and make peace with others.

Nehemiah also knew that, on other occasions, *there is a time to give in.* He allowed others to save face and knew it was important to give in on a few nonessentials (Nehemiah 5:10–11). It is always best in our own relationships to lose a few little, insignificant battles in order to win a much bigger war. Nehemiah was not showing weakness by allowing others to have their way in nonessentials. He was showing strength.

Why is allowing others to have their way in nonessential matters wise, and how is it a show of strength?

NOVEMBER 11

TRUE RELIGION

Pure and undefiled religion before God and the Father is this: to visit orphans and widows in their trouble, and to keep oneself unspotted from the world.
JAMES 1:27

In today's verse, did James mean that proof of a pure religion is occasionally paying some people a friendly visit? Not at all. James chose two of the most recognizably needy groups of people: orphans and widows. Remember, in the first century there were no life insurance policies or Social Security benefits, no orphanages or retirement homes. If the breadwinner died, orphaned children became victims of the street, often abused and traded by slave owners. Widows had no social standing, and some turned to immorality to provide for themselves. As Christians, we are to show mercy and kindness to people in such great need, especially to those who can never reciprocate.

James's command to visit those in need is a call to look in on or to inspect. The Greek word literally means "to care for" these individuals. The word means much more than paying a simple visit to these people. After all, a true sign of Christian character is a genuine concern for anyone in need.

Who are the "orphans and widows" in your life—literally or figuratively—and how can you make an effort to care for them?

NOVEMBER 12

Do Your Part to Salvage Broken Relationships

Pursue peace with all people, and holiness,
without which no one will see the Lord.
HEBREWS 12:14

Most broken relationships can be salvaged. I am a firm believer in reconciliation. But everyone must do their part. We live in a culture where more and more go from one relationship to another, repeating a process that leaves broken hearts and battered dreams in its wake. When relationships break down, too many people simply cut what they could not untie, like an old shoelace. No matter how much may have been invested in someone, it seems easier for some to junk the relationship and move on to the next. We do not do that with our automobiles. We make a major investment in a car, and if it doesn't start one morning, what do we do? If we can't fix it, we call for help. We pinpoint the problem and get it fixed. If that is good sense for an auto repair, why isn't it good sense for relationships that have years of investment behind them? There are too many deposits of love and time invested in a relationship to just junk it when it sputters.

How can you do your part to salvage a broken relationship?

NOVEMBER 13

Be a Channel of Blessing

Freely you have received, freely give.
MATTHEW 10:8

Anyone who has visited the Holy Land has likely been struck by the stark contrast of the two inland bodies of water in the state of Israel—the Sea of Galilee in the north and the Dead Sea in the south.

The Sea of Galilee is teeming with life, abundant with all types of thriving aquatic life. It is often crystal clear and a beautiful blue in color.

The Dead Sea has earned its name for a reason. It is dead! No aquatic life whatsoever is found in its waters, and the sulfuric smell arising from it is nauseating.

What causes this difference between the two bodies of water? The Dead Sea only has an inlet. It takes in but does not give out. But the Sea of Galilee has both an inlet *and* an outlet. It not only receives; it gives away. So it is with the vibrant believer who not only receives God's fullness but also gives it away—and then, like the Sea of Galilee, is constantly being refilled with the Spirit.

How does giving away what you receive from God help you stay spiritually vibrant?

NOVEMBER 14

Facing Death in a Biblical Way

Precious in the sight of the Lord is the death of His saints.
PSALM 116:15

Everyone must face death, and today's scripture gives us comfort as we remember that God knows and cares about this eventuality. People deal with their mortality in different ways. Some *flee* it, even freezing their bodies, hoping medical breakthroughs can bring them back to life in the future. Others *forget* it, assuming the inevitability of death will somehow go away if they don't think about it. Then there are those who *fear* it, living spiritually or emotionally paralyzed with no hope or security in Christ. But there are others, like David, who *face* it. Realizing their days are already numbered in eternity, they have no fear of death because they know the Lord is with them. David said, "I walk through the valley of the shadow of death" (Psalm 23:4). He didn't rush toward it. Nor did he crawl, seeking to postpone it as long as possible. He was not dragged toward it kicking and screaming. He simply walked, comforted by the fact that God was with him, and he was not alone.

How do you think about death?

Call Anytime

Call to Me, and I will answer you, and show you great and mighty things, which you do not know.
JEREMIAH 33:3

Did you know that God has a telephone number? It is Jeremiah 33:3, and He invites you to call Him anytime—and He promises to always answer. But there is more; when you call on Him, He will show you amazing things that have never even entered your mind. This verse holds one of the most amazing promises in all the Bible. When you call Him, you never get put on hold. You never have to listen to a voice message. You never get a quick text reply saying, "Sorry. I can't talk right now." He never fails to answer your call—and He answers in a way that far exceeds your most hopeful and optimistic expectations.

"Call to Me." What a simple invitation. God invites you into His throne room of prayer. We are not referring here to reciting ancient prayers of other people by rote or through rituals. We are talking heart-to-heart communication with the One who knows what we have need of before we even ask.

What can Jeremiah 33:3 teach you about God's faithfulness in answering prayer?

Think Before You Speak

But I say to you that for every idle word men may speak, they will give account of it in the day of judgment. For by your words you will be justified, and by your words you will be condemned.

MATTHEW 12:36–37

Social media platforms are making verbal communication a dying art. The majority of communication today takes place via smartphone or computer. But whether spoken or typed, words have power. They can bless or break; they can help or hurt.

Too many children have heard a frustrated parent say, "You are worthless and will never amount to anything." And the children believed it, allowing those words to shape their self-image and determine their self-worth. Other children have had parents affirm them: "You are important, and God has something for you to do that no one can do quite like you can." These children believed that message and ultimately acted on it.

Words define us: They reveal what is in our hearts. They have power to heal or to hurt, to help or to hinder. Many years ago I heard a simple, yet profound comment that I have never forgotten: "You never have to take back what you don't say!"

What are some of the most powerful words that have been spoken to you or about you? How did they impact you?

NOVEMBER 17

Total Commitment in Relationships

But Jesus said to him, "No one, having put his hand to the plow, and looking back, is fit for the kingdom of God."
LUKE 9:62

Total commitment in relationships takes four steps. The first step is *openness*. And this is often the most difficult step, especially since any long journey always begins with the first step. Committed friends have no agendas hidden from each other. They are open in their relationships with each other.

The second step is *obligation*. Committed friends sense a responsibility for one another. They always stick up for each other and rush to the other's defense when the need arises.

The third step in crossing this river is *objectivity*. They get the big picture. They return favors. They always see past themselves to the importance of reciprocation.

The final step is *optimism*. Committed friends believe the best about each other, stay positive, and always do more than is expected in their relationship. They bring out the best in each other. It only takes a little to be above average in this respect.

Why are the four steps of total commitment important in relationships?

The Source, Course, and Force of Our Prayers

For through Him we both have access by one Spirit to the Father.
EPHESIANS 2:18

When you pray, the entire Godhead—the Father, the Son, and the Holy Spirit—is at work.

The *source* of our prayer is the Father. All true prayer begins when we claim our relationship with Him: *our Father.* And the only way we can truly call Him Father is to be born again into His forever family: "As many as received Him, to them He gave the right to become children of God, to those who believe in His name" (John 1:12). We are all God's creation, but we are not God's children without faith in Christ.

The *course* of our prayer is the Son. There is no access to the Father except through Jesus the Son: "There is one God and one Mediator between God and men, the Man Christ Jesus" (1 Timothy 2:5). Access to the Father is not through a priest, church, or anything or anyone apart from Jesus Christ.

The *force* of our prayer is the Spirit because He always prays according to God's will (Romans 8:26–27).

How does it encourage you to understand the source, the course, and the force of your prayers?

NOVEMBER 19

The New Birth

Nicodemus said to Him, "How can a man be born when he is old? Can he enter a second time into his mother's womb and be born?"

JOHN 3:4

Conversing with Nicodemus, Jesus went directly to the point: "Unless one is born again, he cannot see the kingdom of God" (John 3:3). And Nicodemus, the brightest man in Jerusalem, didn't understand. "How can I?" he must have wondered aloud.

Jesus' message applies to you and me. It is not an option. It is an imperative. We who desire to see and to enter the kingdom of God *must* be born again. The apostle Paul later described this as being "transformed" (Romans 12:2). We get our English word *metamorphosis* from this single compound Greek word. The picture is of a caterpillar spinning a cocoon around itself and later emerging as a new creation, a beautiful butterfly. Similarly, we experience a new birth when we recognize our sin, repent of that sin, and trust in Christ alone to forgive us.

A person can't be born a second time physically, but Christ can take out your old heart and put in a brand-new one. The new birth is God's gift to you. Receive it.

How would you explain to someone what it means to be "born again"?

NOVEMBER 20

THE FINAL PAYMENT

For it is not possible that the blood of bulls and goats could take away sins.
HEBREWS 10:4

Leviticus is an Old Testament book we tend to quickly skim over when reading through the Bible. It can appear monotonous with its detailed minutiae of the sacrificial system of burnt offerings in Jewish worship. Yet it provides us a most vivid foreshadowing of Christ's work of atonement and is the foundational offering in the Torah to understanding Christ's own sacrifice for us.

All the multiplied thousands of animal sacrifices in the Old Testament never took away a single sin. Today's scripture makes this crystal clear. They served to simply cover sins until Christ, the perfect sacrifice, came to take away all the sins of the world. Old Testament sacrifices covered sins until the final payment to remove *all* sin would be paid on a hill called Golgotha, outside the city walls of Jerusalem. Jesus came to Earth to do the Father's will, and that obedience took Him to His own place of execution where He became the final sacrifice for sin.

Why do you think it is important to understand how the Old Testament sacrificial system laid a foundation for Jesus' sacrifice?

NOVEMBER 21

God's Word Is Inspired

And the words of the Lord *are flawless, like silver purified in a crucible, like gold refined seven times.*

PSALM 12:6 NIV

Paul wrote to Timothy that "all" Scripture (2 Timothy 3:16) is inspired by God. This little three-letter, one-syllable word is extremely inclusive. King Solomon framed it such: "Every word of God is pure" (Proverbs 30:5). Note that he said "every word," not "some words." Earlier his father, King David, said, "The law of the Lord is perfect" (Psalm 19:7). Though we might find more worth in reading the Sermon on the Mount in Matthew 5 than we find in reading the long list of unpronounceable names in the genealogy found in Matthew 1, each word of each verse in the entire book is equally inspired. We can rest in God's promise that the Bible will abide forever because of its *supernatural origin*. All Scripture, every word of every verse of every chapter, is God breathed, inspired by Him. Since, unlike all other books, the Bible originates with God and not with man, it "stands forever" (Isaiah 40:8).

When you remember that the Bible is inspired by God, why does it give you confidence no other book can give?

NOVEMBER 22

Head vs. Heart

But the natural man does not receive the things of the Spirit of God, for they are foolishness to him; nor can he know them, because they are spiritually discerned.

1 CORINTHIANS 2:14

The Bible remains a sealed book until God's Spirit opens its truth to us. We may gain a head knowledge of Jesus, but we will never be able to develop heart knowledge, spiritual discernment, until He opens the Scriptures to us (Luke 24:32).

Referring to Jesus, Luke 24:27 says, "Beginning at Moses . . . He expounded to them [the two disciples on the road to Emmaus] in all the Scriptures the things concerning Himself." *Expound* connotes the thought of translating something out of a foreign language. The Bible is really a foreign language to those who do not believe. From Moses to Malachi, Jesus revealed how the entire Jewish Bible speaks of Him. He was the ram on Abraham's altar in Genesis, the Passover lamb in Exodus, the scarlet thread out Rahab's window in Joshua, David's good shepherd in Psalms, the suffering servant in Isaiah, and the fourth man in the midst of the fiery furnace in Daniel. No wonder the two disciples' hearts began to burn within them (v. 32). He was doing the talking, and they were doing the listening.

How does knowing that Jesus was foreshadowed so many times in the Old Testament expand your faith?

NOVEMBER 23

TAKE TIME TO BE GRATEFUL

Let us continually offer the sacrifice of praise to God, that is, the fruit of our lips, giving thanks to His name.
HEBREWS 13:15

Along the journey to Jerusalem, Jesus came upon a colony of ten lepers isolated from everyone they knew and loved due to the contagious nature of their hideous disease. Luke 17:11–19 tells this story. They shouted to Him for mercy as He passed by. He stopped, told them to go show themselves to the priests, and they were healed as they obeyed. They all were cleansed of their disease, but here the similarity ends.

Only "one of them . . . returned" (v. 15) in thanksgiving. We are not told his name. He belongs to that vast throng who live their beautiful lives and perform their selfless deeds in often anonymous ways. We may not know his name, but he is shouting to us today, "Get back to Jesus. Be grateful. Give thanks for all He has done for you."

Jesus looked at him and said, "Arise, go your way. Your faith has made you well" (v. 19). Along your own journey, remember that the God of this universe wants your thanks.

How can you express your thanks to Jesus today for all He has done for you?

NOVEMBER 24

SINS OF OMISSION

Therefore, to him who knows to do good and does not do it, to him it is sin.
JAMES 4:17

When we hear the word *sin,* we usually think of sins of commission—willful, outward acts that violate God's law and love. But our problem is not just doing what we shouldn't (sins of commission) but in not doing what we should (sins of omission). Doing wrong is sin; not doing right is a sin too. It is a sin to tell an outright lie. It is also a sin to know the truth and not tell it.

If you miss rewards in heaven, it will not only be because of sins of commission but also because of sins of omission. And knowing the gospel but not embracing it is the most serious of all the sins of omission. Jesus said, "He who believes in Him is not condemned; but he who does not believe is condemned already, because he has not believed in the name of the only begotten Son of God" (John 3:18).

Embrace the gospel and all it means today and every day.

If you can identify any sins of omission, what stops you from taking action?

NOVEMBER 25

Jesus, Our Rallying Point

Wherever you hear the sound of the trumpet, rally to us there. Our God will fight for us.

NEHEMIAH 4:20

Nehemiah was neither a preacher nor a prophet. He was a civil servant, an ordinary guy who rebuilt a broken city and, in the process, restored a lot of broken hopes. During the process of rebuilding the walls of Jerusalem, Nehemiah had a rallying point for his entire team. He kept a trumpeter always close and constantly by his side. His instructions were the words of today's scripture.

All across our world today, there are all kinds of men and women aiding in Christ's rebuilding process, repairing breaches and restoring what has been destroyed. They are preachers, missionaries, teachers, laborers, laypersons—and they are scattered all along the wall. In some places, the ranks are thin. But we all have our own Commander in Chief, the Lord Jesus Christ, and He is the rallying point for all of us under His service. One day we will hear His trumpeter give the final trumpet sound. We will lay down our tools, leave our workstations, and rally around Him when He comes to receive us as His own.

How does Jesus serve as a rallying point for you and the people you work alongside in His kingdom, even if not in full-time vocational ministry?

The Prayer of Thanks and Praise

Enter into His gates with thanksgiving, and into His courts with praise.
PSALM 100:4

You cannot enter the throne room of prayer until you go through the gate of thanksgiving. We pause to thank God for material blessings: our homes, cars, shoes, all that we have. We then give thanks for our physical blessings: eyes, minds, hearts, health. Next, we thank God for particular people in our lives who cause us to be better than we might be otherwise. Finally, we thank Him for spiritual blessings like love, joy, peace, and our own salvation. Thanksgiving has a liberating effect. When Jonah offered a prayer "of thanksgiving," he was liberated from the belly of a fish (Jonah 2:9–10).

Once we have entered through the gate of thanksgiving, we can now stand in the "courts with praise." Here we let Him know how much we love Him and praise the Lord for His attributes: goodness, patience, mercy, holiness, love. While we thank God for what He does, we praise Him for who He is.

How does adding thanksgiving and praise
to your prayers increase your faith?

NOVEMBER 27

Bring Out the Best in Others

Having confidence in your obedience, I write to you, knowing that you will do even more than I say.
PHILEMON V. 21

If there is one thing that can always be said about the apostle Paul, it is that he was optimistic. He saw an answer in every problem instead of a problem in every answer. He was also savvy enough to know that it is hard to feel good about someone else when we do not feel good about ourselves. He let Philemon know that he believed in him and that he was confident he would do the right thing regarding Philemon's runaway servant, Onesimus. This optimistic approach on Paul's part yielded amazing results. It would bring out the best in Philemon.

We bring out the best in others when we let them know we believe in them and are confident they will do even more than is asked or required. This spirit of optimism is a major step in achieving the fruition of commitment in our relationships. Committed friends believe in each other and come through for one another when the chips are down. In fact, as Paul revealed, they always do what is expected of them—and then some.

How can you bring out the best in someone you know?

CHRIST BUILDS HIS CHURCH

And I also say to you that you are Peter, and on this rock I will build My church, and the gates of Hades shall not prevail against it.
MATTHEW 16:18

This promise from the lips of our Lord that He will build His church, and nothing—not even the gates of hell—can stand against it, comes on the heels of one of the most misunderstood of all Jesus' claims and statements. Peter had just made the "great confession" that Jesus was indeed "the Christ, the Son of the living God" (Matthew 16:16). Then Jesus looked him squarely in the eyes and said, "You are Peter, and on this rock I will build My church" (v. 18). For centuries the Roman Catholic Church has proclaimed that Christ built His church on Peter, whom He called the "rock." However, the language of the New Testament suggests something different. The neuter noun in Greek suggests that it was Peter's confession that Jesus is Lord that was the rock on which Christ would build His church, not Peter himself. And thus, for two millennia, every time someone comes to Christ making a confession of their faith in Him alone, Christ lays another stone into the building of His body, the church.

Why can't the gates of hell stand against Christ's church?

NOVEMBER 29

Respond with Prayer

But I say to you who hear: Love your enemies, do good to those who hate you, bless those who curse you, and pray for those who spitefully use you.
LUKE 6:27–28

It was the worst of times and the best of times for the early church. The disciples had watched the agony of the crucifixion, been with Jesus during those postresurrection days, and watched Him ascend back into heaven from the Mount of Olives. Soon they came under tremendous persecution. And the early church was exploding in growth. Peter and John were arrested and, upon their release, were commanded by the authorities "not to speak at all nor teach in the name of Jesus" (Acts 4:18). Their first inclination in response to this was not to plan or plot but to pray. Peter and John knew Jesus' teachings and perhaps remembered the words of today's scripture.

Luke, the writer of today's scripture, also wrote the book of Acts. He recorded in Acts 4 one of the greatest prayer meetings in all of history. The secret of the early church was that they were a people of prayer. When persecuted, they knew not to seek revenge but to pray.

When have you responded with prayer when you weren't treated well, and how did the situation turn out?

NOVEMBER 30

Blessings for the Righteous

For You, O Lord, will bless the righteous; with favor You will surround him as with a shield.

PSALM 5:12

In addition to the blessing for the righteous in today's scripture, we also read throughout Scripture the blessings of others who practice righteousness, such as in Isaiah 32:17; Proverbs 21:21; Matthew 5:6, and others. Psalm 92:12 says they will "flourish." What a promised potential is ours! To "flourish" sets in motion a chain reaction. It means to sprout, to grow, to thrive, to blossom. In the Christian life we sprout, then we grow, then we thrive, and finally we blossom in our faith. All that is wrapped up in the promise God gives to those of us who practice righteousness.

We search for purpose and peace in so many places and practices. But these are the fruits of a much deeper root. It is not our performance for Christ but our position in Christ that enables us to "flourish like a palm tree." No wonder Jesus said, "Seek first the kingdom of God and His righteousness, and all these things shall be added to you" (Matthew 6:33).

What are some of the blessings of righteousness you enjoy?

DECEMBER

Sow Encouragement

Do not be deceived, God is not mocked; for whatever a man sows, that he will also reap.
GALATIANS 6:7

Most likely, there are people in your world who have lived months, perhaps years, without anyone, anywhere, at any time affirming them. Although they may never articulate it, they are looking for it, longing for it. Instead of saying, "I wish someone would affirm me today," begin looking for someone you can affirm, and watch the biblical principle of reaping and sowing come into effect. Someone you know just might be hanging by a thread with hope almost gone. It just may be that if you don't reach out to them with a word of hope and encouragement, no one else in their entire world ever will. The problem in so many interpersonal relationships is found in the fact that many of us are simply reactive and too few of us are proactive in this area. The very ones we are hoping will affirm us just might be the very ones hoping we will affirm them. Be proactive. Take the initiative. Do something. Reach out to that someone.

How can you sow hope and encouragement into the lives of the people around you?

DECEMBER 2

DECEITFUL DESIRES

If you do well, will you not be accepted? And if you do not do well, sin lies at the door. And its desire is for you, but you should rule over it.
GENESIS 4:7

The word *desire* means "a strong urge, a craving of the soul." There is nothing inherently wrong with desire. Desires can be productive and beneficial when we satisfy them within the laws God prescribed for our well-being.

James wrote about selfish desires: "When desire has conceived, it gives birth to sin; and sin, when it is full-grown, brings forth death" (James 1:15). When the internal source (desire) and the external force (deception) come together, sin is conceived. When we begin to desire something outside of God's boundaries and we take the bait when it comes by, conception takes place, and sin has taken root. Sin grows and at some point bursts out into the open.

When a selfish desire enters the mind and takes root, we should remove it immediately. To remove those thoughts the very moment one passes through your mind, immediately surrender your mind to Christ. Pray, "Lord, my mind is Yours, and my heart is Yours. Please put Your thoughts in me." Open the Bible and feed on God's thoughts.

Why is knowing the Bible so important in recognizing and defeating sinful desires?

DECEMBER 3

How to Deal with Conflict

And there was a great outcry of the people and their wives against their Jewish brethren. . . . And I became very angry when I heard their outcry and these words.

NEHEMIAH 5:1, 6

Unresolved conflicts can do irreparable damage. Long before modern motivational gurus wrote on conflict resolution, Nehemiah successfully dealt with conflicts that existed among members of his team and threatened the rebuilding of the walls of Jerusalem.

Nehemiah began his conflict resolution by backing off. And there was a wise reason to do so. He had, in his own words, become "very angry." He was wise enough to know that when this happens, the best thing we can do is back off and give some "serious thought" (v. 7) to the situation. This phrase in our English Bibles translates two Hebrew words meaning "to counsel or give advice" and "the inner man, the heart." Nehemiah was literally saying, "I backed off and listened to my heart. I took counsel with my heart." And in so doing he found a course of action that ultimately led his people back on the walls and back to the business of rebuilding.

In what situation in your life might backing off be your best course of action?

DECEMBER 4

By Grace Through Faith

For by grace you have been saved through faith, and that not of yourselves; it is the gift of God.
EPHESIANS 2:8

The gift of God's grace is conditional on our transferring our faith to Christ alone for our salvation. These words make me want to shout this verse: "Through faith . . . not of yourselves . . . the gift of God!" The following verse attests that it is not of works "lest anyone should boast." Our faith is the channel through which salvation flows from God to us. It is *through* faith.

Paul's repetition of the truth that salvation is "not of ourselves" and "not of works" (v. 9) brings emphasis to his point that it is the "gift of God." In some other faiths, people do extreme things—even give their lives—in feeble attempts to please their gods and be ushered into heaven. But it is "by grace . . . through faith . . . not of yourselves; it is the gift of God." God is offering His free gift of eternal life to any and all who will simply believe by faith in Christ alone.

How do grace and faith work together in salvation?

DECEMBER 5

Take Responsibility in Relationships

Instead of being motivated by selfish ambition or vanity, each of you should, in humility, be moved to treat one another as more important than yourself.
PHILIPPIANS 2:3 NET

When relationships are broken, our general tendency is to see ourselves only as the offended party. And this is exactly at the heart of why some of us live a lifetime with broken relationships discarded along our path of life. Few of us really want to admit that we are the offending party. In our minds, the problem is usually someone else's fault. Few of us are keen on taking personal responsibility for breakdowns in our relationships. We have been programmed since our childhood to point the finger of accusation at someone else. But isn't there a little of runaway servant Onesimus, the one who returned to Philemon in humility, in all of us? Could it be that we have something to learn from him?

Onesimus went back! And he did so with sincere remorse and regret that led to genuine repentance. Philemon had no choice but to receive him and let the party begin.

How might you need to take responsibility for a relational problem?

All You Need

Our fathers ate the manna in the desert; as it is written, "He gave them bread from heaven to eat."

JOHN 6:31

Every experience the Israelites had in the wilderness holds a lesson for those of us living in this dispensation of grace.

It took only a month after passing through the Red Sea for the food supplies to run out for the hundreds of thousands of Israelites traveling toward their promised land. Hunger set in. The kids were crying. The parents were complaining, questioning Moses' leadership. He must have been feeling like Philip on the Galilean mountainside when Jesus asked him, "Where shall we buy bread, that these may eat?" (John 6:5). Just when Moses was desperate for a solution, God was there with a promise: "I will rain bread from heaven for you. And the people shall go out and gather a certain quota every day" (Exodus 16:4). And true to His word, for the next forty years, God fed His people in this way . . . every morning . . . all they needed.

When have you been desperate for a solution and found God to be there for you with a promise?

DECEMBER 7

Play No Favorites

My brethren, do not hold the faith of our Lord Jesus Christ, the Lord of glory, with partiality.
JAMES 2:1

James took a firm stand against prejudice, against coming to a conclusion based only on an external appearance. James warned, "Don't do that. Don't show partiality or favoritism based on what you see on the outside."

James's warning here was not to those in the political or social arena; he was specifically addressing the church. Our Lord Jesus never looked at outward appearances but instead on the heart. Jesus is still not impressed by how many goods we have accumulated, whom we know, or how high we have climbed up the social ladder. Jesus had as much respect for the poor, unnamed widow offering her two pennies as He did for wealthy Joseph of Arimathea.

But the people James was addressing apparently flattered the rich in hopes of getting something from them. So James said, "Stop this prejudicial behavior. Don't show favoritism." We are never more like Jesus than when we look to the heart of others instead of on their outward appearance. Prejudice shouldn't have a leg to stand on in the Christian faith.

In what situations have you witnessed favoritism in the church? What can you do to correct it?

DECEMBER 8

It's Just a Shadow

Yea, though I walk through the valley of the shadow of death, I will fear no evil; for You are with me; Your rod and Your staff, they comfort me.

PSALM 23:4

David indicated that he walked "through" the valley. In other words, death was not his final destination. It was only a brief sojourn, a temporary passage. He knew this path was not a dead end. The believer does not walk "in" the valley and stay there. We who have placed our trust in Christ walk "through" the valley. It is just a short and temporary passage from this life into eternal life.

There is tremendous comfort in Psalm 23:4 that death is simply a *shadow*. Note carefully that David said this is the valley of the "shadow" of death. No believer ever walks through the valley of death, simply the "valley of the shadow of death." And even in the physical world, we can walk *through* shadows; they can't harm us. The Lord Jesus walked through the valley of death for us—for three days and three nights. Then He emerged alive again from the empty tomb exclaiming, "I have the keys of Hades and of Death" (Revelation 1:18).

Why is death only a shadow for believers in Jesus?

DECEMBER 9

Being Sent

Jesus said to them again, "Peace to you! As the Father has sent Me, I also send you."
JOHN 20:21

Isaiah prayed to God, "Here am I! Send me" (Isaiah 6:8). Only after recognizing God's holiness and his own helplessness, and after experiencing the confession that brought a fresh cleansing from his sin, did Isaiah hear clearly God's call to service. He did not respond to the Lord with merely, "Here I am," indicating his physical location. He said, "Here am I," revealing his willingness to serve. Next followed the passionate request, "Send me."

We read in today's scripture that we are sent. And God still asks the question He asked Isaiah: "Whom shall I send, and who will go for Us?" (v. 8). Catch a fresh glimpse of who God really is and you will see yourself for who you really are. Then, with true confession and repentance, you will, like Isaiah, find a new beginning and hear clearly His voice asking, "Whom shall I send?" And, once you hear it, make Isaiah's prayer your very own: "Here am I! Send me."

What were the three things Isaiah had to experience before hearing and answering God's call?

DECEMBER 10

Bridled by the Master

For we all stumble in many things. If anyone does not stumble in word, he is a perfect man, able also to bridle the whole body. Indeed, we put bits in horses' mouths that they may obey us, and we turn their whole body.

JAMES 3:2–3

If you have ever bridled a horse, you know that the bridle that slips over the horse's head and behind its ears has a bit, a metal bar that goes in the horse's mouth and lies on top of its tongue. When the rider wants the horse to stop, he pulls back hard on the reins, and the bit presses down on the horse's tongue. The rider who controls the horse's tongue can actually control the horse's whole body. A horse controlled by a bit can be of great use, but an unbroken horse can do great damage. Just as a horse needs to come under its master's control, our tongues need to come under our Master's control. A horse can't bridle itself. The one who mastered it puts the bridle on.

Try as we might, we can't control our tongue through our own efforts. What we say actually originates in our hearts, not our mouths. When we yield ourselves under the control of our Master, the Lord Jesus Christ, our speech can honor Him and bless others.

How easy or hard is it for you to control your tongue?

DECEMBER 11

HONESTY AND OPENNESS

Therefore, putting away lying, "Let each one of you speak truth with his neighbor," for we are members of one another.

EPHESIANS 4:25

Honesty and openness are key ingredients to sustaining lasting relationships. We never have to be afraid of the truth. It always wins in the end, and it can set us free (John 8:32). We live in a culture where many people guard against opening up to anyone. There are a lot of paper faces on parade—that is, masks that some people wear in relationships and refuse to take off. This is what makes relationships a risky endeavor. Some people put up a shield, constantly on guard against becoming vulnerable to anyone else. This built-in fear results in too many of us not taking the risk and stepping out in openness.

Not many take relational risks today. They spend their time calculating why others enjoy productive relationships and excusing why they cannot. Relationships are a risky business. Ironically, the very thing we sometimes seek to keep covered up when conversing with others is often the very thing, if we were open, that would attract others to us. Build a bridge of openness today with someone you know, and you will be on the way to building more committed relationships.

How have you seen honesty and openness lead to more committed relationships?

DECEMBER 12

God's Word Is Profitable

All Scripture is given by inspiration of God, and is profitable for doctrine, for reproof, for correction, for instruction in righteousness, that the man of God may be complete, thoroughly equipped for every good work.

2 TIMOTHY 3:16–17

Today's scripture is a powerful passage about the effect of God's Word on our spiritual journeys. Paul wrote that God's Word "is profitable for doctrine, for reproof, for correction, for instruction in righteousness, that the man of God may be complete, thoroughly equipped for every good work." It is the Word of God that sustains the believer along the journey of the Christian life (Matthew 4:4). We begin our journey with "doctrine," proper teaching that shows God's plan of salvation and sanctification. What if we veer off the path? It becomes profitable for "reproof" of our sin. But He doesn't leave us there in defeat and despair; the Bible is profitable for "correction." It provides us a restart. Finally, it sustains us by being profitable to us for "instruction in righteousness." This is one reason God's Word stands forever (Isaiah 40:8), and we can trust it completely.

How have you encountered doctrine, reproof, correction, and instruction in righteousness in God's Word?

DECEMBER 13

A Hoarder's Misery

Come now, you rich, weep and howl for your miseries that are coming upon you! Your riches are corrupted, and your garments are moth-eaten. Your gold and silver are corroded, and their corrosion will be a witness against you and will eat your flesh like fire. You have heaped up treasure in the last days.

JAMES 5:1–3

There is certainly no condemnation of wealth in today's verses. Many of our heroes in the Bible were very wealthy individuals. The real issue with wealth is not in having it but in how we *get* it, *guard* it, and *give* it.

The way we handle our money can bring "miseries" upon us. The word conveys that money may bring joy temporarily, but that joy is followed by misery if our money is accumulated by ungodly means, hoarded, or used only for self-indulgence.

How we get money, how we guard it, and how we give it will reveal what is truly in our hearts. It's deceptive to think our security is found in hoarded wealth. It will one day "witness against you." When you stand before the judgment seat of Christ, the question will not be, "How much did you make?" but "What did you do with what you had?" What a tragedy to come to the end of life and have treasure laid up for this world only.

What types of miseries have you seen come to those who hoard their wealth?

DECEMBER 14

God with Us, for Us, and in Us

I am with you always, even to the end of the age.
MATTHEW 28:20

The name *Immanuel* is a translation of two Hebrew words expressing "God is with us." *God* with us. Not some prophet or teacher or holy man. But God Himself clothed in human flesh—*with us*! He came to where we are so we could go eternally to where He is. God . . . always with us.

God—that is majesty. With us—that is mercy. God—that is glory. With us—that is grace. He came to be with us, to give us what we never deserved and to *not* give us what we did deserve.

He could not be Jesus without being Immanuel. That is, to save us, He first had to come and be with us, taking on human flesh. At Bethlehem we see God with us. At Calvary we see God for us. At Pentecost we see God in us.

How does knowing that God is with you help you cope with life each day?

DECEMBER 15

Speak His Name

And she will bring forth a Son, and you shall call His name
Jesus, for He will save His people from their sins.
MATTHEW 1:21

The name *Jesus* is a transliteration of the Hebrew name *Joshua*, which means "Jehovah saves." His very name, Jesus, tells us of His mission when He came from heaven to earth—to "save His people from their sins."

Jesus is our Lord's intensely personal name. Have you noticed how difficult it is for some people to say this name, Jesus? They find it much easier to refer to Him as God or Lord or Christ or "the Man upstairs." But there is something about speaking the name Jesus. Say it now. Out loud. Jesus is His most personal name, and only those who truly know Him in the free pardoning of their sin find it easy to speak His name.

He came to save you from your sins. Open your heart to Him, for He said, "I came to seek and to save those who were lost" (Luke 19:10, author's paraphrase).

Why is speaking the name of Jesus so powerful?

DECEMBER 16

Potential for Greatness

But you, Bethlehem, in the land of Judah, are not the least among the rulers of Judah; for out of you shall come a Ruler who will shepherd My people Israel.

MATTHEW 2:6

Think of it. Of all the places for the Messiah to be born, God chose Bethlehem. One would have thought it might be in a much more prominent place, like Jerusalem. Bethlehem reminds us that in God's economy the small shall become great, and the last shall be first. Bethlehem was a place of potential, and even though you may feel insignificant, like Bethlehem, so are you!

As the Lord looks at you, He doesn't see you for what you are but for what you could become. This is the message of Bethlehem. God did not come to Caesar's palace to be born, nor to Herod's court. He arrived quietly, almost unannounced in a seemingly insignificant village.

God is reminding you today that in His eyes you have potential for greatness. See yourself as a Bethlehem. You, too, are a person of potential.

How does the story of Bethlehem give you hope about your potential for greatness?

DECEMBER 17

Inconvenience or Providence?

Declaring the end from the beginning, and from ancient times things that are not yet done, saying, "My counsel shall stand, and I will do all My pleasure."

ISAIAH 46:10

Long centuries before His birth, the prophets foretold that Christ would be born in Bethlehem. But how? Joseph and Mary resided seventy miles north, in Nazareth. God put the whole world in motion to fulfill His Word. A decree went out from Caesar Augustus that everyone was to go to the place of their family lineage to pay taxes. So Joseph, because he was of the line of David, left Nazareth with his very pregnant wife on a long journey of inconvenience.

Many of the things in our lives that on the surface appear inconvenient may just be the hand of God's providence getting us to our own Bethlehem. Bethlehem reminds us that what God promises, He performs—no matter what. Bethlehem is a place of providence, and so are you.

What promises of God are you waiting for Him to perform in your life?

DECEMBER 18

Soul vs. Spirit

Mary said: "My soul magnifies the Lord, and my spirit has rejoiced in God my Savior."
LUKE 1:46–47

Mary, realizing that the long-awaited Messiah was now alive and growing in her very womb, began to pray. Her first impulse was not to fear but to pray. She poured forth a prayer of praise and rejoicing. Her impulsive prayer emerged from her soul ("My soul magnifies the Lord") and it emanated from her spirit ("my spirit has rejoiced in God my Savior").

There is a difference between the soul and the spirit. Your soul is the seat of your emotions. The soul is what connects us to each other on the human level. It is also what gives life to the body. Without it the body dies and decays.

The spirit, on the other hand, is what connects you with God in the spiritual dimension. With the soul we are alive physically, and it is with our spirit that we come alive spiritually when we put our faith and trust in Jesus Christ. The soul comes alive when we are born. The spirit comes alive when we are born again.

How do your soul and spirit work together in your prayers?

DECEMBER 19

God Uses Ordinary People

Then Joseph, being aroused from sleep, did as the angel of the Lord commanded him and took to him his wife.
MATTHEW 1:24

Joseph is the one person in the story of Christ's birth who is seldom mentioned and never quoted, yet the entire narrative hinges on his faithfulness. Mary is quoted. As are Elizabeth, Zacharias, the shepherds, the wise men, Herod, Simeon, and even the angels. But there is no record of anything Joseph ever said.

We have hymns and songs about Mary, the wise men, the shepherds, the angels, even the star. But look in any hymnbook, and you will not find a song about Joseph.

There is a reason God chose Joseph to mentor and raise His own son. He was faithful. Each time God sent him a message through an angel, he obeyed immediately (Matthew 1:18–25; 2:13–15; 2:20–22). Our legacy from this forgotten man at the manger is not in what he said but in what he did. The entire story hinges on his obedience to God.

What impresses you most about Joseph, though we don't have a record of a word he spoke?

Life Is About Worship

Glory to God in the highest, and on earth peace, goodwill toward men!
LUKE 2:14

It is difficult to imagine any greater contrasts than what we see at the Nativity. Common, smelly shepherds and sophisticated wise men bow down. Worship flows from everyone toward the child.

They were different socially. Shepherds were low on the socioeconomic scale. Wise men were so socially acceptable they entered the king's palace.

They were different educationally. Shepherds had no formal education, while the wise men were famed for knowledge.

God is telling us that no matter who we are or where we are from, any and all can come to Christ and worship Him. All of life, first and foremost, is about worship. Those at the manger were not there simply admiring this child. They were worshiping Him. Make sure worship is a priority each and every day.

How can you prioritize worshiping God today?

DECEMBER 21

Family Is Important to God

So it was, that while they were there, the days were completed for her to be delivered.
LUKE 2:6

Look in the middle of the Nativity and you find a little family. God entrusted His own Son to a human family, just like yours. He could have circumvented the family, but He didn't. God put His own stamp of approval on the family.

Family is important to God. Think about it. He instituted the family long before He did the church. He placed His own Son in a family with relationships and domestic responsibilities. So Jesus was raised in Nazareth in a family unit.

Later, while hanging on the cross, Jesus spotted Mary and instructed John to care for her. Jesus was a family man. His was a blended family, when you think about it. Family is precious to Him.

The Nativity has a family in the middle of it for good reason. God is pro-family. Jesus has His own unique way of drawing families together.

What are some ways you can show God's love to your family today?

DECEMBER 22

Ponder These Things

But Mary kept all these things and pondered them in her heart.

LUKE 2:19

Mary. A young girl playing in the streets of Nazareth with her friends one day, and finding she is pregnant the next, though a virgin and unmarried. Her initial response? "How can this be?" (Luke 1:34).

After Jesus was born, it all began to sink in; Mary "pondered" all these things in her heart. The word picture is of a cake, with all the ingredients in a bowl, being stirred up. She was putting it all together, stirring it up in her mind . . . the prophecies . . . the angel's message . . . the virgin birth.

She knew baby Jesus' chubby little hands would never be adorned with expensive gold or silver rings. They were destined for other things, like touching lepers, forming clay out of spittle for blind eyes, and eventually being pierced with Roman spikes. But she also knew that millions of us would follow in His steps. She "pondered" all these things and kept them to herself.

What are some things you can ponder in your heart about Jesus to build your faith?

DECEMBER 23

Make Room for Jesus

And she brought forth her firstborn Son, and wrapped Him in swaddling cloths, and laid Him in a manger, because there was no room for them in the inn.
LUKE 2:7

These words grab my heart more than any others: "She . . . laid Him in a manger." Not a nice little wooden cradle like we see in a manger scene. But a rock-hewn cattle trough in a cave-like stable where sandals squashed in the dung as people walked, and the nauseating smell of the animals filled their nostrils. She laid Him in a manger. Think of it. Sickness, disease, death were likely possibilities.

How desperately alone from family and friends Mary must have felt when she realized the babe would be born far away from home. In her hour of pain, her bed was straw in a stable, and when the baby was born, she herself, with trembling fingers, "wrapped Him in swaddling cloths, and laid Him in a manger."

"No room" was not just the message of Bethlehem but the theme of Jesus' life. Yet it is those who find Him and make room in their hearts for Him who understand the true message of why He came.

How can you make more room in your heart and life for Jesus?

DECEMBER 24

FROM HEAVEN TO HELPLESS

Therefore, when He came into the world, He said: "Sacrifice and offering You did not desire, but a body You have prepared for Me."
HEBREWS 10:5

What a step—from the splendor of heaven to the womb of a woman and finally to a stable in Bethlehem. There is so much behind the words "a body You have prepared for Me." God is Spirit, and yet He stepped into a body of flesh to identify with you and, ultimately, to be your sin bearer.

This is condescension of the first and finest order. God became as helpless as a tiny seed planted in the womb of a young virgin girl, then as helpless as a baby totally dependent on someone else's care.

Look at Mary. To paraphrase Max Lucado, "She is in labor . . . her back is aching . . . her feet are swollen . . . she is sweating profusely . . . and having rapid contractions. The baby's head appears as she groans and pushes Him into the world. And He arrives!" God in flesh has come to visit us: "a body You have prepared for Me."

How does Jesus' coming to earth in a human body demonstrate His love for you?

DECEMBER 25

Center Your Life on Christ

Nor is there salvation in any other, for there is no other name under heaven given among men by which we must be saved.
ACTS 4:12

I love Rembrandt's portrayal of the Nativity. One great beam of light falls upon the baby Jesus so that all the other participants are somewhat shrouded in shadow. He wanted nothing to take away from the significance of Christ.

All of life should center on Christ. And primarily, Christ alone. Not only is He the center of the Nativity scene; He is the center of all of human history. His birth divided all of human history into "before" and "after" Christ. And if you don't believe this, just think about it at the end of the year when you change your calendar. His birth points the way for all men and women to see that the road to our eternal home is through Him.

If the Nativity were your own life, who or what would be in the center?

DECEMBER 26

The Power of Praying Scripture

So when they heard that, they raised their voice to God with one accord and said: "Lord, You are God, who made heaven and earth and the sea, and all that is in them, who by the mouth of Your servant David have said: 'Why did the nations rage, and the people plot vain things? The kings of the earth took their stand, and the rulers were gathered together against the Lord *and against His Christ.'"*

ACTS 4:24–26

In Acts 4 the early disciples found themselves in a situation David had prophesied seven hundred years earlier and recorded in Psalm 2:1–2. The "kings of the earth" (Herod), the "rulers" (Pontius Pilate), the "nations" (the Gentiles, Romans), and the "people" (the Jews). They prayed this passage, and praying the Scriptures caused them to see that God was in charge. Their prayer continued, acknowledging that what was happening was only because of what "Your hand and Your purpose determined before to be done" (v. 28). These early believers prayed with power because they knew the Scriptures and used them when they prayed. They offered the Word back to God. They stood on it. They believed it. They claimed its promises as their own. Nothing enables the believer to pray with power like Scripture memory and standing on God's Word when we pray.

When have you prayed the Scriptures, and what was the result?

DECEMBER 27

Prone to Wander

Brethren, if anyone among you wanders from the truth, and someone turns him back, let him know that he who turns a sinner from the error of his way will save a soul from death and cover a multitude of sins.
JAMES 5:19–20

As Christians we are responsible not only to Christ but to one another—for helping to bring back any fellow believers who have wandered from God's truth (the sound doctrine of God's Word).

Sadly, our first reaction to learning that someone has fallen is to rush to the phone and ask, "Did you hear about . . . ?" We may be better known for our pointed fingers of accusation than for our earnest desire to help those who wander from the truth.

Once we are born again, it's good to know our relationship with God can never be truly severed, and that we can come back to Him and start again. We can recognize our mistakes, return to the intersection where we made the wrong turn, and take the better path. Repentance is the key that opens the door of restoration with God.

How do you respond to believers who have wandered away from the truth of God's Word?

DECEMBER 28

The Purpose of Stewardship

Honor the Lord *with your possessions, and with the firstfruits of all your increase.*
PROVERBS 3:9

Our finances generally mark the position of our spiritual pilgrimage in the arena of trusting God. Solomon, who wrote today's scripture, knew you and I would be no further along in our walk with God than the point in which we have learned to trust and acknowledge Him (Proverbs 3:5–6) with our possessions.

What is the purpose behind the stewardship of our possessions? The simple answer is found in the first three words of today's scripture: "Honor the Lord." As believers, this should be our single most important goal in life. Motivation is a telling factor in our stewardship. Some give because they are motivated by *guilt*. They give because they know they ought to do so. Others are motivated by *grudge*. These people give because they feel like they have to do so. And then there are those who find God's promise because they are motivated by *grace*. That is, they give out of deep appreciation and love for God and because they want to do so. In this way, they honor the Lord.

In what ways can you honor the Lord with your possessions?

Praying for Courage and Confirmation

Now, Lord, look on their threats, and grant to Your servants that with all boldness they may speak Your word.
ACTS 4:29

Power in prayer involves being specific. Peter and John, referred to as "Your servants" in today's scripture, were the object of threats, imprisonments, beatings, even death. The Lord had warned His disciples that they would have tribulation in the world (John 16:33). So how would they now pray in the face of great persecution? They prayed specifically.

First, they prayed for *courage*, boldness in preaching (Acts 4:29). They realized that their greatest danger was not from without but from within. So they didn't flee to some monastery to escape the world; they prayed to be bold. They needed supernatural courage to overcome their fears.

They also specifically prayed for *confirmation* (v. 30). They asked God to confirm their new faith with miraculous manifestations that superseded human explanation. And He did!

Let's not hesitate to ask God specifically for courage and/or confirmation when we need them.

In what situation have you needed courage or confirmation, and how did God respond?

DECEMBER 30

YOUR LIFE IS LIKE A PALM TREE

The righteous will flourish like a palm tree, they will grow like a cedar of Lebanon; planted in the house of the LORD, they will flourish in the courts of our God. They will still bear fruit in old age, they will stay fresh and green.

PSALM 92:12–14 NIV

Palm trees are mentioned several times in Scripture. Psalm 92:12 says the righteous person will "flourish like a palm tree." Out of more than sixty thousand species of trees, why would the Lord choose the palm tree to picture how the righteous person flourishes? Let's focus on two reasons. First, the palm tree is a fruit-bearing tree, and it bears its fruit all year long, not simply seasonally. The righteous person is like the palm tree in this respect. He or she is "ready in season and out of season" (2 Timothy 4:2) and is consistent in faith, bearing fruit that remains throughout the year.

Second, the palm tree has a way of turning what is bitter into what is sweet. Palm trees are often found in the terrain near salt water. They have their own way of being nurtured by the brackish, bitter salt water and turning it into delicious and sweet date palms. The righteous man may experience some of the most bitter experiences of life but, at the same time, turn them into blessings for themselves and others.

As a righteous person, how is your life like a palm tree?

God's Grace Is Sufficient

My grace is sufficient for you, for My strength is made perfect in weakness.
2 CORINTHIANS 12:9

Even though God did not relieve or remove Paul's thorn in the flesh (2 Corinthians 12:7), He did something better. He gave him *a promise*: "My grace is sufficient for you, for My strength is made perfect in weakness." God's grace is always enough—more than enough—for whatever need we may face. After all, grace is best defined as getting what we do not deserve. This is what distinguishes grace from mercy. Mercy is not getting what we do deserve. God is rich in grace and showers us daily with blessings we do not deserve.

Perhaps your heart is heavy, and you have your own "thorn in the flesh" distracting you. James 4:6 reminds us that "He [God] gives more grace. . . . God resists the proud, but gives grace to the humble." Whoever you are, whatever your circumstance, wherever you may reside, and with whomever you may have conflict, you can rest and rely on the promise that God's grace is sufficient.

How have you found God's grace to be sufficient for you?

Mission:Dignity

All the author's royalties and any additional proceeds from the Code series (including *The Promise Code*) go to the support of Mission:Dignity, a ministry that enables thousands of retired ministers (and, in most cases, their widows) who are living near the poverty level to live out their days with dignity and security. Many of them spent their ministries in small churches that were unable to provide adequately for their retirement. They also lived in church-owned parsonages and had to vacate them upon their vocational retirement as well. Mission:Dignity tangibly shows these good and godly servants they are not forgotten and will be cared for in their declining years.

All the expenses for this ministry are paid out of an endowment that has already been raised. Consequently, anyone who gives to Mission:Dignity can be assured that every cent of their gift goes straight to one of these precious saints in need.

Find out more by visiting www.missiondignity.org or call toll-free 877-888-9409.

ABOUT THE AUTHOR

O. S. Hawkins, a native of Fort Worth, Texas, is a graduate of Texas Christian University (BBA) and Southwestern Baptist Theological Seminary (MDiv, PhD). He is Chancellor and Senior Professor of Pastoral Ministry and Evangelism at Southwestern Baptist Theological Seminary. He is the former pastor of the historic First Baptist Church in Dallas, Texas, and is President Emeritus of GuideStone Financial Resources, the world's largest Christian-screened mutual fund serving 250,000 church workers and Christian university personnel with an asset base exceeding $20 billion, where he served as president/CEO from 1997 to 2022.

Dr. Hawkins is the author of more than fifty books, including the bestselling "Code Series" with over two million in print, including *The Joshua Code: 52 Scripture Verses Every Believer Should Know*; *The Bible Code: Finding Jesus in Every Book in the Bible*; *The Christmas Code: Daily Devotionals Celebrating the Advent Season*; and *The Easter Code: A 40-Day Journey to the Cross.*

He preaches in churches and conferences across the nation. He is married to Susie and has two daughters, two sons-in-law, and six grandchildren. Visit him at OSHawkins.com and follow him on X @ OSHawkins.

THE Spirit CODE
40 Truths About the Holy Spirit That Every Believer Should Know
O.S. Hawkins
ISBN: 978-1-4002-4643-4
One hundred percent of the author's royalties and proceeds go to support Mission:Dignity—a ministry providing support for impoverished retired pastors and missionaries.
THOMAS NELSON
Since 1798

1 MEET THE HOLY SPIRIT

Allow me the privilege of introducing you to the Holy Spirit. Perhaps there has never been another person as misrepresented and misunderstood as He. He is not some mysterious, nebulous force that can be equated to the famous *Star Wars* saying, "May the Force be with you." Nor, for those who know something of the Bible, did He show up on the scene for the first time on the day of Pentecost in an upper room on Mount Zion in the city of Jerusalem.

Let's begin with a foundational statement: The Holy Spirit is God. One of the foundational truths of orthodox Christianity is the belief that God is one and yet He eternally exists in three persons: Father, Son, and Holy Spirit. In theological jargon this is called the Trinity, three in one, and it is a great mystery. It has been revealed to us in various ways through the Bible but can be challenging to wrap our minds around. I have come to the conclusion that if I could understand all there is to know about the Godhead in my own limited mind, there would not be much to it. It is simply a theological truth that manifests itself from the first chapter of Genesis to the end of the book of Revelation, and because it is rooted in sacred Scripture, must be taken by faith. Many have attempted to explain the reality of the Trinity through metaphors and analogies, but none of them are completely valid.

Some believe that the Father is the God of the Old Testament, the Son, Jesus Christ, is the God of the Gospels, and the Holy Spirit is the God of the book of Acts and the rest of the New Testament. But this is heretical thinking. Jesus did not just show up in the manger at Bethlehem. He was from the beginning. Neither did the Holy Spirit just show up at Pentecost. He was there from the beginning. We cannot separate the Godhead. The Father, the Son, and the Holy Spirit are one . . . three in one. They always have been, and they always will be.

We cannot separate the Godhead. The Father, the Son, and the Holy Spirit are one . . . three in one. They always have been, and they always will be.

There are 31,102 verses in the Bible, and the Holy Spirit shows up in the first two: "In the beginning God created the heavens and the earth. The earth was without form, and void; and darkness was on the face of the deep. And the Spirit of God was hovering over the face of the waters" (Genesis 1:1–2). He was there way back in the beginning at creation, "hovering over the face of the waters." In fact, there has never been a time when the Holy Spirit was not here manifesting the mighty presence and power of God.

The Father, the Son, and the Holy Spirit all were active in creation. It is said of the Father that "in the beginning God created the heavens and the earth" (Genesis 1:1). It is said of the Son that "In the beginning was the Word. . . . All things were made through Him, and without Him nothing was made that was made" (John 1:1, 3). So that we might never be confused as to the identity of this "Word," John went on to add, "The Word became flesh and dwelt among us, and we beheld His glory, the glory as of the only begotten of the Father, full of grace and truth" (John 1:14). Further, as mentioned above, the Holy Spirit, being a member of this triune God, was there as well, doing His part in the creation event.

Repeated in every Jewish synagogue all over the world in every Sabbath service is the Shema, the Jewish confession of faith: "Hear, O Israel: the Lord our God, the Lord is one!" (Deuteronomy 6:4). This confession is immediately followed by what Jesus referred to in the New Testament as the greatest commandment, "You shall love the LORD your God with all your heart, with all your soul, and with all your strength" (Deuteronomy 6:5). As followers of Christ, our Messiah, we affirm this truth—the Lord is one! Yet Scripture is clear in revealing that this one God is manifested to us in three persons: the Father, the Son, and the Holy Spirit. The apostle Paul made this crystal clear in his benediction to the church in Corinth: "The grace of the Lord Jesus Christ, and the love of God, and the communion of the Holy Spirit be with you all" (2 Corinthians 13:14).

Jesus made this emphatic claim in dialogue with the Jews when He said bluntly, "I and My Father are one" (John 10:30). Earlier, at Jesus' baptism in the Jordan River, Matthew recorded, "When He had been baptized, Jesus came up immediately from the water; and behold, the heavens were opened to Him, and He saw the Spirit of God descending like a dove and alighting upon Him. And suddenly a voice came from heaven, saying, 'This is My beloved Son, in whom I am well pleased'" (Matthew 3:16–17). As Jesus, the Son, stood in the waters of baptism, the Father spoke from heaven, and the Spirit descended like a dove.

Then as Jesus was about to physically leave us and just

before He ascended, He left us with a Great Commission: "Go therefore and make disciples . . . baptizing them in the name of the Father and of the Son and of the Holy Spirit" (Matthew 28:19). Thus, we join our Jewish friends in confessing the Shema, "The LORD our God, the LORD is one!" But we understand that this God is the great Three in One, manifesting Himself to us in all His glory as the Father, the Son, and the Holy Spirit.

We will discover in these pages that the Holy Spirit has always been at work in our lives. It is He who convicts us, converts us, commends us, commands us, consoles us, and comforts us. It is He who ultimately completes us. We will get to know the Holy Spirit who knows everything there is to know about us. He is an essential part of our journey toward finding the fullness of joy in life.